Dear Friend,

I am pleased to send you this copy of *Biography of God* by my good friend Skip Heitzig. Skip is a bestselling author and the senior pastor of Calvary Church in Albuquerque, New Mexico.

This practical book uses the Old and New Testaments to introduce the God of the Bible, answering some of the most common questions people have: Does God exist? What is He like? Where is He now? Since the Bible tells us that we are made *"in the image of God"* (Genesis 1:27, ESV), there is nothing—or no one—more important to study and know than Him. I pray this book will draw you, or a loved one, closer to God, your Maker.

For more than 70 years, the Billy Graham Evangelistic Association has worked to share the Good News of Jesus Christ throughout the world by every effective means available, and I'm excited about what God will do in the years ahead. If you would like to know more about our ministry, please contact us:

IN THE U.S.:
Billy Graham Evangelistic Association
1 Billy Graham Parkway
Charlotte, NC 28201-0001
BillyGraham.org
info@bgea.org
Toll-free: 1-877-247-2426

IN CANADA:
Billy Graham Evangelistic
    Association of Canada
20 Hopewell Way NE
Calgary, AB T3J 5H5
BillyGraham.ca
Toll-free: 1-888-393-0003

We would appreciate knowing how our ministry has touched your life.

May God richly bless you.

Franklin Graham
President

BIOGRAPHY
of
GOD

BIOGRAPHY
of
GOD

SKIP HEITZIG

HARVEST HOUSE PUBLISHERS
EUGENE, OREGON

This *Billy Graham Library Selection* special edition is published
with permission from Harvest House Publishers.

Cover designed by Skip Heitzig's team.

Published in association with William K. Jensen Literary Agency, 119 Bampton Court, Eugene, Oregon 97404.

For bulk, special sales, or ministry purchases, please call 1-800-547-8979. Email: Customerservice@hhpbooks.com

Biography of God
Copyright © 2020 by Skip Heitzig
Published by Harvest House Publishers
Eugene, Oregon 97408
www.harvesthousepublishers.com

ISBN 978-0-7369-7773-9 (pbk)
ISBN 978-0-7369-7774-6 (eBook)
ISBN 978-1-593-28695-8 (BGEA edition)

Library of Congress Cataloging-in-Publication Data

Names: Heitzig, Skip, author.
Title: Biography of God / Skip Heitzig.
Description: Eugene, Oregon : Harvest House Publishers, 2020. | Summary:
    "The Biography of God offers a personal encounter with God-one that is
    uplifting, instructive, and practical for every area of life. This is a
    very conversational-style book that inspires, encourages, and enables
    readers to know God better"-- Provided by publisher.
Identifiers: LCCN 2020018196 (print) | LCCN 2020018197 (ebook) | ISBN
    9780736977739 (trade paperback) | ISBN 9780736977746 (ebook)
Subjects: LCSH: God (Christianity) | God (Christianity)--Knowableness. |
    Spirituality--Christianity.
Classification: LCC BT103 .H45 2020 (print) | LCC BT103 (ebook) | DDC
    231--dc23
LC record available at https://lccn.loc.gov/2020018196
LC ebook record available at https://lccn.loc.gov/2020018197

Printed in the United States of America

20 21 22 23 24 25 26 27 28 / BP-RD / 10 9 8 7 6 5 4 3 2 1

This book is dedicated to my grandchildren,
Seth Nathaniel Heitzig and Kadence Joy Heitzig,
both of whom are uniquely crafted by the personal God of
Scripture written about in these pages. It is my deepest hope
that they will walk closely with Him to fulfill
His design for their lives.

ACKNOWLEDGMENTS

I want to acknowledge the team I have around me that makes all my work possible. It's true that alone we can do little; together we can do much. Solomon nailed it when he wrote, "Two are better than one… a rope made of three cords is hard to break" (Ecclesiastes 4:9-12). It's true in daily life, and it was true in the writing of this book.

Thanks to my wife, Lenya, who understands the power of the printed word as well as the spoken word; to my son, Nate, whose contemporary insight is always helpful; to my personal assistant, Laney Dennis, whose steady support makes writing times possible; and to my local publishing team, Quent, Brian, and Lorin, for insights, revisions, and great ideas. I also have a large church staff that is creative, competent, and energetic to follow God's call; they inspire me.

I am indebted to Dr. J.I. Packer for his book *Knowing God*, and equally to Tim Stafford, who wrote *Knowing the Face of God*. These two unique contributions to my early spiritual journey fed my hunger to know the God who revealed Himself in creation and Scripture.

I am most grateful to the God of the universe, who revealed Himself unselfishly through the person of His Son, the Lord Jesus Christ. He interrupted my life when I was turning eighteen. I'm so glad He did, and I am still learning what it means to walk with Him.

CONTENTS

PREFACE:
ABOUT THE COVER ART

The work on the cover of this book is derived from *Woodcut for Die Bibel in Bildern*, 1860, by German artist Julius Schnorr von Carolsfeld (1794–1872). It shows God the Father in power and splendor, a personification of His glory.

Von Carolsfeld was part of the Nazarene Movement, comprised of German Romantic artists driven by a yearning to highlight Christian themes whose work revolved around biblical subjects. He is best remembered for his Picture Bible, published between 1852–1860.

Many throughout history have tried to portray God via artistic means. An image like von Carolsfeld's is creative and beautiful—but limited. It has to be. No person can capture the grandeur of God on canvas, in marble, or engraved on stone or wood. No artistic work can encompass the enormity and essence of God; we can only paint to comprehend, never to apprehend.

Using art to depict God is purely an imaginative endeavor. In employing art on the cover of *Biography of God*, my intention is not to suggest what God looks like or that God the Father is a man (much less an old man, subject to the ravages of time). Jesus, after all, said God is Spirit (John 4:24). Rather, I hope to make a point as to the overarching intention of the book: to render a description of God that is both biblical and beautiful, helping you as the reader to better comprehend our awe-inspiring Creator.

LET ME INTRODUCE YOU

Who is God? What is He like? Is He even there at all? What does He want? Why doesn't He make Himself more available...especially to me?

These were the questions that peppered my mind as a youngster. The memory is still fresh: Around twelve years old, I stood in my backyard on a sunlit morning, burning a small amount of trash for my mom (those were the days when air quality management in California wasn't a huge concern). As the smoke wafted upward, I felt almost transported back in time to Old Testament days, when the priests sacrificed offerings in the temple. I started to think about this simple three-letter word: G-O-D. So easy to say! So hard to understand!

Thoughts about God imposed themselves on me as a youngster, bumping into my everyday activities like an uninvited panhandler. I began wondering if it was possible to know for sure if God existed, and if so, could I know Him the way I knew my mom and dad? Yeah, I went to church with my family and heard the standard answers. But that wasn't enough for me. I wanted more.

An unfed hunger grew inside me to discover the divine presence. Was God an imaginary idea concocted by people throughout time as a convenient way to understand their own existence? Or had God revealed Himself first, breaking into human reality from the outside-in? If God was real, what did He do all day? Did He have any hobbies? Could we make Him happy, sad, or mad? What did He look like? Such are the common thoughts of a child.

A kindergarten teacher once assigned her class to draw a picture of something that was important to them. Each of the children got to work, and scrawled images of parents, pets, sports, and rainbows began to appear. Johnny sat in the back, head down, working diligently. All the other kids turned in their assignments, but Johnny drew on, feverishly scribbling with furrowed brow.

His teacher noticed and asked, "Johnny, what are you drawing?" Without looking up, Johnny replied, "I'm drawing God."

Smiling, the teacher said, "Well, Johnny, no one knows what God looks like."

Without missing a beat, Johnny looked up. "They will when I'm through."

I can't help but chuckle at Johnny's confidence—a child's belief that he knew what God looked like. If Johnny were an adult, we'd call his claim arrogant, and we wouldn't be wrong. So as I sit down to write a book about God, I want to make it clear that I'm not pulling a Johnny. In fact, I still sometimes feel like I did as a twelve-year-old boy in my backyard in California. I've been teaching the Bible for more than thirty-five years, and following Jesus for even longer, but the last thing I would presume is that I know all there is to know about God—let alone make any sort of claim to that effect.

The truth is, I'm just a fellow traveler on redemption's road. Like any Christian, I have access to the same information, the same documents, and the same God as anyone who has given Jesus control of their life. My hope is to offer a fresh perspective—something like a biography of God. By definition, a biography is an account of someone's life written by someone else. It's a nonfictional literary narrative that draws upon available evidence to present a life story. That's what we have in the Bible. Forty different authors penned sixty-six books over a period of fifteen-hundred years, creating a book with a singular focus: God and His interactions with humankind. They wrote freely about God—who He said He is, what He is like, and what He wants and doesn't want. In essence, they painted a portrait of our Maker.

The more I learn about God, the more I realize there is yet to know. It's not that we can't be clear about certain important aspects of Him—His existence, His nature, His personality—but He is not like us. He is wholly *other*. God is beyond human ability to fully comprehend, and people much wiser than I have said as much. But that doesn't mean we can't be curious about God. And it doesn't mean we can't apprehend Him—wrap our minds and hearts around Him—to some degree. I believe that He *wants* us to know Him and has designed our world in such a way that it points us to Him. And He wants us to know Him more and better. That's why He gave us a guide.

In this book, I want to use the Bible to introduce you to God. You may know Him well, or hardly at all. You may think you know Him when actually you only know ideas and facts *about* Him. Either way, you've probably dealt with the kinds of questions I asked as a kid and that all of us ask at some point: Does God exist? What is He like? Where is He now? Are there multiple paths that lead to Him? Is there anything God can't or won't do? What's the deal with holiness? What's all this talk about a personal relationship with God—and how is that even possible with an invisible, all-powerful being? I've had these questions too—and I wanted answers. This book is the result of my lifelong searching, seeking, and finding.

There are three reasons I'm writing this book. First, because these questions are *universal*. Everyone at some point deals with the question of God—whether He exists or not, and if He does, whether He can be known. From children to adults, from the most illiterate to the most philosophically astute, we all look for a cause higher than ourselves—and many have weighed in on the search, writing books or making films, music, or art to try to express their thoughts about God. Down through every generation, every thinking person has wanted to discover if it's possible to know God.

That leads me to the second reason: because studying God is *inspirational*. If in fact we are made in God's image, and if we identify ourselves as children of God, there is nothing more edifying than to study God Himself. Because God is so far above and beyond us, seeking to know Him elevates us. Nothing so expands the soul of a human being as the investigation of the divine. As the apostle Paul wrote, "Set your mind on things above, not on things on the earth" (Colossians 3:2).

> Nothing so expands the soul of a human being as the investigation of the divine.

That doesn't mean we should shirk our everyday responsibilities. Taxes still have to be paid, votes still must be cast, bills must be taken care of, health still requires restoration, relationships still need attention. The Bible speaks to all of those daily concerns with wisdom and insight—and yet it always reminds us to turn our eyes heavenward. To carve out time to read this book, to check it against the Bible and your own experience, to ponder God is a form of relief from this world's tyrannical urgency.

I believe you'll discover that when you turn your thoughts from yourself—your needs, your troubles, your issues—to God and His ways, you'll find relief from stress and anxiety. Your problems won't go away, but they will seem a bit smaller *and* you will see the silver lining, the light of hope, the possibility of better days ahead.

Finally, the third reason I'm writing this book is because knowing God is *consequential.* There's far more at stake if you get this wrong than anything else. The great risk of getting the God issue messed up is that it can mess up everything. Mortimer J. Adler, longtime editor of the Encyclopedia Britannica and co-curator of the 54-volume *Great Books of the Western World* series, was asked why the longest of the many fine essays housed in that collection was about God. His response? "Because more consequences for life follow from that one issue than any other."[1] I've discovered that almost every problem for which I and my fellow clergy members have counseled people stems from an inadequate view of God. For someone who says, "I'm lonely," it could be that he doesn't fully understand the accessibility of God. If someone complains, "I'm useless, incompetent, worthless," maybe she needs a fresh reminder of God the Father, whose love fueled the greatest possible redemption. Those trapped by their sin have likely lost sight of God's holiness or His available power. Even in the church, Christians suffer from an insufficient view of God. That's the root of almost all our troubles.

Therefore, learning about and knowing God is the most practical of all pursuits. "Disregard the study of God," says J.I. Packer, "and you sentence yourself to stumble and blunder through life blindfolded, as it were, with no sense of direction and no understanding of what surrounds you." He elaborates,

> We can only truly know God on His terms, based on who He says He is and what He has done to make relationship possible.

> As it would be cruel to an Amazonian tribesman to fly him to London, put him down without explanation in Trafalgar Square and leave him, as one who knew nothing of English or England, to fend for himself, so we are cruel to ourselves if we try to live in this world without knowing about the God whose world it is and who runs it.[2]

But we must be realistic and cautious. One of the greatest struggles any of us has is to come to terms with God. There is danger here— for the believer who thinks he has God all figured out, for the seeker who seeks God without really looking for Him, and for the skeptic who tries to create a God that matches his feelings about the world. We can only truly know God on His terms, based on who He says He is and what He has done to make relationship possible. With that in mind, I'm writing this book for those three categories of people: the saint, the seeker, and the skeptic. Whatever you consider yourself to be now, you may find yourself moving among all three of these categories.

But you'll also find that getting to know God better, wherever you're at, is worth your time and effort. In these pages, you will find biblical answers to many of the questions people ask about God. We'll consider what the Scriptures of the Old and New Testaments say about Him—and if you can trust the Bible to tell you the truth. We'll sit down for a cup of coffee, as it were, with the God who is holy and incomprehensible and intimate and merciful. We'll peer into the mystery of the Trinity, the enigma of Father, Son, and Holy Spirit, each a distinct Person but also a single and singular God. And I'll let you in on something truly crazy and wonderful: how you can be God's friend. You may be surprised to find out that a relationship with you is what He wants.

My hope and prayer is that you'll be able to form a picture of God as a result. Not an image per se, but a portrait of His character, a soul sketch of the powerful yet personal, almighty yet all-loving God of the universe. There's a lot at stake here—your hope and happiness now, and your peace and security in eternity. That's why I want you to read this book—so you can have an encounter with the One who knows you better than anyone ever will. I want you to meet your Maker.

Chapter 1

CAN GOD BE KNOWN?

A man sat by a hospital bed, stunned by its emptiness. Moments before, it had been filled with the love of his life, her body broken and bandaged, but her heartbeat beeping steadily on the monitor. He never saw the car that put her there, sometimes wasn't even sure how long they had been in the hospital. Was it hours or days? People came and went, doctors and nurses, friends and coworkers, the kids (though he couldn't stand to have their eyes bore into his, asking questions to which they already knew the answers).

A chaplain even stopped by, wearing one of those collars, asking permission to pray. He had shrugged. He wasn't a praying man, wasn't the kind to turn over responsibility to someone he couldn't even see. But after the chaplain left, a thought hung in his mind: *What if I'm wrong?*

She had never opened her eyes. He had leaned in, trying to hear her breathe, desperate for the flutter of an eyelid, the twitch of a finger—anything to show she was still there. His wife lay right in front of him and he didn't know whether he would ever see her smile again, hear her voice, feel her fingers wrap around his as she had once confidently promised him, "You'll get better. You can beat this."

She had been wrong. He couldn't beat the drinking, couldn't will his way to sobriety. But that wasn't entirely fair to her. He had been careless with one of the most precious people in his life. He forced himself to remember everything she had said, even the part that wrecked his view of himself, the world, his whole life. "You'll get better. You can beat this...if you will just trust God."

He never left her, never was out of hearing, until just now. They had given him time with her, after her heart stopped, after the paddles and carts and monitors has been rolled out. Now the bed was empty and his heart was wrung out like an old washcloth. She had believed, had wanted him to, but he couldn't honestly wrap his mind around the concept of an eternal, all-seeing, all-knowing, yet seemingly always-absent God. Now he remembered—the times he caught her praying on her knees in the closet, eyes shut and hands raised. He had heard her murmur his name, the kids' names, people whose names he didn't know—all directed, as near as he could tell, toward the shoe rack.

He wasn't angry—yet. He knew he would be, would feel the rage of being deprived, would want to aim it like an arrow somewhere. He knew the sadness was coming, like a tsunami after an earthquake. But now, there was no anger or sorrow—only the question.

What if I'm wrong?

He knew, above all else, that this was what he would have to deal with in the days and years ahead—and how he answered it would mean everything.

Two Great Realities

You never know the moment you will come face to face with the question of God. Will it be when you're young, or when you're old? Will it happen in the wake of tragedy, or in the stillness of an unguarded moment? Will it come after a lifetime of religious service, in a season of stark survival, or during an ongoing battle of intellectual resistance? Whenever or however it happens, the moment is coming when you must do business with God, either taking Him seriously by responding to His overtures, or pushing Him away into the background and turning up the volume of your inner voices. No matter how smart or careful you are, how determined you are to chart your own course, you're going to reach the end of yourself.

But when you get to that isolated place, accessible only to you, you're going to find that you're not alone. In fact, you'll learn that you never were. When the weight of that reality settles on you, will it crush you, or will you let yourself be unburdened? To know for sure, you'll have to answer this question: *What if I've been wrong about God?* As the seventeenth-century mathematician Blaise Pascal once insisted, you have far more to lose if you're wrong about God than if you believe in Him and He doesn't exist!

What if God does exist? What if He can be known? What if He already knows you and loves you deeply? What if He is pursuing you the way lovers pursue each other, the way fire consumes oxygen, the way a mother pulls her child from the street? What if your Maker wants more than anything to meet you? If you want answers to those questions, you're going to need one thing: faith.

> Faith calls what is invisible *fact* and what is not readily apparent *guaranteed.*

Hebrews 11 is a well-known New Testament chapter that's all about faith. It recounts a who's who of Old Testament figures, praising them for their faithful journeys through life with God, sort of like a Hall of Fame of faith. These were lives covered with enough "fingerprints" to point to the invisible God who left those fingerprints. The chapter begins by providing a definition of faith: "Now faith is the assurance of things hoped for, the conviction of things not seen" (v. 1 ESV). Faith calls what is invisible *fact* and what is not readily apparent *guaranteed.*

So in asking the question "Can God be known?," Hebrews 11 gives us the answer: "Without faith it is impossible to please Him, for he who comes to God must believe that He is, and that He is a rewarder of those who diligently seek Him" (v. 6). Let's camp on this text for a moment, for this verse points to two great realities and two subsequent responsibilities. The two great realities: God exists and God is personal. They go hand in hand with two great responsibilities: faith and pursuit. Let's start with the first: to come to God, you have to "believe that He is"—that is, that He exists.

Taking God Out of the Equation...

The most fundamental question in the universe is, Does God exist? I asked it as a twelve-year-old; everyone asks it at some point. And everything hinges on the answer—origin, purpose, meaning, hope. The Russian novelist Fyodor Dostoevsky brought up the issue in his 1880 masterwork *The Brothers Karamazov*. Through his characters, he posed the question that he himself had long struggled with—the question of God. As Smerdyakov (a true atheist) in essence says to Ivan (an on-and-off atheist), "If there is no God, then everything is permitted."

The implications of this statement are ominous. Without God to provide protective boundaries to human intellect and ingenuity, our best impulses are subject to corruption and decay. And yet Dostoevsky's statement resulted from the work of many brilliant thinkers of his day—some of whom (and many since) took his statement as permission to promote atheism.

The classic argument that God is a cosmic killjoy is off the table if He doesn't exist. Not only is there no more good cop, bad cop thinking in play, but there is no cop at all. If God doesn't exist, then we populate this planet by chance. There's no design, no purpose. Dostoevsky's probing statement became a license for mankind to run with the ball, so to speak. Just read this summary of the most influential thoughts of his day, views that still hold sway:

- If God doesn't exist, then Ludwig Feuerbach was right when he said that God is a mere projection of our humanity.

- If God doesn't exist, then Karl Marx was correct to assert that the material is all that matters; Christianity is merely a reflex of capitalism.

- If God doesn't exist, then Friedrich Nietzsche made sense when he said that our existence is senseless and useless.

- If God doesn't exist, then Sigmund Freud was right when he dismissed God as an infantile illusion that should be discarded.

Tower of Babel, anyone?

If there is no God—if all these thinkers were right and we're all alone in this universe—then what's the point? If we're not here by the design and purpose of a higher being, then all that's left is what we can make of life. And the human track record suggests constant industrial and technological advancement coupled with spiraling depression and despair.

As novelist and philosopher Jean-Paul Sartre said, "Dostoevsky once wrote: 'If God did not exist, everything would be permitted'; and that, for existentialism[1] is the starting point. Everything is indeed permitted if God does not exist, and man is in consequence forlorn."[2] In other words, the first thing that is permitted if God doesn't exist is despair. Left alone to our own devices, we will lose hope. In fact, hopelessness is the logical conclusion if there is no God.

Sartre claimed that God is a shackle that keeps mankind from taking responsibility for his own actions: "What man needs is to find himself again and to understand that nothing can save him from himself, not even a valid proof of the existence of God."[3] Imagine that—facing an undeniable proof that God exists and remaining unchanged.

The self-deception Sartre accused Christians of practicing is far more evident in his own insistence that man has it within himself to be the agent of his own change, his own salvation. If that's so, what are we waiting for? There have been more than enough intelligent, well-intentioned people to provide a solution to humanity's problems. And yet our capacity to warp good into evil has remained a

constant throughout history. It would seem that we are either unin-
terested in or incapable of solving our issues.

What some call freedom morphs into their own imprisonment
and despair; as one quipster noted, "The more you do as you please,
the less you are pleased with what you do." Despair is the frequent
companion and colleague of nihilism, the belief that values are false
inventions based on era and culture, and that life, therefore, has no
meaning. In contrast, the Bible says that God is a safeguard, protecting us from the terrible results of our unadulterated freedom and
providing relief from them.

The French philosopher Albert Camus wrote that nihilism is
"the experience of the loss of absolute values...The nihilist response
to this 'Everything is permitted' is not simply despair, but 'the
desire to despair and to negate.'"[4] In other words, in a world without boundaries of any sort—a world of the complete freedom that
people often say is their most inalienable right—we won't just feel
despair; we will seek it out and embrace it.

We can see the ripples of nihilism and existentialism extend
throughout history and into the present day. In *Macbeth*, Shake-
speare wrote, "Life...is a tale, told by an idiot, full of sound and fury,
signifying nothing!" Actor Nicolas Cage gave voice to this emptiness when he said, "I wonder if there's a hole in the soul of my generation. We've inherited the American dream, but where do we take
it?"[5] Bruce Springsteen said, "I have spent my life judging the distance between the American reality and the American dream."[6] I
wonder if that distance is the width of a God-shaped hole.

...and Bringing Him Right Back In

Denying God's existence doesn't provide answers, but if God
does exist, then a whole other host of questions follow: What is God
like? What does He want? What does He love and hate? An honest
exploration of the evidence will enable us to find those answers—
to the extent that I'll even say that it takes more faith to be an atheist than to believe in a personal God.

I've met many intellectually honest atheists. I like it when I do. They grapple with the whole God question with sincerity, but I've found that a lot of them haven't done their homework. They hold their position not for lack of intellectual satisfaction, but for moral reasons. If they open themselves up to the existence of God, they realize that it means they're accountable to Him. They would have to let go of certain positions on issues or personal habits, and they would rather hang on to what's right in front of them than trust that God has something better for them. As someone well put it, an atheist cannot find God for the same reason a thief can't find a policeman: because he's not looking for Him (or he's looking to avoid Him at all costs).

Ravi Zacharias spoke of a visit to the Wexner Center for Performing Arts in Columbus, Ohio, described by *Newsweek* as "America's first deconstructionist building."[7] Divided red brick turrets, disruptive white scaffolding, and free-hanging columns attached at the ceiling but not at the floor are all supposed to reflect the senseless and incoherent nature of life. When this was explained to Zacharias, he had only one question of the man who designed the building: "Did he do the same with the foundation?"

The goal of the deconstructionist is to break down meaning through bizarre experimentation in everything from philosophy to literature to art and architecture. But just as an avant-garde architect might play around with elements but not break the building code for safety reasons, so one cannot run away from God without violating their own well-being.

Albert Einstein believed in God, though not "in the known God of the Bible, but rather in the mysterious God expressed in nature." For him, the wonders of the natural universe pointed to the hand of a divine being, but that being, "whatever name we give him—creative Force, or God—escapes all book knowledge."[8] While I certainly wouldn't dream of going to toe-to-toe with Einstein in theoretical physics, I beg to differ. For me, Einstein embodies the view that faith and reason are incompatible; he believed in God until he grew up and applied science to the universe.

In trying to explain his reverence for the wonders of nature, Einstein used God as a metaphor for the order and design of the natural world—something he acknowledged was beyond human capacity to engineer or even fully grasp. But for Einstein, God was not personal, not interested in peoples' lives or issues or hearts. However, the second great reality Hebrews 11 introduces us to says otherwise.

God Can Be Known—Personally

Not only does God exist, but He is personal. Notice how the writer of Hebrews framed it: "He is a rewarder of those who diligently seek Him" (11:6). God can interact with those whom He has made. He is able to love, to reward, to care for those who sincerely pursue Him. He has personality. And if we're honest, we hunger for Him to be that way. We long to know and be known by our Maker. That was the apostle Paul's heart cry, even after thirty years of serving and walking with God—"that I may know Him and the power of His resurrection, and the fellowship of His sufferings" (Philippians 3:10).

Years ago, a book title leaped off a shelf at me, and my heart lunged right back toward it. It was J.I. Packer's *Knowing God*, which has over and over fed my desire to know God more personally and intimately. Having the privilege of sitting down for breakfast with Packer in Amsterdam, I thanked him for his great contribution to my faith and then got to know, albeit casually, the author who helped me know God better.

In that great book, which has sold more than a million copies, Packer strikes at the heart of the issue for many of us when he writes, "Ignorance of God—ignorance both of His ways and of the practice of communion with Him—lies at the root of much of the church's weakness today."[9]

I winced at this simple statement, struck by conviction, but then felt it pulling me onward, birthing an insatiable hunger to know

God more. I became determined to know God's ways and to walk in His company, all the while feeling like the apostle who admitted, "Not that I have already attained, or am already perfected" (Philippians 3:12).

Because you now know that I fall easily for simple titles, let me confess to another. *Knowing the Face of God,* by Tim Stafford, became a companion in my life for a time as well. In the book, Stafford admitted that he didn't have problems finding intellectual fulfillment in God or evidence of God's power at work. His faith wasn't dry, nor did he lack appropriate emotions toward God, but he still wasn't satisfied:

> On a human level, Christianity was more than I had hoped for. It was the human-to-God level I felt shaky about. I wanted more. I have come to realize that I was not alone in my longing...such questions aren't usually voiced. When they are—when the conversation moves to the subject of knowing God—listeners grow suddenly quiet and attentive. For a long time I thought this was a disapproving silence. I now know that it is the silence that falls on a room of hungry people when someone talks of food.[10]

Acknowledging our hunger to know God, which I am convinced most everyone has, leads to an important question: How do you have a personal relationship with God? After all, there's no one like Him. Such a complex and unique being as God can't be easy to know! Even though evidence of His personality exists all around us, He can't be seen. Every buck stops ultimately with Him, and yet He still knows all the details of your life. But the fact of the matter is that God wants to be known—that's a major theme of the Bible, evident in these two great realities: He exists, and He is personal.

So how do we get to know Him?

Two Great Responsibilities

The fact that God exists means we are bound by certain

responsibilities. Once we can say, "Okay, God is real and He wants me to know Him," then we must first respond with faith. Remember Hebrews 11:6: "Without faith it is impossible to please Him, for he who comes to God must believe that He is, and that He is a rewarder of those who diligently seek Him." Belief is essential to knowing God.

We All Put Faith in Something

Many people today have made science a religion. Their mantra is "Empirical knowledge frees us from superstition and religious nonsense." But they worship at the altar of facts, which will fall short eventually, as any scientist will admit. At some point, logic and science no longer serve to enlighten us. They become tyrants, shackling us to a finite existence, a world that will someday end. The philosopher Søren Kierkegaard talked about how our thoughts can get tangled in our heads and hearts, leading to skepticism. Nothing could be more liberating than to make a deliberate, committed move toward God—even when we don't have answers to all our questions. Kierkegaard called this a leap of faith. I prefer to see it as a reasoned "next step."

Kierkegaard wasn't suggesting that we can believe whatever we want to. How many times have you heard someone say, "That's my truth"? As he explained in his essay "The Present Age," Kierkegaard meant that each of us must make a deeply personal commitment to seeking the truth, and when we find it, we must stick to what we find. This leap of faith, then, isn't a blind jump into further uncertainty, but an open-eyed step forward based on the truth we have found.

At some point in your spiritual journey, you will be required to take that next step of faith toward God. Why? Well, as it stands right now, we can't see God or hear His voice. Yet His "fingerprints" are all around us—in nature, in the moral law imprinted on all of humanity, in our internal longings. But the common external guideposts that govern all relationships, such as vocal tones, body language, and facial expressions, are absent.

One day we will see Him face to face and hear His voice audibly. When you're in heaven, you won't need faith any longer. You'll be right there with God. But not yet, not now. So, as Paul noted, "We live by faith, not by sight" (2 Corinthians 5:7 NIV). We can and should examine the evidence that reveals God to us, but we should do so with the understanding that all the evidence in the world means nothing without the will to believe it.

Faith is more than mere acknowledgment. To move from seeing God as an impersonal "higher power" or "great spirit" or "the man upstairs" to loving Him as your Father in heaven takes a paradigm shift in how you see yourself in relation to Him. It's one thing to acknowledge the existence of God; it's quite another to trust in that God. It's like skydiving: It's one thing to acknowledge the greatness of a parachute while sitting in a training session on the ground; it's another to jump out of a plane with nothing but that parachute strapped to your back! Faith is betting your eternal life on Jesus Christ.

Risking a Leap into Life

A skeptical physician was once tending to his patient, a strong lifelong believer in Christ. After he concluded his work-up, he said to her, "You know, I just don't get the whole faith thing. I suppose I believe in God, and I'm pretty convinced that Jesus was real, but I've still got my doubts. It just feels like something is missing."

"Here's the difference," she responded. "I've known that you're a good doctor, skillful and thorough. I have always thought that if I got sick, you'd be around to help me. But a week ago, everything changed. When the cancer came, I let you cut into me and

> Whenever we examine information about God or evidence for His existence, there comes a point where we must choose to believe or not.

remove some things I can't pronounce and give me some medicine I still don't fully understand. My trust in you went from theoretical to actual. I once believed in you hypothetically; I have now come to trust you concretely."

Faith isn't just accepting that there is a problem and that God is a spiritual doctor who can cure you in some abstract way. Faith requires receiving the remedy. Whenever we examine information about God or evidence for His existence, there comes a point where we must choose to believe or not. When we activate our faith, that pleases God.

Belief unlocks the door to knowing God. But it's more than just that initial entrance, that first leap of faith; rather, it's a life of faith. It's an ongoing process of belief, built on daily acts of faith in different stages of life. Every day we jump out of the airplane, so to speak; every day we submit to the doctor's procedures. Faith is putting all our eggs in God's basket.

That's why faith takes humility. We can never know everything there is to know about God. God is infinite; we are finite. God is transcendent; we are tethered to time and space. Though we may take almost every opportunity we can to learn about God in His Word, from other Christians, and through the challenges life brings our way, He will always be beyond our human ability to fully grasp or understand. And we should be good with that. He wouldn't be God if He wasn't way beyond us. There's always something new and wonderful to learn about Him, enough to fill the eternity we'll spend with Him one day.

The Oldest Mistake in the Book

But some people make the mistake of being prideful. They think they've got God figured out. They have an idea of God and they stick with it, despite evidence to the contrary. Some see God as benevolent, if maybe distant, smiling down and approving of all our choices as long as we're sincere in making them. But if they read the

Bible long enough and walk with God far enough, they will discover another side of the divine nature.

They'll read all those inconvenient passages in Scripture that speak of God's holiness, justice, and wrath—and it shocks them. "God hates sin? Hell is real? Jesus will judge us all?" Those facts can be hard to accept. At that point a person must make a choice: to keep on following God with a more fully-orbed view, which will require faith, or abandon such troublesome Bible verses in favor of their previously held (and idolatrous) view of God.

In *Your God Is Too Small*, J.B. Phillips came up with a great list of all the different versions of God that people want to believe in.[11] I'll add my concerns about each parenthetically. They included the Resident Policeman (who wants to worship a cosmic killjoy?), the Parental Hangover (how can we have a mature faith when God is our mental embodiment of our parents' shortcomings?), the Grand Old Man (though many love this winking "it's-just-a-little-sin" fellow, he is not God), Meek-and-Mild (a growing faith requires seeing God as "not safe but good"), and the Managing Director (who can find comfort in a God who set the wheels of this overwhelming universe spinning, then went on a permanent coffee break?), among others.

> God wants us to get past our tendency to limit Him...He is always greater than our present concept of Him.

These are not God as He is, but God as we want Him to be. They're all limited views of a limitless God. We sell God short when we call Him our conscience or old-fashioned or a myth, or see Him as an escape from our problems, or worse, as a reflection of our upbringing or remnant of our childhood. God wants us to get past our tendency to limit Him, our attempts to wrap our minds around Him and get Him down on paper. God is infinitely greater that our bottom line, and He is always greater than our present concept of Him.

Embrace the Tension

As you read this book—and more importantly, as you read the Bible—you will encounter God in ways you didn't expect. The thought will strike you that God is different from the idea you had of Him. Some of His ways will surprise you with joy or relief, and others will shock or even challenge you. Every new discovery will require you to grow in your faith, to accept what you don't fully grasp, to take the limits off God even as you develop a broader framework of your life as a believer. Turning away is always an option, but avoiding the fullest picture we can obtain of God is turning away from faith.

So when it comes to knowing God, you may need to take a step of faith. Embrace the tension. You may need to say, "I don't know God as well as I thought I did, and I'm willing to change." When we seek God by taking well-reasoned and reasonable steps, He will be pleased, and we will be rewarded; God doesn't require a shot in the dark. But when we accept that a step of faith is a necessary response to the God who exists, who knows and cares for us, we'll be ready for the second great responsibility: pursuit.

The Joy of Pursuit

The writer of Hebrews tells us that God rewards those "who diligently seek Him" (11:6). God wants you to pursue Him. Isn't that true of any relationship? Whether you're married, dating, or single, you want someone you care about to care about you—not only to know you exist but to think you're worth getting to know. Any healthy relationship requires mutual pursuit, and relationships stagnate when the pursuit is abandoned.

Over and over, the Bible tells us not only that God can be found and known but that He loves it when we seek Him. King David told his son Solomon to get to know God: "If you seek Him, He will be found by you; but if you forsake Him, He will cast you off forever" (1 Chronicles 28:9). David put a similar thought in song: "There is truly a reward for those who live for God" (Psalm 58:11 NLT). The prophet Jeremiah shared God's promise to the faithful seeker: "You will seek Me and find Me, when you search for Me with all your heart" (Jeremiah 29:13). We all know Jesus's familiar guarantee that asking leads to receiving, seeking to finding, and knocking to opening (Luke 11:10). We are to seek God, and He will respond. James made the math simple: "Draw near to God and He will draw near to you" (James 4:8). Relationships are about the pursuit.

In all of this, though, we are talking about our response to what God did first. Our pursuit of God is our answer to His initial pursuit of us. God made the first move; He always does. As "Prime Mover" of the universe, He expects an honest response. "Don't bargain with God. Be direct...This is not a cat-and-mouse, hide-and-seek game we're in" (Luke 11:10 msg). He does not play games with us. If we are able to seek Him, it's because He came after us first. "We love Him because He first loved us" (1 John 4:19). He made the first move, revealing Himself in a number of ways we'll explore in the pages ahead. That revelation demands a response. After all, Jesus didn't tell us to casually snack after righteousness; rather, we are to "hunger and thirst" for it (Matthew 5:6). When we do, He will satisfy us.

Your pursuit ought to be an intentional, committed response to a God who intentionally committed Himself to you in Christ. When you look at the list of people in Hebrews 11, the Hall of Faith, that's the thread woven throughout each of their lives: faithful pursuit in response to the God who is and who cares.

What is your chief pursuit, your master passion? What do you want more than anything else in life? Only you can answer those questions. And you need to. Surveys, polls, and research all point to the typical answer: People want to be happy. The Declaration of Independence touts our right to the pursuit of happiness, along with life and liberty. Faced with the uncertainties of their children's future, most parents admit they just want their kids to be happy. Let me tell you something that might surprise you: God wants you to be happy too.

How we go about pursuing happiness is the key. At some point, we all look for it in the wrong places, in human relationships and accomplishments and accumulation, and surprisingly, even within the church itself. Now, education may open opportunities, money may buy certain comforts, and status may purchase a type of satisfaction. But God made you, and He knows what it takes to make you truly happy.

Hardwired to Know God

The psychiatrist Carl Jung thought of God as an unknowable reflection of the human condition. As he considered the impact of this on the mind, he said, "About a third of my cases are suffering from no clinically definable neurosis, but from the senselessness and emptiness of their lives. It seems to me, however, that this can well be described as the general neurosis of our time."[12] What Jung called neurosis, I call refusing to deal honestly with God. Only God can truly satisfy our souls. He hardwired us to be empty without Him.

I grew up with a friend named Tony, a talented and determined guy who set goals personally and professionally and achieved them at a young age. I liked his carefree, caution-to-the-wind attitude in life and was always amazed by his drive, charisma, and Midas touch in business affairs. I'll even admit to a tinge of jealousy. He had it all: homes, property, exotic cars, and a string of well-connected friends. But to look at him today is to take a sobering look at the future of any who, like Tony, would do life without God. Ask him how he's doing, and he'll tell you, "I'm miserable. I've run out of goals." We can point out the comparatively shallow nature of living to get more material things, but even the loftier goals of the men I mentioned earlier in this chapter pan out the same way—or worse.

People can only satisfy themselves to the limits of their capacity. Whether our goals are material like Tony's, psychological like those of Freud or Jung, social like Marx's classless society, or scientific and naturalistic like Einstein's theories, all of them are limited to what the human mind—even the most brilliant—can achieve. But God has no limits. He made you and knows what you need to be happy.

Furthermore, God promises rewards to those who pursue Him. One of those rewards is satisfaction—the fulfilling contentment of being what you were created to be. Remember, the more you do as you please, the less you are pleased with what you do. If you make life all about you, you'll never be satisfied. But the more you do what pleases God, the more pleasure He will give you in that pursuit. That includes taking care of all the things you need on an everyday basis. "Seek first the kingdom of God and His righteousness, and all these things shall be added to you" (Matthew 6:33).

Augustine confessed, "You have made us for yourself, and our heart is restless until it rests in you."[13] If God is your chief pursuit, your master passion, He will take good care of you. If you give Him an honest chance, He will provide what you truly need—meaningful relationships, daily provision, perseverance with hope. He knows everything about you, including this essential truth: Without Him, you are lost. Beyond the restlessness and hunger for more that we all feel at some point, God is waiting to calm your soul. Let God be God to you, and it's all going to work out.

I know you have questions. That's good—I'm glad you do. How else could you have a meaningful life? I hope to give you solid, biblical answers to some of the most common ones. But know this: You can know God. "The secret things belong to the LORD our God, but those things which are revealed belong to us and to our children forever" (Deuteronomy 29:29). Commit yourself to act in faith as you encounter Him, believing that He wants you to know Him better. Let's open the door—there's Someone I want you to meet.

Chapter 2

IS ANYONE UP THERE?

Proofs for God's Existence, Part 1:
Ontological and Cosmological

I used to hate watching *The Wizard of Oz*. I know it's a classic and that it was the great breakthrough movie of 1939 when color film was made popular to a world that mostly knew black and white. But tell that to a little kid who was scared stiff by the flying monkeys swooping down to snatch their terrified prey! Who could sleep after seeing that? Nightmares were a guarantee.

But aside from that, the movie had its merits. You may recall the scene when Dorothy, her dog, Toto, and her three friends approach the Great Oz. Intimidated by his appearance, an enormous frightening head that floats in the midst of flames and speaks with a thundering voice, they fall back. But then Toto pulls a nearby curtain aside, revealing a man pulling levers and speaking into a microphone.

The man notices these uninvited interlopers, leans into the mic, and Oz bellows, "Pay no attention to that man behind the curtain!" But how can they not? They can't just *unsee* the charade played out in front of them. The man behind the curtain is the explanation for everything they had seen and heard outside that curtain. This new evidence reveals the truth—that Oz didn't really exist. They would have to look past their disappointment and try to find a new way home.

Is Anyone Up There?

We all reach a point in our lives where what we thought was true—the things we base our lives on—turns out to be not enough. Our failures overwhelm us, our successes underwhelm us, and we're forced to question what we've believed in. Some people have tried to follow God only to realize there was no guarantee of peace and quiet. Others have never bothered with God, but when life or circumstances get hard, they're forced to acknowledge, usually in desperation, that He exists.

Both kinds of people (and the myriad in between) must at some point come face to face with a serious line of questioning: How can we *know* that God exists? How do we know God isn't a fabrication of our mental state or a projection of our deepest desires and worries? How can we be certain that God isn't merely a fictional hope concocted by those who can't stand the thought of being alone in the universe?

The Wizard of Oz aside, I remember looking up at the stars as a kid, wondering about God. "Are You really there? Do You really exist? And if You do, how can I *know* that You exist?" I've since discovered I wasn't alone in my curiosity. It's human nature to want proof—something to hang on to that bolsters our belief (or the lack of it). Even most believers, if they're honest, can relate to Isaiah, who said to the Lord, "Truly, you are a God who hides himself" (Isaiah 45:15 ESV). Isaiah was affirming that most people want to worship a God they can see, touch, and display.

> It's natural to wonder where God is, or what He is doing, when hard times darken every horizon.

This is especially true in the midst of suffering. What bothered Job most about his painful season of loss was the seeming absence of God. He opined, "Look, I go forward, but He is not there, and backward, but I cannot perceive Him; when He works on the left hand, I cannot behold Him; when He turns to the right hand, I cannot see Him"

(Job 23:8-9). There can be a fine line between hope and despair when you're hurting. It's natural to wonder where God is, or what He is doing, when hard times darken every horizon.

Blurred Perspectives and Embedded Truth

When suffering bleeds into our otherwise peaceful lives, our theology tends to get fuzzy. Elie Wiesel discovered that. In his book *Night,* he describes gruesome scenes he witnessed as a Jewish teenager at Birkenau concentration camp during the Holocaust. Not only did countless people lose their lives there, but, as Chuck Swindoll put it, Wiesel's idea of God was murdered there too.[1] Something died in his soul. The prize-winning author Francois Mauriac, who wrote the foreword to Wiesel's book, noted, "For [Wiesel], Nietzsche's cry expressed an almost physical reality: God is dead, the God of love, of gentleness, of comfort...has vanished forevermore."[2]

Yet for most of us, if we're honest, a part deep inside us seems to know that God is there. Or at least we highly suspect that He is. Even Job, though confused by God's apparent absence in his suffering, affirmed,

> I know that my Redeemer lives, and He shall stand at last on the earth; and after my skin is destroyed, this I know, that in my flesh I shall see God, whom I shall see for myself, and my eyes shall behold, and not another. How my heart yearns within me! (Job 19:25-27).

Really, we want to know that we know. We would like some evidence. We're hoping the case is stacked in God's favor. In fact, we are wired to think this way: God "has planted eternity in the human heart, but even so, people cannot see the whole scope of God's work from beginning to end" (Ecclesiastes 3:11 NLT).

The French mathematician and philosopher Blaise Pascal (1623–1662) recognized this desire for proof as a consequence of humankind's need for God, driven by the fallout from sin. His description of this need has since been characterized as a "God-shaped hole"—an emptiness in each of us that only God can satisfy. Pascal understood that we look for God in all the wrong places and in all the wrong ways, and unless we find God Himself, the void will never be filled.

But if we are going to honestly investigate whether God exists, we have to be open to what we find. Years ago, I read a story from *The London Observer* that speaks to our tendency to believe in the most convenient view available, to be satisfied with less than the full truth. As we try to fill that God-shaped hole, sadly, a poor fit is good enough for many people.

> A family of mice lived in a grand piano. They enjoyed listening to the music that came from the Great Player. They never saw the Great Player but they believed in him anyway, because they enjoyed the music that came from the piano.
>
> One day, one of the little mice got especially brave. He climbed deep into the bowels of the piano and he made an astonishing discovery: the music did not come from a great player. Rather, the music came from wires that reverberated back and forth. The little mouse returned to his family, tremendously excited. He informed his family that there was no Great Player who made the piano music; rather, there were these long, thin vibrating wires. The mice abandoned their belief in a great piano player. Instead they took on a mechanistic view—that the music was a purely natural phenomenon.
>
> Soon, another one of the little mice got especially brave. He climbed up even further up into the piano. To his amazement, he found that the music did not come from reverberating wires, but rather from little hammers that struck the wires. It was those hammers that really made the music. So he returned to his family with a new description of the source of the music.
>
> The mice rejoiced that they were so educated that they understood that there was no great piano player, that the music came from little hammers that struck the wires. They

did not believe that there was a player playing the piano. Instead, they believed that their understanding of the universe explained all of reality. But the fact is, the Player continued to play his music.[3]

In spite of what the mice believed, the Great Player existed. In the face of all their discoveries and rationalizations, he continued to be the source of the music they heard and enjoyed. In the same way, God's existence doesn't depend on our belief. Yet we use our limited human understanding to define God in terms we can manipulate; all we like mice have gone astray. But even if we rule God out of our equations, He continues to exist, to play His tune that orders the universe, and He persists in pursuing us.

And God doesn't demand that we not ask questions about Him and the universe we inhabit; in fact, I think He would rather we dig in deeply and really ponder the evidence. Like the mice in the bowels of the piano, He wants us to make certain discoveries. But unlike the mice in the piano, He wants our observations to lead to right conclusions. He wants us to be open to what we find.

We All Want Answers

Maybe you're thinking, *Skip, you're wasting my time. I've never really had any doubts about God. I believe He exists.* If that's the case, I commend you for your belief, but you're in the minority. Most of us have had doubts about God's existence at one time or another. If you haven't, someone you know or will know has—your siblings or kids or grandkids, a neighbor or coworker or classmate—and the Bible tells us to be ready to give a reason for what we believe. So I hope you will be prepared. I hope you will allow this book to help make you ready.

I was abruptly awakened to this need to be prepared during my first week of college. Having come to Christ in the summer after I graduated from high school and having spent that summer wrapped in the warm womb of Christian fellowship and Bible study, I was birthed into the cold bright lights of intellectual antagonism on the first day of my integrated zoology class.

My professor publicly challenged my beliefs in front of my classmates. I stood alone as he announced his goal to overturn my naïve religious delusions throughout the course of the semester. He failed, but his hostility stayed with me, like a fading bruise. In the months and years to follow, things didn't get any easier. My undergraduate studies in radium physics, human anatomy, and clinical practice all came with professors who were blatantly unsympathetic to my Christian worldview. Surrounded by agnostics, atheists, skeptics, and a few nominally religious hangers-on, I found myself in a deep crisis of faith.

I needed good answers. I needed to know far more than *what* I believed in. I needed to know *why* I believed it, and I needed to be able to articulate that to others. I came to a place in my thinking where, if I couldn't find any good answers to satisfy me intellectually and share with others persuasively, I wasn't interested in just going along for the ride. That crisis led to a discovery—several, actually.

Not only did I find good answers, but I also found that faith was easier for some when certain obstacles were removed. Some people are predisposed to reject Christianity on intellectual grounds. A little bit of preparation on your part, using reason to explain the issues, could go a long way in preparing their hearts for a faith commitment. The apostle Peter said it best: "If someone asks about your hope as a believer, always be ready to explain it" (1 Peter 3:15 NLT). And Jude added, "Show mercy to those whose faith is wavering" (Jude 22 NLT).

So what evidence is there that God exists? In this chapter and the next, we'll look at what's called God's general revelation: clues from the cosmos and our own consciences about God's existence. In particular, we'll look at four proofs.

The Skies Speak: General Revelation

It's usually a good idea to start at the beginning, so that's what we'll do with God. The first two verses in the Bible tell us, "In the beginning God created the heavens and the earth. The earth was without form, and void; and darkness was on the face of the deep" (Genesis 1:1-2). The words "without form" and "void" (*tohu* and *bohu* in the original Hebrew text) mean there was emptiness, like the opposite of reality. They indicate that the primeval world was vacant and desolate, utterly uninhabitable and undesirable, until God made something out of nothing.

Some people can't swallow that last line—*What do you mean God made something?* Their philosophical predisposition biases them against any notion of God in explaining the existence of the universe. Opting instead to work off the notions of pure naturalism, they elect to believe that *no one plus nothing equals everything.* Make no mistake—that is also a position of faith, albeit sorely misplaced and lacking in sound reasoning!

First Proof: To Be or Not to Be (The Ontological Argument)

That opens the door to one of the first proofs of God's existence: the ontological argument. Yikes, right? Philosophers like to come up with fancy names for these proofs. When I studied philosophy in my graduate coursework, I realized that philosophers often talk about things they don't understand, and they make it sound like it's your fault! Sometimes, though, they touch on subjects worth discussing. And with a little help, we can understand the terms they use.

Ontology is just a way of talking about the existence of things. It addresses a simple but deep question: Why does *something* exist instead of *nothing?* The simple answer is because God wants it to. But of course, we humans have seldom settled for the simple answer.

It's one thing to ask, "Do I exist?" because here you are, asking the question, which shows that you exist. It's another to ask, "How do I exist?" or "Why do I exist?" In philosophical terms, we would say, "What is the *nature* of my being?" The *how* and *why* point us toward two options: a purpose-filled existence or a meaningless journey into nothingness. That second position is the upshot of atheism. But if our existence does have purpose and meaning, it begs the question: Who gave those to us?

The Ancients Try to Uncover God (and Fail)

The ancient Greeks—guys like Parmenides, Plato, and Aristotle—were some of the first to really dig into thinking about our existence. At first they kept it simple: Everything breaks down into two categories, being and nonbeing. In other words, something either *is* or it *isn't*. Then, Parmenides (b. 515 BC) posited that everything that *is* exists as part of one big reality. Reality is all there is and all that has ever been. Nonreality—anything existing outside of our reality—isn't even a possibility.

So if God exists, that would put Him in the same reality as us, which would mean He isn't a being who transcends us. A higher being would have to exist outside of this reality, but Parmenides said this is impossible. Everything just *is* and that's how it is. Not a very satisfying view of the universe, is it?

Plato (c. 428–327 BC) argued for more possibilities than that. He believed that nonbeing was a possible state of existence. He was trying to establish how humans might be different from God. But his claim doesn't help us prove God's existence because you can't say that "nothing" (nonbeing) is how we differ from each other or God. "If I exist, and God exists, what's the difference?" *Nothing*. So there's no difference between us and God? Yeah, that's not going to work.

Aristotle (384–322 BC) said that there are, in fact, higher beings who are different from us by nature. But these beings only exist metaphysically. They function almost like ideals, traits we aspire to have. They have no physical form and there's no interaction between us and them, so whether they exist or not doesn't really matter. And even if they do exist, they can't be known. So that's another dead end. Are you still with me? Good! Keep reading.

Medieval Guys Talk About God's Greatness

In the eleventh century, the Italian monk Anselm of Canterbury made a two-part argument for God's existence. First: By definition, God is the greatest thing we can possibly think of; He is perfect. But if He only existed as a thought, He wouldn't be the greatest. That leads to the second part of the argument: God therefore must exist in reality. And if His existence depended on a cause, He would not be the greatest being we can possibly think of. So God has no cause; He is uncaused. To sum up, if God is an uncaused reality, He must exist. In philosophical terms, God's perfection makes Him a necessary being. Some critics of Anselm's day, however, weren't willing to concede that such a perfect being could possibly exist. And so the dance went on.

After centuries of inquiry that led nowhere, Thomas Aquinas (1225–1274) moved the question in a meaningful direction. He argued that all beings have essence and existence. Essence is *what* they are (human, for example). Existence is *that* they are (as opposed to not being). In the case of humans, because we are finite (we have a beginning and an end), our existence is different from our essence.

For example, our bodies show our existence, but our souls contain our essence. But for God, because He is an infinite being, existence and essence are the same thing. That's what makes Him unique; that's what makes Him different from us.[4] If all this philosophy is giving you a headache, hang in there! This will become clearer when we look at the remaining arguments for God's existence. Keep in mind that it's one thing to think God could possibly exist, and another to believe that He actually exists. Even if we use logic and reason to build watertight arguments about God, a person can still choose not to take the step of believing in God. That's the step that matters most, no matter how many flights of stairs we take to get there.

We're Confused, but God Is Not

For all the different ontological arguments that have developed over the centuries, God doesn't tie us into pretzels when it comes to whether He exists or not. The Bible doesn't get lost in the philosophical woods. Genesis 1:1 just assumes that God exists: "In the beginning, God..." Scripture doesn't wrestle with different questions; it leaves it up to you to decide, based on evidence and faith, what you believe. But some people just won't be satisfied with the simple truths that God exists and that something exists rather than nothing because God said, "Let there be..." For His own reasons and purposes, God chose to create us. His decision, His will, are why something exists instead of nothing.

Even after wrestling with the ontological argument for God and coming to the logical conclusion that we exist because of God, how do we know that He is really out there? After all, we know we're here. So where is God? Philosophers can do all the mental gymnastics they want, but in the end, we want something we can sink our teeth into—a proof or argument that has hands and feet in the real world.

At this point, it's not a question of whether we exist. We're dealing with what our senses perceive—land and sky, people, animals and plants, thoughts and feelings. We know they exist. But how do all these things point to God? That moves us to the next proof for God: the cosmological argument.

Second Proof: How Did This Ball Get Rolling? (The Cosmological Argument)

Cosmology is the study of the universe and its origin. For the Christian believer, it includes the argument based on creation. Cosmology looks at the world in terms of causes and effects. There has to have been a reason for everything that exists—everything we see, hear, smell, taste, touch, and feel. Philosophers call this the first cause, and the argument is that wherever there is a thing, there must have been a preceding thought; wherever there is a thought, there must have been a thinker.

We look at everything we see and ask, "Where did it come from?" It's the classic question of the chicken and the egg. Every cycle has to start somewhere. When you consider every observable object in the universe, even taking into account the things you can't see, like atoms and particles, you eventually come to the question, "Who or what caused all this?" And if you answer "God," the buck stops there because nothing caused God. As Anselm noted, He is the uncaused Cause.

Again, these thoughts have been whirling around in human minds for millennia. Plato and Aristotle both reasoned back to an uncaused Cause, and other great thinkers built on their thoughts— Maimonides, Anselm, Aquinas, Descartes, and Spinoza. A German mathematician, Leibniz, started with the ontological question but gave a cosmological answer: "The first question that must be asked is: Why is there something rather than nothing?"[5] And he came to an answer: *Something* only happens with sufficient reason.

Nothing Comes from Nothing

As the renowned philosopher Julie Andrews noted in *The Sound of Music*: "Nothing comes from nothing, nothing ever could." Okay, she's actually a renowned soprano and Oscar winner, but she was onto something, wasn't she? Nothing can come from nothing, so why is there something? According to everything scientists and philosophers have discovered, something can't come from nothing. Atheists hate this truth because it means that the universe exists, in whatever form it exists, because a higher power chose to make it.

Perhaps you've heard about the Christian and atheist who were walking through the woods when they came upon a big glass sphere eight feet in diameter. The Christian asked, "Where did this come from?" The atheist said, "I don't know, but someone must have put it there." They both agreed. Then the Christian said, "Suppose this globe was a little bit larger—say, sixteen feet in diameter rather than eight. Will it still need a cause?" The atheist said, "Of course it will need a cause. If little globes need causes, then bigger globes need causes." The Christian nodded and said, "All right, what if the sphere was eight thousand miles in diameter and twenty-five thousand miles in circumference?" The atheist saw the trap that was coming and said, "Sure, I guess it would. If smaller spheres need causes and bigger spheres need causes, then enormous spheres would also need causes."

The Christian said, "What if the globe was as big as the whole universe—will it still need a cause?" And the atheist said, "Of course not. The universe is just there."[6] Many atheists mock Christians for saying, "Someone made something out of nothing." But they claim that nothing made everything out of nothing. Here's the point: Both conclusions take faith. But one takes solid evidence and bases faith on it, and the other has to ignore a logical fallacy in order to believe.

> Nature is full of evidence that points to an intelligent designer, not the myriad happy accidents that evolution is predicated upon.

I read about a missionary who said that he tried to explain the concept of evolution to a group of indigenous people in the Amazon rainforest. As he described the process of man descending from apes, he was met with roars of laughter. They were astounded that anyone would believe such a thing! To those who honestly examine the evidence that feeds the cosmological argument, the natives' laughter seems well-founded.[7] Nature is full of evidence that points to an intelligent designer, not the myriad happy accidents that evolution is predicated upon. Any field of honest inquiry—science, philosophy, religion—requires that we follow that evidence.

Playing Red Light, Green Light with the Universe

Is the universe all there ever has been, or did it have a beginning? Astronomers have obsessed over this question but have provided no certain answers, only theories and speculation. That's how we end up with creative but far-fetched ideas like the multiverse (infinite worlds full of infinite versions of you and the choices you make, and probably at least one where you're a mermaid). But even in this theory, where all possible worlds are competing to come into existence, there still had to be a starting point. Even if you believe in the big bang, the original mass existent for the big bang had to come from somewhere. Science is continually producing evidence that strongly supports the idea that the universe had a beginning. The concept of the steady-state theory (once held by scientist and atheist Carl Sagan), which says that the universe is eternal, is a dying one and presents too many problems. As Robert Jastrow, founder-director of NASA's Goddard Institute for Space Studies, put it, "A sound explanation may exist for the explosive birth of our universe; but if it does, science cannot find out what the explanation is. The scientist's pursuit of the past ends in the moment of creation!"[8]

Whether the universe is infinite or finite has definite implications for our view of God. In an infinite universe, there is no God; otherwise, God would just be another being in the universe with us. In that case, God would not be God the way the Bible describes Him, and all of our big questions about life would be unanswerable. That's pretty unsatisfying. The search for a more satisfying answer points us toward a finite universe, something with a beginning and an end. But it seems that many people don't want to go there. We ask, "Is anybody up there?," but many of us don't want it to be God, or at least not the God of the Bible. Like with the glass sphere in the woods, people stop asking questions at a certain point because the answers might lead them somewhere they don't want to go. It's like playing "red light, green light" but refusing to go when God calls out, "Green light!" because you know the path is leading you to Him. But that's exactly where the cosmological argument for God's existence takes us. It takes into account that the universe is limited—that it had a beginning—and that beginning was caused by something beyond its boundaries. The argument can be summed up this way:

The universe had a beginning.

Anything that has a beginning must have been caused by something else.

Therefore, the universe was caused by something else, and this cause was God.[9]

Where Is the Evidence Leading You?

The lifework of scientists is the pursuit of knowledge. One of the main tenets of science is to follow the evidence where it leads. Where is it leading? We're a bit further along scientifically than we were 2,000 years ago. We now know that the universe is expanding. There's some debate as to what the rate of expansion is, but the fact that it's expanding is widely accepted.[10] The laws of physics indicate that whatever can expand will eventually be pulled back together by gravity. So eventually, the universe will collapse into nothingness. Scientists who buy into the big bang theory call this the big crunch. If you go past that point of total collapse, you'll move past the existence of time, space, and matter, perhaps even to a scenario the Bible describes as formless and void.

Speaking of space, time, and matter, you've heard of the theory of general relativity. In part, it says that space and time don't exist without matter. So if matter had a beginning, then time necessarily also had a beginning; thus, the universe is not eternal. Where does that lead us? Back to the beginning—and God. If the universe is not infinite, then it came from somewhere. Something caused it to happen; it requires a first, uncaused cause. No explanation provides a better first cause than God. That's what the cosmological argument boils down to—that God is the cause behind all the effects in existence. And the closer you look at our existence, the clearer that becomes.

This foray into all these philosophical arguments might feel like a long, hard climb so far, but don't despair. We now have two solid arguments that God exists and is active in our world. Review these proofs and anchor them to your heart. Not only will they boost your own faith, but you never know when you'll be able to share them in a conversation with a coworker, relative, or fellow customer in line at the grocery store. Now take a deep breath and let's look at the last two arguments.

Chapter 3

FOLLOW THE CLUES

Proofs for God's Existence, Part 2:
Teleological and Moral Law

Oh good, you're still here! The two arguments from the last chapter (the ontological and cosmological arguments) point to God's existence. Because *He* is, *we* are, along with the universe around us. Our existence depends on His existence. That's the only reasonable conclusion, and God has given us the ability to reason so that we can find the best ways to know Him and tell others about Him.

Remember—especially if you're a Christian—that reason is not a weapon. In using these evidences, you're not arguing people into the kingdom of God; you're just helping remove the roadblocks some people have been using as excuses not to believe in God. You are using reason to *pre-evangelize* those who have objections to accepting Jesus Christ. Paul "reasoned" with Felix (Acts 24:25), an unbelieving leader who was predisposed to dismissing the Christian gospel. Paul also declared to the Roman governor Festus that he was telling him "words of truth and reason" (Acts 26:25). Because unbelievers often have good questions, we should provide good answers. There's nothing wrong with using reason to help people understand truth; in fact, there's everything *right* about it.

Science and philosophy can help lead us down that path, but King David could have told us that. In fact, he did:

The heavens proclaim the glory of God.
　　The skies display his craftsmanship.
Day after day they continue to speak;
　　night after night they make him known.
They speak without a sound or word;
　　their voice is never heard.
Yet their message has gone throughout the earth,
　　and their words to all the world.

God has made a home in the heavens for the sun.
It bursts forth like a radiant bridegroom after his wedding.
　　It rejoices like a great athlete eager to run the race.
The sun rises at one end of the heavens
　　and follows its course to the other end.
Nothing can hide from its heat (Psalm 19:1-6 NLT).

Third Proof: Nature Is Designed
(The Teleological Argument)

As we look at the natural world, we notice it is highly ordered and tuned—as if it had been designed—something David credits to its reflection of God's glory. This leads us to a third line of evidence: the teleological argument, or the argument from *design*. Simply stated, because all design implies a designer, and because the universe reflects intricate design, there must be a Great Designer behind it all. That's what David meant when he said, "The heavens proclaim the glory of God." The ancient Greeks were perhaps the first in the secular world to infer design from observing the universe. Though Plato, Aristotle, and others believed in multiple gods and higher powers, they also reasoned that the world wasn't some kind of cosmic accident.

Believers see that God is confirmed by the splendor of His creation. That word, *splendor*, is one we don't hear too often these days. It speaks of magnificence, luxuriousness, or grandness. The image of royalty or extreme wealth it might conjure doesn't do it justice. As

Job said, "[God] comes from the north as golden splendor; with God is awesome majesty" (Job 37:22). And God, in setting Job straight, invited him to—if he could—become like God: "Adorn yourself with majesty and splendor, and array yourself with glory and beauty" (Job 40:10). God bestows splendor to His creation, which means it has value way beyond whatever science can say about it. Nature is the transcendent work of a transcendent being.

> We don't use science to prove God's existence, but we can observe the way it corresponds with a Christian view of God.

Science always tends to be in the process of catching up with the Bible, but even so, it's a tool we can use to know God better. As C.S. Lewis put it, "I believe in Christianity as I believe that the Sun has risen, not only because I see it, but because by it I see everything else."[1] We don't use science to prove God's existence, but we can observe the way it corresponds with a Christian view of God. In fact, science and faith go hand in hand—something we see in the life of one of history's best-known believers.

An Early Champion for Faith and Science

A young man in the fourth century played the prodigal. Though instructed in the faith of his devout Christian mother, Augustine of Hippo threw himself into partying and living the good life and didn't give a pig's ear about God. He went to school in the great north African city of Carthage, looking to make a name for himself as a philosopher. His beliefs shifted into warped versions of Christianity (Manicheanism and Neoplatonism), but he began to struggle with his lack of control over his fleshly appetites. One day, while walking in his garden, he heard a child's voice telling him, "Tolle, lege; tolle, lege" ("Take up and read"). On a table, he saw a book of Paul's letters he had been reading. He opened it and read the first thing he saw:

Let us walk properly, as in the day, not in revelry and drunkenness, not in lewdness and lust, not in strife and envy. But
put on the Lord Jesus Christ, and make no provision for
the flesh, to fulfill its lusts (Romans 13:13-14).

God's words rocked Augustine's world. He later wrote, "No further
would I read; nor needed I: for instantly at the end of this sentence,
by a light...of serenity infused into my heart, all the darkness vanished away."[2] I mention Augustine because after his conversion, he

> **The greater
> the design, the
> greater the
> Designer!**

became a great champion of orthodox Christian belief, defending the faith against assault
from many pretenders. It was only when he
surrendered his intellect to God that he
found peace—and discovered that intellectual pursuits and matters of faith were
compatible.

It's worth noting that Augustine reasoned from Genesis 1:12
that God made all of creation with the ability to reproduce itself.
He likened this potential to a seed that holds in itself everything it
needs to grow into whatever it is supposed to be—a tree, grass, a
crop. Many things can affect the growth of a seed—poor soil, lack
of water or sun, harsh weather, and so on. But everything a seed
needs to become all it was meant to be is present at the beginning
in a neatly compact package, not by accident but by design. Limited as he was by the scientific understanding of his day, Augustine's
understanding of Scripture was on target. As part of God's creation,
human beings grow from a fertilized seed and are filled with all
sorts of potential. But we're different from animals and plants in
that we have free will, as well as the ability to reason and question
and think of ourselves as more than just physical beings. Free will is
what makes us ask these deeper questions about our existence, all of
which eventually lead us back to God. The greater the design, the
greater the Designer!

The Discoveries of Science Point Toward the God of the Bible

Science and the Bible are not at odds. That's what the eighteenth-century philosopher and apologist William Paley believed. In his classic argument for design, he maintained that someone finding a watch in an open field would surmise that a watchmaker was responsible for its existence, rightly believing that design doesn't happen naturally without outside action. Paley's argument holds: No one would see a watch in a field, a dictionary on a shelf, or a car in a parking lot and assume these accidentally came into existence by themselves.

> Science provides clues that point to God, and faith is able to move beyond what science can offer.

On three different occasions I've visited Mount Rushmore and looked up at those four presidential faces on their granite perch. I have never heard a guide insist that those faces were produced by chance over billions of years. Anyone can easily see that the rock was carved, that designers and artists turned the mountain into a monument. It required purposeful energy to create those profiles. But what about the real-life presidents that those stone carvings represent? Would anyone suggest that Washington, Jefferson, Roosevelt, and Lincoln—each a human being possessing far more intricacy than their stone depictions could ever convey—came about by random chance and natural processes over billions of years? MIT-trained professor Dr. Gerald Schroeder frames the point well:

> Other than sex and blood cells, every cell in your body is making approximately two thousand proteins every second. A protein is a combination of three hundred to over a thousand amino acids. An adult human body is made of approximately seventy-five trillion cells. Every second of every minute of every day, your body and every body is organizing on the order of 150 thousand, thousand, thousand, thousand,

thousand, thousand, amino acids into carefully constructed chains of proteins. Every second; every minute; every day. The fabric from which we, and all life, is built, is being continuously rewoven at a most astonishingly rapid rate.[3]

To suggest that such a complexity of activity is the result of fortuitous occurrences of accidental circumstance is absurd. Randomness is simply not a satisfying explanation for the existence of the natural world. One scientist figured that the odds of a one-celled animal coming about by pure chance would be 1 in $10^{40,000}$. The odds for an infinitely more complex human being to emerge by chance are too high to calculate![4]

Christians don't have to be afraid of science; in fact, the church should make an ally of it. You can combine science and faith without sacrificing an ounce of integrity in either area. Science provides clues that point to God, and faith is able to move beyond what science can offer. Science can only appeal to reason. Faith can also appeal to reason, but it can then move beyond reason into mystery—that is, past sheer logic and reason's ability to explain, acceptable only based on other proof. The apostle Paul saw the merit of this distinction. He addressed both the idea and impact of design when he wrote to the Christians in Rome:

> [The unrighteous] know the truth about God because he has made it obvious to them. For ever since the world was created, people have seen the earth and sky. Through everything God made, they can clearly see his invisible qualities—his eternal power and divine nature. So they have no excuse for not knowing God (Romans 1:19-20 NLT).

A two-hour drive south of where I live, the Very Large Array near Socorro, New Mexico, listens to the universe. Each of its twenty-eight antennas is an eighty-two-foot dish with eight receiving monitors. This facility has made discoveries about everything from ice on Mercury to supermassive black holes.[5] The advancements made possible in science are fascinating, but what's really behind humankind's interest in deep space? Could it be a search for intelligence beyond the earth, for answers that can explain the way things are here? I can't help but wonder if researchers expect to find God out there among the quasars and Einstein rings, far away and otherwise engaged.

But we don't have to go nearly that far to find God. David's point in Psalm 19 is that God has already shouted His message through the stars we can see from the ground. An honest look at creation itself should convince us of the Great Designer's presence and genius. When you look at a constellation or a sunset, a cloud formation or a shooting star, you're looking at God's creativity. And if the art before your eyes is that glorious, what must the Artist be like? This is why Paul said that people have no excuse for not recognizing God. The universe itself is the canvas of God's splendor.

The Devastating Power of a Fine-Tuned Universe

As we observe the universe, we notice patterns—in galaxies, a chameleon's spiraling tail, wind-made ripples on water or sand, honeycombs, sunflowers, the spiral of a pinecone's scales, spider webs, snowflakes. Certain patterns are so common that they're predictable—even if the examples are uncommonly beautiful. Did these patterns just happen that way, or were they made that way on purpose? And if they just happened by chance, why is our environment on earth so well-suited for the kind of life we find here?

Scientists often speak of these favorable conditions as the fine-tuning of the universe. We live in the so-called Goldilocks zone— the habitable zone where everything is *just right*. Not too close to the sun to burn up, not too far to freeze. Just enough oxygen in our nitrogen-rich atmosphere to keep us breathing comfortably. A moon just far enough away to create regular tides and biorhythms. An axis tilted at such an angle that we

> The fine-tuned universe is one of the most compelling arguments for God's existence.

have four seasons. The examples go on and on, and to explain these remarkable conditions by naïvely saying, "It just so happened" is almost hilariously myopic.

In our finely tuned universe, everything matters—from the location of celestial bodies to the distance between atoms. Jupiter, for example, absorbs a huge amount of cosmic waste that would otherwise hit us. The asteroid belt beyond Mars does similar work. That protective function extends from planets to the unseen energy responsible for most of the stuff in the universe. Scientists have concluded that even the spiral shape of the Milky Way galaxy plays a crucial role in sustaining life on Earth.

The fine-tuned universe is one of the most compelling arguments for God's existence. More than just encouraging anyone predisposed to put faith in an intelligent designer, it has the power to devastate anyone trying to refute such design exists. Some of modern history's most influential atheists have pivoted their entire belief system after confronting the truth of life and how it defies all odds to exist.

The Wonder and Risk of Following the Evidence

Antony Flew was an atheist's atheist. For fifty years, he argued rigorously against God and Christianity, even debating before the Oxford Socratic Club (whose president was C.S. Lewis) and delivering papers on the inherent flaws of trusting in Christ. Many atheists looked to Flew as a hero, providing grist for the mill and fodder for their cannons.

But in 2004, he shocked his followers with a simple but unequivocal statement that the universe must be the work of an intelligent designer. What changed his mind? The study of DNA. Flew said,

> By the almost unbelievable complexity of the arrangements which are needed to produce (life), that intelligence must have been involved in getting these extraordinarily diverse elements to work together. It's the enormous complexity of

the number of elements and the enormous subtlety of the ways they work together. It is all a matter of the enormous complexity by which the results were achieved, which looked to me like the work of intelligence.[6]

Flew even admitted, "I now believe that the universe was brought into existence by an infinite Intelligence." These statements sent massive shockwaves reverberating through the hallowed halls of higher learning. For decades, Flew had stated that the burden of proof for God's existence was on the theists, those who believed in God. But the evidence of the basic building blocks of life overwhelmed him and changed his mind.

A single DNA molecule, the building block of all life, caries the same amount of information as an encyclopedia volume or a massive dictionary. To use Paley's analogy, no one seeing an encyclopedia or dictionary lying in a field would ever hesitate to believe it was the product of intelligence. Its degree of complexity points to design, not a billion-year-long course of evolution. You don't look at a painting, read a poem, or listen to a concerto and say, "Wow, how cool that all this just randomly formed into this specific composition!" Antony Flew looked at the complexity and function and form of DNA and realized, "This isn't random. This had to have been made with purpose, on purpose." He followed where the evidence led him, which prompted him to ask, in his words, "Has science discovered God?"[7]

Other scientists have followed suit, some exchanging atheism for belief in God and others following long-held Christian convictions, but without forsaking scientific principles. Among them are the director of the human genome project, Frances Collins; astrophysicist Jennifer Wiseman; theoretical physicist Freeman Dyson; and Nobel Prize winners such as neurochemist Sir John Eccles and chemist D.H.R. Barton, who said, "God is truth. There is no incompatibility between science and religion. Both are seeking the same truth."[8] Robert Jastrow, NASA's Institute for Space Studies developer, said, "For the scientist who has lived by his faith in the power of reason, the story ends like a bad dream. He has scaled the mountains of ignorance; he is about to conquer the highest peak; as he pulls himself over the final rock, he is greeted by a band of theologians who have been sitting there for centuries."[9] Someone is up there, and He is patiently awaiting those who take the long path—a journey painstakingly cluttered with unmistakable clues.

Fourth Proof: We All Possess a Moral Compass (The Argument for Moral Law)

The final clue pointing to God's existence moves us away from the huge cosmos and into the human conscience. All human beings on Earth, no matter their culture, country, language, or education, share a common feature: We all have a moral compass. We possess a basic idea of what is right and wrong. Granted, this can vary from people group to people group. Customs and current values depend partly on social conditioning. But built into the fabric of a human being is an anchor of morality, the idea that things should be a certain way.

We're often not aware of moral law as such. But from the time we are children we can recognize when something is unfair. This is what prompts one nation to rise up and defend a poorer, more helpless nation against oppressors, or a child to protect a school friend from a bully. This moral compass is at the heart of every major public policy issue today, from abortion to euthanasia to same-sex marriage to capital punishment. We may not agree on what is right and wrong with each of these issues, but we all have a sense that there *is* a right and wrong inherent in them.

How Do We Know Right from Wrong?

Where did this sense of right and wrong come from? Why is it so universally felt? Even the agnostic or atheist will say, "Look at this world—there's evil everywhere. Things aren't fair. From natural disasters to disease to unbridled greed, inequity and injustice are all around us." They are unwittingly articulating the existence of moral law. Often they'll conclude from that sense of wrongness that because evil exists, God cannot. If God is a moral being, and there is immorality, God can't exist. But think about it: When someone says something is wrong, how can they know that? They can't, unless they're appealing to a standard that is said to be right. That's the moral law. Morality, this sense of ethical decency and principled goodness, involves comparison. If I show you a picture of Mother Teresa and a picture of Adolf Hitler and ask you who is the better person, you know the answer instinctively and factually, unless you grew up in a censored society or maybe took a really weird philosophy course in college.

In the same way, you can't say there's injustice unless you are appealing to a standard of justice. That requires belief in a higher standard of truth and decency and goodness. And where did that standard come from? Because all people are conscious of a moral standard or law, that implies there's a moral Lawgiver.

C.S. Lewis, an Oxford scholar and one-time stout atheist, was converted by this reasoning. He said, "My argument against God was that the universe seemed so cruel and unjust. But how had I got this idea of *just* and *unjust*? A man does not call a line crooked unless he has some idea of a straight line."[10] This is what the apostle Paul meant when he said, "The truth about God is known to them instinctively" (Romans 1:19 TLB).

A Modern Champion of Faith and Science

Francis Collins was the head of the Human Genome Project, which aimed to map the full extent of human DNA. I caught wind of this brilliant scientist's spiritual awakening when I spotted his book *The Language of God* in an airport newsstand. This Presidential Medal of Freedom recipient grew up agnostic and became ardently atheistic as his scientific career advanced. But then he read *Mere Christianity*, and C.S. Lewis's arguments influenced him. Collins was compelled to be intellectually honest. He realized that he had drawn conclusions about God without examining all the data, a cardinal scientific no-no.

I was able to speak directly to Collins about his spiritual life after hearing him speak at a medical conference. He confirmed in person what he had written in his book about the eye-opening journey he had undertaken: "I had started this journey of intellectual exploration to confirm my atheism. That now lay in ruins as the argument from the Moral Law (and many other issues) forced me to admit the plausibility of the God hypothesis...Faith in God now seemed more rational than disbelief."[11]

Your conscience tells you there is a God. Otherwise, you wouldn't ask the question, "Is there a God?" That question is instinctive, part of your makeup. Dogs don't ask that question, nor do cats, frogs, or dolphins. But people do. However, that doesn't mean some of us don't fight our instincts. As Paul said,

> What happened was this: People knew God perfectly well, but when they didn't treat him like God, refusing to worship him, they trivialized themselves into silliness and confusion so that there was neither sense nor direction left in their lives. They pretended to know it all, but were illiterate regarding life (Romans 1:22 MSG).

People continue to hold science in higher esteem than what their own hard-wiring tells them, but as NASA pioneer Dr. Wernher von Braun observed regarding science's many proofs for God's existence, "Must we really light a candle to see the sun?"[12]

Follow Paul's thoughts as he forged his way through this argument:

> Even Gentiles [think of Gentiles here as agnostics and atheists], who do not have God's written law, show that they know his law when they instinctively obey it, even without having heard it. They demonstrate that God's law is written in their hearts, for their own conscience and

thoughts either accuse them or tell them they are doing right (Romans 2:14-15 NLT).

In other words, the conscience of every person tells him or her that there is a right or a wrong. That's our default setting. It's how God wrote our software. However, the conscience can become calloused, hardened, and desensitized by every decision we make that goes against the moral law. In that sense, the worst thing that can happen when you lie or cheat is to get away with it. If you don't get caught, you may never feel driven to repent—and continued lack of repentance only hardens your heart.

But generally speaking, the value systems in almost every culture dictate that certain actions are wrong—for example, murder, theft, or adultery. The argument from moral law says that the existence of God is the best explanation for this phenomenon.

Fifth Proof: The Argument from Experience

Up to this point, all the arguments I've articulated (and you've patiently waded through) are objective evidences; that is, they can be understood by analysis and are based on facts. They can be examined and evaluated by anyone. Inquirers can discover them by an honest search in the fields of philosophy, natural science, and moral law.

This next argument, however, is a subjective one. That is, it cannot be evaluated by *all*—only by *you*. I am talking about your own experience with God. I saved this one for last because your experience can't be relied on all by itself—that's the beginning of the slippery slope of moral relativism. When everyone determines their reality based on "their truth," the idea of objective truth gets waylaid.

Some people claim to have had extraordinary experiences that cannot be objectively corroborated. I've had people insist to me that they had been abducted by aliens, and it's as good an explanation as any for the way they are. The same goes for those who have seen

Jesus's face in a tortilla. Some will say that these experiences prove that God exists (or that aliens do, or whatever it may be). Now, I'm not saying these people don't believe what they're saying. But the sheer subjectivity and randomness of their experiences undermines the credibility of their argument.

Subjective experience apart from objective analysis isn't enough to arrive at truth. For example, someone might tell you, "I smeared a rotten banana all over my head and it changed my life. Now I have peace, joy, and can communicate with monkeys." Well, that may be a valid experience for that person. But is there anything objective that we can tie this experience to that's provable? For instance, how many people throughout history have smeared rotten bananas on their head and walked away saying, "I have peace and joy and I can talk to monkeys"?

By contrast, the Christian experience has been shared by many. Scores of people for generations have shared remarkably similar testimonies, no matter their country of origin, culture, background, or age—in a nutshell, they say, "I have received Jesus Christ as Savior, and this is how He changed my life." That story has been repeated over and over for the past 2,000 years by people whose behavior and thoughts have undergone a radical about-face, and who were then willing to lay down their lives for the cause of Christ.

Eye to eye with death—in the arena, at the stake, at gunpoint—and given the chance to go free if only they would recant, these believers refused. Subjective belief unanchored in objective truth doesn't withstand such weighty scrutiny. Mere stubbornness or an iron will are more likely to melt away when faced with such a bottom-line consequence. We're only human, right?

The logical conclusion is that these people must have been saved by the same God through the same Savior by the same grace, the same truth, the same gospel. Changed lives are themselves a proof that God exists. When subjective experience can be tied to objective evidence, it only fortifies the argument for God's existence. That personal knowledge, however, must go beyond the evidence of general revelation and anchor itself in the specific character, nature, and will of God Himself. And thankfully, God has revealed Himself specifically, in a written revelation so compelling that anyone who reads it would have to consider that God is not just interested in relationship but driven by it.

Chapter 4

NOW IT GETS PERSONAL

Proofs for God's Existence, Part 3:
Specific Revelation

We still haven't answered the question posed in the first chapter: *Who is God?* Giving reasons for God's existence is a good start, but we must probe deeper. Once we concede that He does indeed exist, we must then ask, What kind of God is He? And why not a *she*? Why do we refer to God in the male gender? Where do we get the notion of God as a supreme being who created the world and maintains it, even interacting with human lives? Does this come from deep within us, or is it simply the result of cultural conditioning and parental influence? Or does it come from an outside source (like the Bible) that is testable and therefore can be counted as reliable? Can the sixty-six books that comprise the Christian Bible be trusted to tell us about God, the human condition, and our future?

In high school, I remember some seniors wearing what I considered dorky smiles on their faces while carrying Bibles around campus. The West Coast revival known as the Jesus movement was in full swing, and it seemed like everyone was getting caught up in this latest of fads. I viewed all the activity skeptically and didn't want to have anything to do with it. One afternoon I even tried talking one of these Jesus people *out* of being a Christian. But within six months of that day, I found myself believing in Christ and experiencing the power of a transformed life. That summer after graduation, God would become personal to me.

To really know the God who exists, we need more than His general revelation. Augustine noted that even unbelievers know something about the earth, heavens, and other elements of this world. They can observe the patterns and motions of celestial bodies, the seasons that produce life on earth, and the predictable eclipses of the sun and moon. But while these may point us to the existence of God, they are in and of themselves not enough to reveal exactly who God is.

We've spent the first few chapters of this book establishing some bedrock truths about God: We can know that He exists and that He is powerful and creative. And we can do so without so much as cracking open a sacred book like the Bible. The path of reason will lead any observer of the universe to that conclusion. But without the guidance of the Scriptures, any further conclusions about the nature of God would likely be faulty. After all, God is much more than just a cosmic watchmaker.

Let's Get Specific

For example, contrary to the opinions of many of history's leading scientists and philosophers, God not only can be known—He *wants* to be known. God is personal and relational. We can see that from the many times God refers to Himself using male pronouns—but not because God is a man. God doesn't have a body; He is Spirit (John 4:24). We know He has all the qualities belonging to both male and female, since He made us in His image (Genesis 1:26-27). Men and women are equal in value before Him. In portraying Himself so often as a father, God is making Himself relatable to us. I don't know why He chooses to be Father and not Mother, but the Bible describes God as King, Father, Husband, Master, and Father of Jesus Christ. God incarnated Himself as a man, and we see the metaphor of the church as the bride of Christ. Paul called the mystery of marriage—of the union of husband and wife—a reflection of the relationship between Christ and the church (Ephesians 5:22-32).

Whatever the deeper meanings and implications of those parallels are, we know without a doubt that God desires unity with us.

To allow us to get to know Him, God not only gave us general revelation (what nature reveals about Him) to get our attention, but special revelation (what He said to and through various people in the Bible) to provide us with specific instruction about Himself. If we are going to discover anything about God's character beyond His glorious creative power, we're going to need more than what we can ascertain from observing nature.

King David spent many of his early years outdoors as a shepherd, and he declared that God's creation reveals His handiwork (Psalm 19:1-6). His is a poetic description, not a scientific text, but it is nonetheless clear that when we marvel at the sun, moon, and stars, we are bearing witness to God's designing hand. That's general revelation—what God has revealed about Himself in the natural world that we can infer using reason and deduction. This type of revelation is plainly available to all humans. No one is ignorant of it. As Paul said,

> Ever since the world was created, people have seen the earth and sky. Through everything God made, they can clearly see his invisible qualities—his eternal power and divine nature. So they have no excuse for not knowing God (Romans 1:20 NLT).

> **In the Bible, God has decided to reveal everything that humanity needs to know about Him, including what He has done for us and expects from us.**

And Paul himself appealed to this when he spoke to a crowd of Jewish and pagan people in Lystra, saying that God "has not left himself without testimony: He has shown kindness by giving you rain from heaven and crops in their seasons; he provides you with plenty of food and fills your hearts with joy" (Acts 14:17 NIV). So all people of all times can know that God exists, that He is intelligent, and that He is transcendent. But that's only part of the story.

God is so much more, which David made clear when he shifted in Psalm 19 from God's natural creation to God's written revelation:

> The instructions of the Lord are perfect,
>   reviving the soul.
> The decrees of the Lord are trustworthy,
>   making wise the simple.
> The commandments of the Lord are right,
>   bringing joy to the heart.
> The commands of the Lord are clear,
>   giving insight for living.
> Reverence for the Lord is pure,
>   lasting forever.
> The laws of the Lord are true;
>   each one is fair.
> They are more desirable than gold,
>   even the finest gold.
> They are sweeter than honey,
>   even honey dripping from the comb.
> They are a warning to your servant,
>   a great reward for those who obey them (Psalm 19:7-11 NLT).

David made sure his readers understood that God reveals Himself both generally and specifically. Generally, God shows He is there through the cosmos, cause and effect, and human conscience. Specifically, He reveals Himself through Scripture, the Savior, and history—His story. In the Bible, God has decided to reveal everything that humanity needs to know about Him, including what He has done for us and expects from us.

But Is It Personal?

Hold on! A book—the Bible—is the way to know God? How personal is that? To some this feels highly *impersonal*. It's like God wrote a letter telling us He's in charge, then He stepped away as the absentee landlord of the universe, never to be heard from again. How can you have a personal relationship with someone like that? Plus, so many different interpretations could be spun from reading such a book through the lenses of various backgrounds, experiences, and understandings. Leaving us a book, of all things, seems inefficient and detached.

Not so, I'll argue. All throughout the Old Testament, God certainly told humanity about Himself, but He also informed people that He was going to come to them. Over and over, through hundreds of prophetic passages, God told His people that He would send a Messiah who would show them *exactly* what God was like. That Messiah was Jesus.

Jesus, therefore, is the ultimate special revelation. The Old Testament anticipated Him, then He showed up on earth, doing miracles and preaching and teaching to show people exactly how He fulfilled the prophecies of the Bible. The author of Hebrews put it this way:

> Long ago God spoke many times and in many ways to our ancestors through the prophets. And now in these final days, he has spoken to us through his Son. God promised everything to the Son as an inheritance, and through the Son he created the universe. The Son radiates God's own glory and expresses the very character of God (Hebrews 1:1-3 NLT).

That seems like a pretty roundabout way for God to make Himself known, using nature to give hints, then prophecy to point to a brief but powerful visitation. But have you ever considered that God *wanted* to establish His existence, nature, and character like that? Like it or not, God chose to disclose Himself mainly though a long-distance letter. Why might He do so? I can think of two reasons.

The Ultimate Fact-Checker

The first reason is because using recorded prophecy has certain advantages. For example, when advance writers like the prophets commit their predictions to writing, those predictions can eventually be either authenticated or debunked. So when the prophets in the Old Testament announced a coming Messiah, they predicted where He would be born, what tribe of Israel He would come from, where He would live and minister, the kind of death He would die, the miraculous nature of His life, and His physical resurrection.

Either those things happened or they didn't. If they didn't, then the predictions are easily discredited as false. But if they did, then the predictions serve to authenticate the validity of Scripture and further endorse the person they predict. Because it's humanly impossible for a person to arrange the tribe and town he will be born into, the chance of any of those predictions being fulfilled becomes minuscule.

Bible prophecy isn't just a bunch of good guesses made by a bunch of good guessers. The predictions made in Scripture are layered with multiple contingencies and features that can't be known in advance and can't be controlled—at least by humans. Thus, the accurate fulfillment of those predictions is a huge confirmation of the divine authorship of Scripture, since there's no way those prophecies could be fulfilled by pure chance, even given 100 billion years!

Fire Insurance or Something More?

A second reason God may have chosen to reveal Himself through a book is because so much is at stake. You can snub the Bible, insisting that it's only one of many holy books filled with myths and stories, and definitely not the inerrant Word of God. But what if you're wrong? What if the Bible really *is* the truth? I contend that you have much more to lose than I do if *I'm* wrong.

This was Pascal's challenge. As the seventeenth-century French physicist and philosopher wrote in his book *Pensées* (or *Meditations*), "If we [Christians] are right, we gain everything, and lose nothing. If we are wrong, we lose nothing and gain nothing. Therefore, based on simple mathematics, only the fool would choose to live a Godless life."[1] Pretty basic, right? If God exists, we who are believers in Christ go to heaven and nonbelievers go to hell, and their loss is infinite. If, however, God does not exist, believers and nonbelievers alike gain nothing and lose nothing. Pascal suggested that when we weigh the options, the clear and rational choice is to live as though God does exist.

So let's consider this letter from God we call the Scriptures and discover why it's a crucial part of getting to know who He is.

Get It in Writing: God Revealed in Scripture

Why does God reveal Himself specifically? Because general revelation alone is not enough. General revelation (also called natural revelation) speaks of the existence and glory of God; it reveals an intelligent, powerful, and transcendent deity. Yet it is insufficient for us to actually know God. You can know all about a person's accomplishments without knowing their thoughts and feelings and beliefs—who they are as an individual—just as you can gather only so much about who an artist is from their art. To truly get to know the artist, you would need to meet them, to talk and interact with them, to laugh and reflect on life together. With God, that's where specific revelation comes in. And the first type of specific revelation is Scripture.

When David described the special revelation of Scripture, he used words like *perfect, trustworthy, right, clear, pure, true,* and *fair*. Here's his point: Nature can speak eloquently and powerfully to the existence and glory of a creator. But if you want to know Him personally, you're going to need more. You're going to need something special to know this unique being we call God, and that knowledge can only be found in the Bible—the written revelation and self-disclosure of God.

Why do you need more than nature? Because though the heavens speak eloquently, they leave a lot out. The stars, the moon, and the sun speak of the glory of God, but they don't tell you anything about the love of God, the plan of God, or the sacrifice of God. Special revelation fills in the blanks left by general revelation. If you want the full scoop, you've got to get it from the book, the owner's manual, the account of God's work through history as inspired by God Himself through the hands of human writers.

But don't other great faith traditions and religions have written scriptures, sources of divine revelation, as well? Muslims have the Qur'an and Hadiths, Hindus point to the Vedas and Upanishads, Buddhists make reference to the Tipitaka, Mormons to the Book of Mormon and the Pearl of Great Price, while Taoists lean on the Dao De Jing. So what makes the Bible special?

Beyond the manuscript evidence for the Bible's veracity and historicity, beyond the archaeological substantiation of people and places found in its texts, is the singular arena of Bible prophecy.

Against the Odds: The Power of Accurate Prophecy

Doesn't it stand to reason that if God desired to communicate with humans, He would want that communication to be verifiable? Wouldn't He want it to demonstrate supernatural evidence of His authorship? This is why, to authenticate His words, God employed prophets. They spoke and wrote down His messages far in advance of their fulfillment (which often took miracles to accomplish even then). The biblical prophetic account is stacked with a huge number of fulfilled predictions, giving us no reason to believe the rest won't also be fulfilled.

Now, the track record of other so-called prophets throughout history is so poor that critics assume the Bible must be wrong. Some skeptics claim that New Testament writers inserted Old Testament prophecies into the story of Jesus after the fact so that it would look like Jesus fulfilled all those predictions. The burden of proof, however, is on those skeptics, and they'll have a hard time proving their claim.

For instance, the Gospels have been shown to be historically reliable. Reputable scholars have traced their origins, matched them against contemporary historical records, verified that we have an accurate record of Jesus's actual words, and rebutted claims of coincidence, contradiction, and significant changes.

Furthermore, much of what Jesus said and did (such as His

claims to divinity in John 5:17-18, 7:28-29, 8:19, 8:58, and 10:30) went beyond the typical Jewish understanding of the Old Testament's messianic prophecies. That means the New Testament writers were interpreting the text according to the facts, not the other way around. For example, the resurrection helped New Testament writers better understand passages such as Psalm 22 and Isaiah 53.

The New Testament authors were also committed to what was written in the Gospels. Why would moral men lie to advance an agenda, and then die for that lie? Again, skeptics are the ones who have to prove their claim. There's no scholarly or historical reason to doubt the accuracy of the Gospels—only subjective refusals to deal with their message.

And if that's the case, we're left with a phenomenal record of fulfilled prophecy. Jesus Christ fulfilled over 300 prophecies about the Messiah in the Old Testament. The odds of Him fulfilling just sixteen of those is 1 in 10^{45}.[2] Just to give you perspective, scientists estimate that there 10^{82} atoms in the universe.[3] I don't know if mathematicians have even come up with names for numbers that run that high. Let's just say that God's prophetic track record shows an incredible level of specificity.

And if prophecy demonstrates that God's Word can be trusted, we would do well to pay attention to what the Bible has to say to us. That's why we can never say something like, "I don't need to go to church and read my Bible; I'm just going to go camping and commune with God, because God is in nature." You can do that, but you won't truly get to know God if that's all you do. General revelation points us toward the fact that God exists. Acknowledging that is a huge step for many, but it's really just the first step toward knowing God. For more, you need special revelation. If we stick solely to general revelation, our tendency is to make up the things we don't know about God. The apostle Peter described the difference:

> We did not follow cunningly devised fables when we
> made known to you the power and coming of our Lord

Jesus Christ, but were eyewitnesses of His majesty. For He received from God the Father honor and glory when such a voice came to Him from the Excellent Glory: "This is My beloved Son, in whom I am well pleased." And we heard this voice which came from heaven when we were with Him on the holy mountain.

And so we have the prophetic word confirmed, which you do well to heed as a light that shines in a dark place, until the day dawns and the morning star rises in your hearts; knowing this first, that no prophecy of Scripture is of any private interpretation, for prophecy never came by the will of man, but holy men of God spoke as they were moved by the Holy Spirit (2 Peter 1:16-21).

Peter saw things you and I will never see. He walked with Jesus and saw Him heal and perform miracles on a daily basis. He stood on a mountaintop with James and John and watched Jesus become transfigured and shine with a miraculous blinding light. Peter saw firsthand the majesty and might of the Messiah, and it awed him. Read again what he said: "We have the prophetic word confirmed." All the prophecies that point to Jesus, that Jesus fulfilled and will fulfill, are even better and surer than the miraculous works He did.

The Bible is not some optional bonus added on to the Christian experience, to be dusted off for special occasions like funerals and weddings and to be sworn on in courts of law. Remember what Jesus said of its importance: "Man shall not live by bread alone, but by every word of God" (Luke 4:4). God's written Word is central to our lives. Without specific revelation, we wouldn't understand who Jesus is or His mission. He rooted His rescue operation firmly in Scripture, quoting Isaiah 61 and claiming that it was fulfilled in front of the very witnesses to whom He read it:

The Spirit of the Lord is upon Me, because He has anointed Me to preach the gospel to the poor; He has sent Me to heal the brokenhearted, to proclaim liberty to the captives and recovery of sight to the blind, to set at liberty those who are oppressed; to proclaim the acceptable year of the Lord (Luke 4:18-19).

Up Close and Personal: God Revealed in Jesus Christ

It's one thing for God to send prophets throughout history and have them write down the remarkable record that is the Bible. But God went a step further. He wanted to show mankind what He was like, so He came in human flesh, in the form of God the Son. Jesus Himself is the greatest proof of God's specific revelation. The apostle John attested to this when he wrote, "No one has ever seen God. But the unique One, who is himself God, is near to the Father's heart. He has revealed God to us" (John 1:18 NLT).

Think of it like this: We live in a big box that contains the universe. Two things qualify life in this box: time and space (it is always a certain hour, and we are always in a certain place). But we who are inside this box have a suspicion that there must be something more outside the box. And every time someone comes along and says, "I'll invent something about what exists outside our box," a new religion is born.

But we'll never be able to discover what's really outside the box on our own; whoever is out there would have to come inside our box and show himself. That's precisely what God did when He sent Jesus. So, how exactly did He pull this off? How does a transcendent, limitless God communicate with finite, limited beings like us?

> If you want to know what God is like, look at Jesus.

First, God wrote us a letter telling us that He was coming. He spoke to a select group of people—His prophets—giving them messages and instructions to pass on to His people. And those words, written down over the centuries, revealed the plan that He had all along: to take on flesh and become one of us, entering the box so that He could give His life for us and make a way for us to have a personal relationship with Him. That's exactly what Jesus Christ did. When He came, He showed us God!

That's why, if you want to know what God is like, look at Jesus. Don't look anywhere else, because Jesus is unique—"the image of the invisible God" (Colossians 1:15). He is the exact representation of God to us—His love, mercy, and holiness all on display in real life.

So if you want to know what God thinks about sin, listen to Jesus. If you want to know how God feels about love, peace, or family, look at what Jesus said. Without His specific revelation, we'd be left guessing about those things—and the sun, moon, and stars, radiant and glorious though they are, would offer cold comfort. God stepped into human history not only so that we could know Him, but also so that we could become part of His story.

The Record Speaks: God Revealed in History

History—*His story*—is full of evidence that points us to God. All the miracles recorded in the Bible are evidence of God's existence, part of His specific revelation. Sometimes referred to as *evidential apologetics*, biblical miracles help vindicate the case for Christianity and point people to trust in this God of personal power who is sovereign over His creation. The burning bush, the contest between Elijah and the prophets of Baal on Mount Carmel, David's defeat of Goliath—all are part of a mind-blowing catalog of God's interactions in history, proof of His desire that both His people and their enemies should know one thing: there is a God in Israel.

Former skeptic and journalist for the *Chicago Tribune* Lee Strobel borrowed a statement from the late philosopher Richard L. Purtill to define miracles. As Strobel explained, "A miracle is an event brought about by the power of God that is a temporary exception to the ordinary course of nature for the purpose of showing that God has acted in history."[4] Not all reports of miracles are credible or able to be substantiated. But the miracles of Jesus, especially the standout miracle of His bodily resurrection as reported in the New Testament, are corroborated by excellent data. Sources outside the Bible serve to confirm both His death and His resurrection. In short, no other faith tradition has the mountain of evidence to validate claims of the miraculous like Christianity does.

And God's miracles aren't random. Each one serves the purpose of introducing both the recipients and the witnesses to the One who made them and everything around them. David knew this; in essence, he told Goliath, "You're bringing your spear and sword, but I'm coming in the name of the Lord. And as you die, you will know who He is." Then there was Elijah, who prayed before the prophets of Baal, "Lord God of Israel, let it be known today that you are God, and there is no one like You." And when Pharaoh asked, "Who is this God, and why should I pay a lick of attention to Him or let His people go?" God's response came in the form of ten plagues, each a slap in the face to a different false god in the Egyptian pantheon. How's that for an answer, Pharaoh?

Skeptics try to explain these miracles away, but it's a Sisyphean task. Their arguments often end up requiring more of a miracle than the ones God actually performed, and their doubt rolls back downhill, crushing their case.

Taste and See: Personal Revelation

We've considered general revelation, or God revealing Himself in His creation and in the human conscience. We've seen God's special (or specific) revelation in the Bible, the person of Jesus Christ, and feats of history. But let's scale all of this down a bit. Let's set aside science and philosophy and theology for a moment and think practically. Let's get down to where we live.

Part of the more detailed portrait of God that specific revelation paints is a specific requirement: We must respond to Him. If God exists, what are you going to do about Him? What will your response be to such life-defining truth? If Freud and Feuerbach and Marx are correct and we're alone in the universe, then what's the point? That way lies hopelessness. But if they're wrong and the Bible is right, if our consciences and cause and effect and creation tell us about God, we had better do something.

Once God's truth has been revealed to us, we will remain miserable if we don't respond to it. We can get mad about it, and we can call it foolishness and belittle those who cling to it, but we can't ignore it. Here's why: We will each answer to God one day. After all, the Bible says, "It is appointed for men to die once, but after this the judgment" (Hebrews 9:27). If there is a God and if one day we are going to face Him, what are we going to do about that?

> God does not force Himself on us. But He has presented enough evidence, both within us and around us, to keep us from ignoring Him.

That becomes the preeminent question on a personal level. George Bernard Shaw crystallized this beautifully when he said, "The statistics on death are quite impressive. One out of one people die."[5] We get one shot, and then we answer to the One who gave us that shot. The next logical step, then, is to make general and special revelation a personal revelation. That's the meaning of the text we started with in chapter 1: "Without faith it is impossible to please Him, for he who comes to God must believe that He is"—that He exists, that He really is there—"and that He is a rewarder of those who diligently seek Him" (Hebrews 11:6).

God's special revelation shows us that He gave us free will. He does not force Himself on us. But He has presented enough evidence, both within us and around us, to keep us from ignoring Him. We can continue to keep Him at arm's length, acknowledging His existence while maintaining a philosophical or theological distance. But moral law makes that costly—we will constantly be fighting a sense that there is more to knowing God than just knowing that He is.

All this revelation should lead us to seek God—to surrender to Him and say, "You are God and I am not. I want to know You better. Here I am. Lead me." You can know all about the Bible, but you don't graduate from Bible study until you meet the Author. You can know all about the latest scientific discoveries, but you undermine their value until you meet the Creator. And you can insist that you're doing just fine without God, but you will live with a nagging sense that there's something more to life until you meet your Maker.

An atheist spoke to a university crowd. "God doesn't exist," he proclaimed, challenging everyone present to refute the various arguments he had made. "If anyone can prove I'm wrong, come on up," he said. Embarrassed silence echoed back. "Anyone?" he said, permitting himself a triumphant smirk. "Prove me wrong."

An elderly gentleman stood and came forward. Everyone in the crowd knew who he was: a respected member of a local church who used to be the town drunk. The speaker cocked an eye at him and asked, "Well, what's your proof?" The man said nothing. He took out an orange and began to peel it. The atheist's exasperation grew, and finally, arms folded, he exclaimed, "Well? Do you have any proof that I'm wrong?"

The old man slowly ate a segment of the orange, then asked, "How did this orange taste?" The atheist spread his arms. "How would I know? I didn't eat it." The man nodded slowly and said, "Exactly my point. What I have discovered is that I had to taste what Jesus was offering me to know if was any good. And I have found that what He has to offer is very good."

There is no God. Have you looked for Him?

I don't believe in Jesus. Have you investigated Him?

There is a point where our objections and doubts become a crutch. We use them to prop up an unexamined view or, having investigated, to keep God at arm's length. God has revealed Himself in so many ways. If you truly and honestly seek Him and you are open to what you discover, you will find Him—and you will find Him waiting with open arms to embrace you as His child. It's a subjective experience, to be sure, but one tied to an irrefutable objective reality: "Taste and see that the Lord is good" (Psalm 34:8).

Chapter 5

I'M GOD AND YOU'RE NOT: AN ENCOUNTER WITH GOD

Now that we've established that we can know God exists, that He can be known, and that He wants to be known by us, let's consider what it is to know God. Anyone dealing with such an immense subject as *God* must admit that knowing God is far more complicated than knowing anything else. Learning a language, for example, is a difficult undertaking but certainly doable. Knowing a puppy is fairly easy once you understand some basic canine instincts; after a few weeks, the relationship becomes pretty predictable. Having a relationship with a human is thornier because people may hide certain things from you, or change their attitudes toward you.

So what about knowing God? After all, we are dealing with the Creator and sustainer of everything. That complicates things...*a lot*! To know such a being first requires a high level of respect (what the Bible calls "the fear of the Lord") and the realization that our knowledge of Him can only be partial and incomplete. For humans to fully know God is as impossible as a puppy fully knowing its owner. Indeed, the level of our knowledge of God depends more on God than on us—He must decide to disclose Himself to us. I remember J.I. Packer's clear axiom, "The more complex the object, the more complex is the knowing of it."[1] I will say this, though: Despite any challenges we face in getting to know God, His invitation is worth accepting.

Time and Disclosure

Getting to know someone takes both time and disclosure. It requires a willingness to reveal yourself to the other person over a period of time. It's an involved process. The first time I met my wife, Lenya, I was at my previous girlfriend's apartment for a potluck. I saw this radiant beauty across the room and I went over and had a conversation with her. After being taken aback by her firm handshake and bold introduction—"Hi, I'm Lenya!"—I relaxed a bit as we talked about spiritual things. She had just become a Christian. She asked about music, hobbies, and the Bible, and as the evening wore on, I thought, *I want to know this girl better.*

A few days later, I gave her a call and I took her out. Our first date was a concert at church, a good, safe place to meet, and one that took minimal commitment. Our second date was at a nice seafood restaurant, where Lenya ordered chicken and I found out that at that time she hated seafood. I was learning, observing her likes and dislikes. On the third date, I took her to the beach so she could watch me show off my surfing skills, but there were no waves that day. So we ended up talking for hours. As time went on, we shared our backgrounds, family histories, spiritual journeys, and future plans. Time and disclosure were having their way.

I especially remember another dinner, about a year or so later, when we were reconnecting after a period of time apart. We talked at a deeper level about the things of God, what He was showing us, and our hopes, dreams, and aspirations. I was more honest and direct that night, and I felt Lenya was as well. We were now "baring our souls" to each other, and it was deeply satisfying. Shortly thereafter, I decided to go to the next level and ask this girl to marry me.

Now we've spent thirty-eight great years together and I'm still getting to know her. Marriage is a process, a lifelong development of living out what the Bible calls "one flesh." I've learned a lot along the way, discovering that I need to ask the right questions and listen the right way. Building a relationship doesn't happen overnight, but I will say that all the time and effort is worth it.

What Is It Like to Get to Know God?

That's the kind of relationship God wants with you: a singular, intimate experience that grows and develops over the course of your life. This relationship with God (like any relationship) involves *listening* as He speaks to you from His Word and the Holy Spirit interprets it to your soul. It also involves *learning* His attributes—His characteristics, His loves and aversions.

But unlike any other relationship, this involves building a rapport with the most unique being ever, one who is infinitely above us on every level and yet invites us into His presence and fellowship; therefore it requires worship on our part. And then to complicate things, God is invisible—He is outside of our time-space continuum, though very involved in it at the same time. This requires faith on our part. All these factors collide in Exodus 32–34 and will be the focus of this chapter and the next. This passage, which tells the story of God's personal revelation to Moses, is one of the few places in the Bible where God describes Himself, giving a list of His own attributes—those qualities that define Him. I mentioned earlier in the book that Genesis 1:1 assumes God exists and moves directly into a description of Him creating the world. It isn't until these chapters in Exodus that we get a formal introduction, with God telling Moses His personal name and describing His character and attributes.

> What you think about God determines what you think about everything else.

Why is it important that we learn about God's attributes? Because what you think about God determines what you think about everything else. If you get God wrong, your views about everything else will also be skewed: what you think about yourself, what you think about other people, what you think about the world, what you think about what is right and what is wrong. As A.W. Tozer said, "Whatever a person thinks about God is the most important thing about that person."[2]

The amazing thing is that God is thinking about us too. He had enjoyed personal interactions with people before Moses came along. God used to walk in the cool of the day with Adam and Eve in the paradise of Eden. He gave Noah the architectural instructions for building a floating zoo that would save the human race and perpetuate life on earth. God even called Abraham His friend (Isaiah 41:8). But Moses was special, even among that group. God revealed more about Himself to Moses than to anyone else in recorded history. Moses had already enjoyed personal (and powerful) exchanges with God up to this point, but they were limited, and Moses wanted more—*much more*. This story unfolds in four phases: revolt, request, revelation, and response.

Phase 1: Revolt

I call Exodus 32 the "Uh-oh!" chapter because it exposes one of Israel's greatest gaffes. Their mistake here marks one of the lowest points in the nation's history. God had called Moses to go up the mountain to meet with Him, and the people said, "Yes, please go, Moses! God's presence—all that shofar blasting and lightning and thunder and smoke—is terrifying us. We'll just hang out down here."

The sixth time Moses went up the mountain to meet God, the Lord gave him the Ten Commandments, etched in stone by His own hand. Moses was up there forty days and nights (Exodus 24:18). Even from the Israelite camp below, it was the greatest lightshow ever. But the people grew restless and went to Aaron, Moses's brother. "This guy Moses ditched us," they said. "We need some gods to lead us. What are you going to do about it?"

The irony here is thick: Moses was on the mountain receiving God's revelation, but the people turned surprisingly fast to their own imagination and crafted an idol—a golden cow. That's unexpected! During their deliverance from Egypt, they had seen the gods of the Egyptians get a royal smackdown by God's power. So why a golden calf? This isn't all that hard to figure out. Egyptian legend had it that divine lightning struck a cow and transformed it into Apis, a golden bull that symbolized Egypt's power.

While Moses was up on the mountain, the people saw lightning and heard thunder, and this likely reminded them of the legend of Apis. As the earth shook, some of the leaders might have thought, *If these people could see some visible display down here in the camp after those fireworks, it would seal the deal! We've got to make some image of God in His power—what better than a golden calf?* So the cow makes sense. The more fundamental question is why the people would make an image of God at all. It was probably because of that complicating factor mentioned above—*invisibility.*

God is invisible. We all have problems with that at some point. How do you have a personal relationship with someone you can't see, hear, or touch? H.G. Wells explored the problems of being unseen in his classic novel *The Invisible Man.* At first, being able to go around without people seeing you seems pretty cool—but it turns out to be a tricky gift. People don't trust someone they can't see. After all, there's no telling whether an invisible person is lurking nearby or eavesdropping. Over time, the invisible man in Wells' story became more and more warped in his morals and character, partly in response to his inability to have a trusting relationship with anyone. Not a happy ending.

Sometimes we may feel like the little boy who asked his mom, "Is God up there?" His mom replied, "Of course He is." And the boy said, "Wouldn't it be great if He just poked His head out once in a while so we could see Him?" We all yearn for that to some degree. We want visibility; we want manifestation. We relate to Isaiah, who said, "Truly, you are a God who hides himself" (Isaiah 45:15 ESV). Another translation says, "Truly, O God of Israel, our Savior, you work in mysterious ways" (NLT). One of those mysterious ways is that we must choose to believe in Him though we can't see Him.

We can't weigh God; we can't record His voice pattern; we can't photograph Him (though some insist on the far-fetched idea that God's face has been seen in reflections or clouds in certain photographs). To connect in faith to this kind of God is to defy sanity for some, though most of us are okay with it, or we've learned to be. But we still long to see Him, and the Bible promises that one day we will. We are "looking for the blessed hope and glorious appearing of our great God and Savior Jesus Christ" (Titus 2:13). But until that moment, when we see Him face to face, "we walk by faith, not by sight" (2 Corinthians 5:7).

So why is sculpting an image of God such a bad thing? Can't visible reminders inspire us to worship the invisible God? For some people, isn't devotion triggered or enhanced when prompted by a picture or statue? And yet, in the second of the Ten Commandments, God forbade His people to make images of Him. There are two reasons for this. First, there is no image in the universe that can fully represent God. An image could never capture all that He is because He is, by nature, unlimited. An image automatically limits our perception of Him. "To whom then will you liken God? Or what likeness will you compare to Him?" (Isaiah 40:18). The golden calf Aaron crafted may have represented God's power and strength, but it said nothing of His love, mercy, forgiveness, compassion, or justice—all key moral attributes of God's nature, and all absent in this calf-god.

The second reason is that once you have made an image of God, you have created Him in your image, in your limited perception of Him. In this image, you're seeing what your imagination has concocted, not what God's revelation has confirmed. That's why God forbade us from making images of Him—so that we can't guess at His body language or posture; we can't pit one of His attributes against another. God doesn't want us to pin down one part of His nature or character and make an idol of it. We must take Him on His terms, or not at all. That's the implication of the second commandment. Anything else is idolatry and rebellion.

At the heart of every revolt against God's commands is a lame excuse, but when it came to the creation of the golden calf, Aaron's was award-winning: "Don't get so upset, my lord...You know how evil these people are" (Exodus 32:22 NLT). Aaron went on to explain to Moses that he had asked the people to give him all their gold. "When they brought it to me, I simply threw it into the fire—and out came this calf!" (v. 24 NLT). A police officer once handed me a list of actual excuses he had heard on the job. It included such gems as a guy running two straight red lights, then telling this officer, "Hey, it's a V-8—you try and stop it!" But whatever the excuse for speeding on our roadways or worshipping a shiny cow in the desert, the law was broken.

What lame excuse might you or someone you know attempt to give for not coming to Christ or submitting to God's will and purpose? What would constitute a good excuse for ignoring God's offer of salvation? That's a fair question. Many people bring up the fact there have been abuses of position and power within the church, but human error doesn't reflect God's intent to reach your heart.

You can't keep hiding behind those kinds of excuses. There will comes a point when you have to deal with Jesus one on one, no matter what has happened to you or been done to you. The world is full of sinners, and sometimes even the redeemed ones mess up badly. Your heart hungers for comfort, but the perfection you seek can only be found in God Himself, and in Jesus Christ you have God's clear message: "End your revolt and come home, child."

Phase 2: Request

Cleary, for the Israelites to make the golden calf was a debacle and personally upsetting to God Almighty. After the whole fiasco, God told Moses, "I'll send My angel with you, but I'm not traveling with you anymore." He didn't abandon His people, but He knew their stubbornness and hardheartedness would make it hard for Him to be among them. "If I did, I would surely destroy you along the way" (Exodus 33:3 NLT).

To their credit, the people took this news hard, especially Moses. He had a long talk with God, baring his heart to the One who had led him thus far. He begged God not to take His presence away, and then he made a candid and heartfelt request: "Please, show me Your glory" (v. 18). Moses had already experienced God's voice, God's power, and God's presence, but he wanted more.

Moses wanted to actually see God, to catch a glimpse of Him and receive comfort from Him in a personal, intimate way. God agreed—with certain stipulations. Precautions had to be taken so Moses wouldn't die from what would have been an overwhelming display of God's glory. God told him, "I will make all My goodness pass before you, and I will proclaim the name of the Lord before you" (v. 19). But God also told him, "You cannot see My face; for no man shall see Me, and live" (v. 20). He agreed to pass by, shielding Moses from the full impact of His glory and allowing Moses to see His back—"but My face shall not be seen" (v. 23).

You've got to love Moses's heart! He wanted nothing less than everything there was to experience of God. He wanted to see this invisible God up close and personal. When he spoke of God's glory, he used the Hebrew word *kavod*, which means "heavy" in the figurative sense, like the weight of a good reputation or important position. Moses wanted a full disclosure of all that God is—to have the weight of God's majesty press into his human experience. But God made it clear that the effect of that would be a like a bug getting too close to a pest control zapper.

What's interesting about Moses's request is that he had already experienced a lot of God—certainly more than most people had. He heard God speak to him from the burning bush, he saw God manifest His power in the plagues that broke the bonds of Egypt, and he watched God split a passage through the Red Sea so His people could get to safety—and then collapse the same waters on the Egyptian army, thereby securing Israel's freedom. That would be enough to satisfy anyone for a lifetime. So why did Moses ask for this?

Here's why: No matter who you are, how spiritually well-informed you are, or how knowledgeable about theology or conversant in the Scripture you are, this is what you long for at your deepest level: to see God. We all do. Even though we experience some presence of God when we gather at church or when we're alone in prayer and Bible study, we still want God to be visible.

Whenever I travel and have to spend time apart from my family, I miss them. These days I like to look at my iPhone pictures of them, but there was a time when I used to carry actual photographs of them. I would prop up a little frame and photo on the bedside table in a hotel, and even though this was a comfort when we were apart, it was never enough. I would call them just to hear their voices, and while that would tide me over, I still wanted to see them. In some ways, seeing their pictures and hearing their voices only accentuated my sense of loss, making me long for home. I wanted to see them face to face.

Moses's request revealed that he, too, wasn't satisfied. Once you've wrapped your head around the reality of God's existence, you spend the rest of your life wrapping your heart around it. Any deeply stirring experience you have in worship or prayer or reading the Bible was never meant to fully satisfy you. When you get a true taste of God, you will always want more. Our experience of Him here can only whet our appetite for more of Him. Complete satisfaction cannot come until we see Him in person. "When I awake," said the psalmist, "I will see you face to face and be satisfied" (Psalm 17:15 NLT).

I love what Tim Stafford wrote about this yearning to see God up close and personal:

> If Moses could not see what he wanted...then we should not be too surprised at our own sense of incompleteness. Our longing, even our frustration, is nothing to be ashamed of. If anything it is a mark of God's touch. We long to know him completely because we have come to know him in part.[3]

Phase 3: Revelation

If Moses didn't get exactly what he longed for, what did he get?

What could possibly be a concession for a one-on-one with God? What would God deem as the best substitute for Moses's longing to see Him? A game-changing revelation—a statement of character and intent:

> The LORD descended in the cloud and stood with him there, and *proclaimed* the name of the LORD. And the LORD passed before him and *proclaimed*, "The LORD, the LORD God, merciful and gracious, longsuffering, and abounding in goodness and truth, keeping mercy for thousands, forgiving iniquity and transgression and sin, by no means clearing the guilty, visiting the iniquity of the fathers upon the children and the children's children to the third and the fourth generation" (Exodus 34:5-7, emphasis added).

Moses did not see God directly. Rather, he heard God's words—His proclamation of His powerful name and a ninefold description of His character. Twelve other times in the Bible, this monumental moment will be recalled—when God gave His self-declaration to Moses.

When Moses asked to see God's glory, this is probably not what he expected. He didn't get a sign from heaven, a vision, or an apparition of the face of Jesus in some unleavened bread. He got words—glorious words, to be sure, but no fireworks or soul-tingling sensation. It was as if God was saying, "This is all you need." God has a well-documented tendency to give us not what we want but what we need.

We're familiar with the former, but not so much with the latter, which is why we're often surprised by what God does or doesn't do. When the apostle Paul begged God to heal him, God instead replied, "My grace is all you need. My power works best in weakness" (2 Corinthians 12:9 NLT). Paul didn't need a miracle; he needed God's grace to sustain him through his hard times. And God gave Moses words, not wonder; He gave him faith, not sight, essentially telling him, "Believe what I'm telling you about Myself."

When Jesus walked incognito alongside the two disciples on the road to Emmaus, He gave them a Bible study about the Messiah. Afterward, when they realized who He was, they said, "Did not our heart burn within us while He talked with us on the road, and while He opened the Scriptures to us?" (Luke 24:32). They didn't say, "Our hearts burned while He was glowing over there in the corner," or "Our hearts burned while we told Him about what happened in Jerusalem." Their hearts burned while Jesus spoke to them and revealed the Scriptures. What He said wasn't a new revelation but a new application of the old revelation of the Hebrew Scriptures and prophets. That was what they needed.

Everything you need is in the pages of the Bible. This isn't some pastoral cliché; we need to believe that what Peter said is true:

> His divine power has given to us all things that pertain to life and godliness, through the knowledge of Him who called us by glory and virtue, by which have been given to us exceedingly great and precious promises (2 Peter 1:3-4).

God's truest revelation isn't in the miracles He has done or the wonders of His creation. It's in the power of knowing Him through His Word.

A man once saved up all his money to go on a cruise. Every penny he had went toward purchasing his ticket, so he brought food on board, thinking it was the only way he would be able to eat: bread, peanut butter, and jelly. Day after day, he walked by the tables in the ship's restaurants, past the prime rib and lobster, back to his cabin, where he spread a bit of peanut butter on increasingly stale slices of bread and choked them down. Finally, after two weeks, the delicious smells overwhelmed him. He went to the porter and said, "Look, it's the last day of the cruise and I will do

> Everything you need—every tool, every grace, every bit of strength and wisdom for all of life's challenges—is given to you in the Word of God.

anything to eat what's on your menu. I'll wash dishes, swab decks, whatever." The porter laughed and said, "Didn't you know? When you buy a ticket, the food is included." The man had suffered needlessly. The food was already his; in his ignorance, he just hadn't taken advantage of it.

Everything you need—every tool, every grace, every bit of strength and wisdom for all of life's challenges—is given to you in the Word of God. Yet I meet people all the time who are searching for something more in the Christian life. I hear it in their prayers: they want more power, they want more of the Holy Spirit, they want more blessings, they want more glory. They want more, more, more. And God is saying, "It's yours. It's a package deal. You get the ticket to the boat, you get the meal."

Here's my question: Are you as excited about God's words as you are about His wonders? Because the essence of God's revelation to Moses was the list of His chief characteristics, accompanied by His promises to do what only He could do to save those who put their trust in Him.

Phase 4: Response

Even if God's words are all we need, we still want more—but we don't need more. That's why looking at Moses's response is important. After God spoke, "Moses made haste and bowed his head toward the earth, and worshiped" (Exodus 34:8). Another translation says, "Moses immediately threw himself to the ground and worshiped" (NLT). Here's what is noteworthy: Moses did not get what he asked for, but he still worshipped God. After God revealed himself to Moses, we don't see Moses saying, "This is not what I signed up for. I want tingles—I want to be moved emotionally. I want more than just words; I want wonders."

Here's why there's no record of that: After hearing God describe Himself in this list of attributes, Moses saw himself differently. He heard God's words and realized, "That's who God is." And then he worshipped because he saw himself with new insight. His worship, in effect, acknowledged this truth: "It's not about me, is it, God? It's not about what I want or how I feel. It's about You. You are God and I'm not."

Let that last phrase soak in: *You are God and I'm not.* Getting that wrong—often in the form of a reversal that says, "I am in charge, not God"—is our default setting. It's a mistake we have to be aware of, knowing we'll make it unless we are careful not to.

When Moses told God, "Show me Your glory," he was focusing on himself—his ideas about God, his experience of God, his status as a follower of God. We see this egocentric approach to God a lot these days: *What's in it for me? How will I be blessed?* People visit churches and ask, "What do you have to offer?" They want programs and a style of worship music that appeals to them and strokes their sense of self-worth, and a lot of them assume they have so much to offer that any church would be lucky to have them.

But which of your accomplishments could possibly impress God? Which of your degrees indicates you know more than the One who created space, time, and matter? Which of your awards shines a brighter light on you than the attention of the One who is Light Himself? Which achievement overshadows creation itself? Which network connects you to more people than the One who knows everyone and everything, including every thought you've had or ever will have? If you're feeling humbled, that's an appropriate response. The only thing you can offer the Lord is your heart and your worship.

> Wanting to experience more of God is part of loving Him.

I'm Not God; Now What?

In the next chapter, we'll zero in on the attributes of God. As we survey them, our response should be that of worship. For now, I'd like you consider three truths I pray will linger in your mind and heart about knowing the God who has revealed Himself this way.

First, longing is part of loving. Wanting to experience more of

God is part of loving Him. In fact, that's what God responds to—as we've noted, He rewards those who diligently seek Him. In seeking Him, however, know that you won't be fully rewarded until you see Him face to face. There are benefits now, but the ultimate reward is yet to come. Wanting to see His glory is natural, but to protect you, God says, "Not yet." It's a little like when you were a kid, waiting those last few weeks and days for Christmas to arrive so you could open your presents. Those presents are there under the tree—they're yours—but you can't have them just yet. Learn to love the Lord even as you long for Him.

Next, worshipping is better than wondering. Instead of worrying, "Does God not love me? Is that why I don't experience or feel or see more than I do?," focus on who He is. Every time God reveals Himself to you, whether through new knowledge or reinforced understanding, respond by worshipping Him. Because God is saying, "This is what you need, and it is all you need." And when you worship, you're saying, "You're right; it's enough."

Finally, invisible does not mean unavailable. It doesn't matter that you can't see God. What's most important is that God sees you. Let that comfort you as it did David when he wrote, "Where can I go from Your Spirit? Or where can I flee from Your presence? If I ascend into heaven, You are there; if I make my bed in hell, behold, You are there...Even there Your hand shall lead me, and Your right hand shall hold me" (Psalm 139:7-8, 10).

Job came to grips with the same truth.

> I go forward, but He is not there, and backward, but I cannot perceive Him; when He works on the left hand, I cannot behold Him; when He turns to the right hand, I cannot see Him. But He knows the way that I take; when He has tested me, I shall come forth as gold (Job 23:8-10).

When we enter into walking by faith and not by sight, God's availability becomes evident and His invisibility becomes irrelevant.

That understanding frees us to consider who He is, and who He is anchors us in every situation. All our questions fade, our excuses dissolve, and our hearts connect with the One who is calling us. It's a tremendous relief to rest in the truth that He is God and we are not.

Chapter 6

A CUP OF COFFEE WITH GOD: A SHORT AUTOBIOGRAPHY

Several years ago, a series of ads sponsored by the American Humanist Association appeared on Washington, DC buses just in time for Christmas. One of them read, "Why believe in a God? Just be good for goodness' sake," taking a line from "Santa Claus is Comin' to Town." The spokesman for the group, Fred Edwards, said, "Our reason for doing it during the holidays is there are an awful lot of agnostics, atheists and other types of nontheists who feel a little alone during the holidays because of its association with traditional religion."[1]

> The people who enjoy life the most are those who love God the most and realize that He loves them.

The British Humanist Association ran a similar campaign in England, with signs on buses announcing, "There's probably no God. Now stop worrying and enjoy your life."[2] The harangue seemed to be centered on organized religion—in particular, Christians who keep people from enjoying the holidays by trying to make it all about Jesus. But the ads reveal more than the makers likely intended them to: They implied that life is lonely without God, and that belief in God isn't pleasurable and one must seek alternatives to enjoy life.

That first implication is true: Life *is* lonely without God. Back in chapter 2, I mentioned the "God-shaped hole" in every heart. I need to clarify here that God didn't make us with a lack of something;

Adam and Eve were created ready for a fulfilling relationship with their Maker, and humankind was set to follow suit. However, the first couple's choice to follow their own desires over God's introduced sin and led to separation from God. That left us with a gap where our relationship with God used to be—something we were made with that is now missing.

The hole works on two levels: First, it represents a desire for relationship with God that comes from being made in God's image. God lives eternally in community—Father, Son, and Holy Spirit—so it makes sense we would desire community as part of our basic make-up. This is an essential part of us that can only be filled by knowing God. But the hole is also the gap left post-fall—a sin-caused separation that left all of us with something crucial missing from our souls. I experienced it before coming to Christ, and thousands of people I've talked to have as well. We all have a longing to know our Maker. The Bible says we were subjected to emptiness—part of the cost of our sin—and are now waiting with the rest of creation to be redeemed, set free from death and decay (see Romans 8:18-23). Sin punched a hole in every person's innermost being, but God used that deep-seated longing—that need to know Him—so we would wonder why it's there and do something about it (see Acts 17:27).

But the second implication of those atheists' attack ads—that following God means you can't enjoy life—is not true. I've discovered that the people who enjoy life the most are those who love God the most and realize that He loves them. The most compelling people I've ever been around are those who are so in love with God that they believe in and obey Him. They are centered, stable, purposeful, and therefore contented and even captivating. They find God to be the perfect—and only—fit for their greatest needs. Having the hole in the soul filled does wonders for one's outlook!

How do we get to know this God who wants to know us? How do we make sure we're on the right track? This is where the practical part of God's specific revelation comes into play. If you want to know the truth about God, read what He said about Himself—a reliable account that comes down to us through the centuries intact: the Bible.

As previously noted, J.I. Packer stated that ignorance of God "lies at the root of much of the church's weakness today."[3] I agree— but sometimes, to counter that ignorance, all you need is an introduction. And who could be a better source of that introduction than God Himself, in a statement recorded by Moses in Exodus 34? Think of this passage as God's autobiography—a short but complete description of God Himself. In it, God was telling Moses (and us) all the things that He is that we are not. This self-disclosure—God's revelation of His character and nature—is referenced many times later in Scripture. It's as if He sat down with Moses for a cup of coffee and told him about Himself.

So what does God say about Himself? Let's read:

> The LORD came down in a cloud and stood there with him; and he called out his own name, Yahweh. The LORD passed in front of Moses, calling out, "Yahweh! The LORD! The God of compassion and mercy! I am slow to anger and filled with unfailing love and faithfulness. I lavish unfailing love to a thousand generations. I forgive iniquity, rebellion, and sin. But I do not excuse the guilty. I lay the sins of the parents upon their children and grandchildren; the entire family is affected—even children in the third and fourth generations" (Exodus 34:5-7 NLT).

Designation: What's in a Name

As in any good introduction, the first thing God gave was His personal designation, His name: "The LORD, the LORD God," as the New King James Version puts it. When you meet someone, one of the first questions you ask is "What's your name?" And when you learn a person's name, that helps to separate him or her from the general masses of people all around you. It's the tip of the identification iceberg.

My father's name is Louis Frank Heitzig, and when I was born, the fourth of four boys, he told my mother he wanted to give me his name, Louis. He suggested Louis Frederick Heitzig, but my mom said, "Not so fast. I've always liked the name Skip." After a bit of back and forth, I ended up with all four names! Still, as the last in a line of Heitzig boys, I was often called by the one name my teachers knew they would get right—my last name. They knew that one wouldn't change.

In the Bible, a name is far more than an identity tag or a personal parental preference driven by popular name trends. Biblical names denote character, reputation, even a person's authority. It was typical to equate a person's name with that person's nature. In some cases, God told people what to call their children. Other times, the parents chose based on some distinguishing act or trait they saw when the child was a baby. Some people lived up (or down) to their names.

One modern study indicated that young men with unpopular or uncommon names were more likely to end up in jail.[4] That's a word to the wise for those families that might attempt to get too clever with their baby names—the Turners, who might name their little girl Paige, or Mr. and Mrs. Peace, who could call their son Warren, or the Bacon family, who might decide their son Chris should have the middle initial of P. My advice? Just don't.

In Scripture, sometimes parents gave a name because they were hoping for some fulfillment of that name in their child. For example, *Judah* means "praise," showing the hope that this child would grow up to praise the Lord. *Samuel* means "God hears." What a great thought—to want your son to grow up with the knowledge that God is always listening. Other parents named their kids after the circumstances of their birth—for example, the twins Esau and Jacob. Esau was born first and came out red and covered in hair, so they called him Hairy. That's what *Esau* means. His brother came after him, grabbing Hairy's heel, so they called him Heel-Catcher, or "one who stumbles another," *Jacob*. And the younger brother went on to trip up his older brother, tricking Esau out of his birthright as the firstborn. (God later changed Jacob's name to *Israel*, indicating he'd start fighting at God's side instead of against Him.)

In Scripture, you can find hundreds of names for God. Some are compound titles that describe Him, some detail His actions, and some are titles, but every name reveals a special facet of His utterly unique character. *Elohim* means "God the Creator, the strong and faithful one." *Adonai* is "the Lord, our Master," and *El Elyon* is "God Most High." But in Exodus 34:6, in His statement to Moses, God reintroduced Himself by His personal name, Yahweh, which simply means "I AM." That's the name He used when he first met Moses at the burning bush: "I AM WHO I AM" (Exodus 3:14). He told Moses, "This is My name forever, and this is My memorial to all generations" (v. 15).

You might say, "What kind of name is that?" After all, you've never met anyone else named *I Am*. Well, that's fitting, because God is as unique as His name. In Hebrew, "I AM" is *hayah*, which means "to be." For God to say His name is *hayah hayah*—"I AM THAT I AM"—is for Him to call Himself the Self-Existent One, perfectly eternal, the only being with no beginning and no end. It means that He is the only noncontingent Being—His existence does not depend on anyone or anything else.

God wasn't created. He doesn't need anyone or anything—not a helper, counselor, or doctor. No one can tell Him something He doesn't already know. He exists beyond our concepts of time past, present, and future. God is constantly in the present tense—the Great I AM, not the Great I WILL BE or I USED TO BE GREAT. He is both eternal and consistent in who He is.

The fact that God's name is in the eternal present tense tells us something else: He is active in our world. He is *doing*. Far from the deist's view of an impersonal God who made the universe and then stepped away to let it run on its own, free from His interference, the Scriptures reveal otherwise. Over the course of His revelation to Moses, God talks about His relationship to His chosen people: He is gracious, merciful, and longsuffering toward them. He isn't a detached watchmaker, an aloof engineer who set life in motion and moved on to other things. This is a choosing God, a feeling God, an active God, One who is involved in our lives.

The Jews revered the exclusive character of their God, which is why they were very careful when they wrote His name. When you see LORD in capitals in some translations of the Bible, it stands for four consonants in Hebrew, represented as *YHWH* and pronounced most often as *Yahweh*. That's God's name, often called by its Greek equivalent, the tetragrammaton.

God's name is so unique, setting Him apart from every other being in existence, that the Jews didn't want to risk mispronouncing it and somehow marring the holiness of it. So the Masoretes (Jewish scholar-scribes of the sixth to tenth centuries) took the vowels from the name *Adonai* and combined them with the four consonant YHWH, which gave rise to name *Jehovah* in English. *I AM* is as close as we can get to describing the indescribable. That's why we see the name written as *Adonai*, and many Jews simply refer to God as *ha'Shem*, "the Name." There is no name like it.

Description: What Is God's Nature?

When I was a kid, we had a family dentist whose name was Dr. Steel. I can still remember his tiny office down the road from our home with its antiseptic smell perfuming the air. But I especially recall after one particularly painful visit how well Dr. Steel lived up to his name (as in *nerves* of steel). With his tightly cropped military-style haircut and dispassionate, gravelly voice, this dentist didn't appear to care about my discomfort level—he insisted that the *spray* anesthesia he had given me would work as well as injectable Novocain. But it didn't! His name and his character were perfectly matched.

God's name goes hand in hand with His qualities (though on a much better level than Dr. Steel). The power of His name alone is enough to make it clear there is no one like Him. But God granted Moses the privilege of getting to know Him better. So He let Moses in on some of His characteristics. Like a powerful waterfall cascading out of a mountain ledge, God's name is the fountainhead of His attributes, and the river of God's character feeds three springs. Let's call them His beneficial, bountiful, and balanced attributes.

> The LORD passed before him and proclaimed, "The LORD, the LORD God, merciful and gracious, longsuffering, and abounding in goodness and truth, keeping mercy for thousands, forgiving iniquity and transgression and sin, by no means clearing the guilty, visiting the iniquity of the fathers upon the children and the children's children to the third and the fourth generation" (Exodus 34:6-7).

The God Who Is for You (God's Beneficial Attributes)

God chose an interesting first word to describe Himself: *merciful*. If we were to guess, we might think He would first say He was holy, sovereign, or even loving. The root of the Hebrew word translated *merciful* comes from a description of a mother's womb. It carries that sense of maternal compassion, the tenderness toward a child that only a parent can have.

When I first held my newborn son, I was overwhelmed by both love and the weight of responsibility. I also thought of the rotten, heartbreaking things I did to my mom while I was growing up, and as I cradled Nate, I had a new appreciation for her unending mercy and love. Though our kids can drive us crazy, that wellspring of compassion, that sense of wanting to pardon them, to make things right again, never stops flowing. Parental love is remarkably merciful.

Imagine that level of feeling coming from God, who is unhindered by human shortsightedness, criticism, and insecurity. As Oswald Chambers noted, "The love of God is not created—it is His nature."[5] And God had proved His love and mercy to Israel over and over. As we saw in the last chapter, Moses had come down from the mountain to find God's people worshipping a golden calf. Yet He didn't destroy them. The fact that Moses was now meeting with

God a second time demonstrates that God loves to offer second chances and longs to bring His wayward kids back into obedience.

The second quality God used to describe Himself is that He is *gracious*. This word shows up thirteen times in the Old Testament, always with reference to God, and it carries the idea of someone strong helping someone weaker. I'll sign up for that one because God is always using His strength to help me, the weak one—not to bully or harass or oppress me. God treats us well not because we are strong or we deserve it, but because the opposite is true. He gives us what we don't have and don't deserve. That's the whole idea of grace, an attribute fully evident in the Old Testament that comes into full blossom in the New Testament.[6] Paul summed it up when he wrote, "God demonstrates His own love toward us, in that while we were still sinners, Christ died for us" (Romans 5:8).

Toward the end of this chapter we'll see that God is not only merciful and gracious, but also just. For now, I want to mention the key differences between the three. Justice is getting what you deserve. Mercy is not getting what you deserve. Grace is getting what you don't deserve. For example, if a police officer pulls you over for speeding and gives you a ticket, that's justice. You got what was coming to you. If the officer lets you off with a warning, that's mercy—you didn't get what was coming to you. But if the officer gives you the ticket and then pays the fine himself, that's grace. He met the requirements of justice but went beyond even mercy and paid the penalty himself. (That would never happen, by the way, but I trust the point is made.)

On one occasion, when Nate was little, he and his cousin got into a fight and disobeyed my wife, Lenya. In response, she did something very unusual: She took them to the store and bought them a gift! The whole time, Nate was thinking, *When is the other shoe going to drop?* He knew what his mom was doing wasn't right. It didn't make any sense, and it didn't fit any previous parenting paradigms. He wondered when she was going to take away his gift and give him the punishment he deserved. He even asked her, "Are you going to spank me here in the store?" Lenya replied, "I want you to learn a lesson: This is often the way God treats us. Even though my heart is hurt by what you did, not only am I not going to give you what you deserve, but I'm going to give you a gift to show you how good God is to us." This made a huge impact on Nate, and years later, he told her, "Mom, I'll never forget that." That's the effect of God's grace.

The third trait God used to describe Himself is that He is *long-suffering*. Many translations put it "slow to anger," and *The Message* renders it "endlessly patient." God doesn't fly off the handle when you mess up. God doesn't need anger management classes when you rebel. Make no mistake: God's wrath is real, and He will execute judgment on this earth, but He is in no rush to get there.

Think of all the things you see in the world around you that make you mad. Night after night, the latest news breaks our hearts and creates a thirst to see justice done. A gunman unloads his firearm at a crowd, killing women and children. A coworker cuts corners and cheats on his time sheet but gets a promotion. Sometimes the injustice in the world can so overwhelm us that it's hard to see straight, and we may end up lashing out at whoever is nearby, regardless of whether they're the ones making us angry. Our anger can be like that depicted in old cartoons, where a thermometer rises into the "red zone" or a kettle comes to a fierce boil. But that's not God's anger. He's not doing a slow boil, putting up with sin until He loses His temper and then BOOM, the world ends. His wrath is perfectly measured and meticulously timed.

One meaning of the Hebrew word translated *longsuffering* is "long-nosed." The idea is that anger shows up in a person's nose as it turns red and the nostrils flare. The longer the nose, the longer it takes to get mad—like the cartoon thermometer. That's kind of a silly image—to picture God with a nose long enough to last till the end times, but that's helpful for us. As Peter noted, "The Lord is not slack concerning His promise, as some count slackness, but is longsuffering toward us, not willing that any should perish but that all should come to repentance" (2 Peter 3:9). When we ask, "God, when are You going to do something about all this evil?" God says, "I will do something—just not yet." His mercy, grace, and patience will last until the time is right, when as many people as are going to respond to Him have responded. Until that time, His qualities benefit all of us.

The God Who Fills You Up (God's Bountiful Attributes)

Another wonderful fact about God's qualities is that not only are they never in short supply, but they're always overflowing. Jeremiah noted that God's mercies are "new every morning" (Lamentations 3:23). And God told Moses that He is "abounding in goodness and truth" (Exodus 34:6). When we say the aphorism "God is good, all the time; all the time, God is good," we remind ourselves that His goodness flows from Him, into us, through us, and all around us, and it's never diminished. That statement, by the way, originated in Nigeria after a period of great persecution. When we suffer, God steps up even more. He never runs out of goodness and truth, love and faithfulness. That's who He is, and there is more than enough of Him to fill us, satisfy us, and flow out from us so we can show His qualities to others.

> God's love for you never changes...He knows all about you and loves you anyway.

The Hebrew word used in Exodus 34 for "goodness"—*checed*—is sometimes translated "love" or "lovingkindess." Applied to humans, it refers to loyalty, like what we would show to a friend. But whenever this term is applied to God, it speaks of unchanging character and constant love. God's love for you never changes. God is unshakable and *unshockable*. He knows all about you and loves you anyway. He never says, "I loved you more when I knew you less." Psalm 136:1 reminds us, "Give thanks to the Lord, for he is good! His faithful love [*checed*] endures forever" (NLT). Next time you hear that God is good, remember that He has made a commitment to love you *no matter what*!

God also abounds in truth. As Eugene Peterson put it, God is "so deeply true" (Exodus 34:6 MSG). We would say God is reliable and trustworthy. I have a friend we nicknamed Pencil. Whenever he set an appointment, he would always write his plans in pencil because he would change his schedule so often. Whenever he said he would be at a certain place at a specific time, we knew that meant he *might* be at a certain place at a certain time. But when God makes a promise, it's done. It's engraved. You can rely on God to keep His promises.

Some view God through the lens of abrogation—the idea that He can say something one minute and then take it back the next. But with God, there are no takebacks. He always says what He means and means what He says. He doesn't call something evil in one era only to call it good in another. Many people wish He did, because that would allow them to justify their tendency to lean whichever direction the cultural winds are blowing. But if God changed with society's whims, He wouldn't be God. His constancy is what enables us to remain anchored in any era, under every circumstance.

If you've ever gotten mad at God for His constancy in maintaining these good qualities, you wouldn't be the first. Some people are shocked that God could ever be merciful and gracious enough to forgive rapists, murderers, and child abusers. Jonah was angry with God for saving the Ninevites, who had a long history of violence and inhumanity. When God sent Jonah to Nineveh with a message of judgment, Jonah should've been licking his prophetic chops. God was about to bring down the most terrifying, brutal, bloodthirsty regime in the region. *Yes—finally!* Instead, Jonah tried to get as far away from Nineveh (and God's call) as possible. You know how that worked out for him.

When Jonah, bleached by gastric acid and reeking of fish, finally delivered God's warning, what he knew would happen is what did, in fact, happen: The Ninevites repented. Every single one of them. And he hated it:

> Didn't I say before I left home that you would do this, Lord? That is why I ran away to Tarshish! I knew that you are a merciful and compassionate God, slow to get angry and filled with unfailing love. You are eager to turn back from destroying people (Jonah 4:2 NLT).

Jonah called on God to kill him rather than let him live in a world where people as evil as the Ninevites could repent and be forgiven. God had one question for him: "Is it right for you to be angry?" (v. 4).

This scene raises an important question for anyone who identifies as a God follower: Do people see in you a reflection of the character and nature of God? We as believers in Christ often get it backwards, representing an anger we perceive in God that is not at the heart of His nature. We criticize and condemn when God desires to see people turn around and come home to Him. We lack mercy and grace and goodness while acting like we represent God's final say on a matter. But Paul told us to "be imitators of God as dear children. And walk in love, as Christ also has loved us and given Himself for us" (Ephesians 5:1-2).

What gives us the right to separate one of God's attributes from the rest? Why do we act like His truth is the nail and we're supposed to be His hammers? The truth is that God will do the judging—not us. The truth is that we are to be like Jesus, knowing that sin and judgment are real while embracing the mercy of salvation and extending God's grace to everyone we meet. We can and should defend truth, but never without the awareness that we need it as much as the people we're confronting. That's our commission.

I've been told that Antarctica is the healthiest place to live on Earth. No germs can survive there. The winds blow all contaminants northward, to temperatures and environs where they can thrive. But no one is signing up to take a vacation at the South Pole because it's usually 60 degrees below zero.[7] I think we Christians can sometimes become coldhearted in our attempt to make the world germ- and sin-free. *We've got to get all these heathens to shape up.* But God calls us to share His rescue plan in Jesus Christ. And that means imitating His abundant mercy, grace, patience, kindness, and truth by warming up our relationships with patient, steady love—seeking others' highest good the way God seeks ours. He isn't stingy with His gifts, and we shouldn't be either.

The God Who Is Fair (God's Balanced Attributes)

Balancing love and truth is perhaps the greatest challenge of a Christian's daily life—but God Himself is our model. After giving Moses His beneficial and bountiful attributes, God concluded His self-disclosure with a statement of theological and judicial balance:

> Keeping mercy for thousands, forgiving iniquity and trans-gression and sin, by no means clearing the guilty, visiting the iniquity of the fathers upon the children and the children's children to the third and the fourth generation (Exodus 34:7).

God began by again reminding Moses of His mercy, His *checed.* Why the repetition? Because His love and mercy is not just for Moses or Israel, but for "thousands"—it is for all people, a truth that resonates throughout Scripture. Jesus said that He came because God loved the whole world, and Peter echoed this when he said, "I see very clearly that God shows no favoritism. In every nation he accepts those who fear him and do what is right" (Acts 10:34-35 NLT).

We must always remember that God loves to forgive people. That's what motivated Him to send Jesus to the cross. Forgiveness is humankind's greatest need, regardless of our differences. In God's love, there is no place for distinctions in race, ethnicity, gender, age, and so on. We're all on equal footing before Him. We all need forgiveness for our sin, and there is only one way to be forgiven by God: through Jesus Christ. When we realize our need and come to Him as we are, with no excuses, He welcomes us with open arms.

But notice the balance in God's statement to Moses. On one hand, the Lord said He "[forgives] iniquity and transgression and sin." On the other, He says He will not clear "the guilty." But everyone is a sinner and therefore everyone is guilty. So which guilty ones will God forgive, and which will He not forgive?

God has a big eraser for anyone who will admit their sin and turn from it; He will forgive it all. But flip that coin and you'll see the other side of His beneficial and bountiful love: God is holy and just. He can't renounce His justice and let sin go unchecked. He must judge it. He must deal with it. That's the balance of His nature. We are all guilty of sin, and God does not forgive or excuse it just because we want Him to, or because we've lived good lives and have done good things.

This is how it works: Either you will accept that Jesus Christ was punished for your sin, or you will be punished for your sin. Those are the only two options. You can let Jesus become the sin-bearer for you and it's over—your sin is wiped from God's record books. Or you can bear your sin yourself and it is never over. God is willing to get rid of iniquity and transgression and sin, but only on His terms.

The last part of God's self-disclosure bears a closer look: "Visiting the iniquity of the fathers upon the children and the children's children to the third and the fourth generation." That means it's God's nature to forgive but not to remove the consequences of sin. Some misunderstand this verse to mean that God punishes children for their parent's stupidity or sin. But that would be unjust. God does not do that. He judges each person individually.[8] After all, "'Do I have any pleasure at all that the wicked should die?' says the Lord God, 'and not that he should turn from his ways and live?'" (Ezekiel 18:23).

While each of us stands or falls based on our own relationship with God, He still allows the natural consequences of sin to play out in our lives and the lives of those we love. That's what God meant when said He would "lay the sins of the parents upon their children and grandchildren" (Exodus 34:7 NLT). Our sin affects those closest to us. Things like abuse, addiction, and infidelity cause suffering not just in the lives of those who do them, but also in the lives of their loved ones—particularly their children, who will likely feel the effects of these sinful actions as they grow up and have their own children. It's tragic.

However, because God is longsuffering and merciful and gracious, He often uses suffering to draw people to Him. He doesn't write us off for making bad choices or being stupid or ignorant. He will save anyone who turns to Him. If you're still breathing and you turn from your sin, you can be forgiven.

> God won't always be what you want, but He will always be what you need.

And that takes us full circle to Jesus Christ. Just as the name God mentioned to Moses spoke of His nature, so the name of Jesus tells us who we're dealing with. *Jesus* simply means "God saves." In Hebrew, it's *Yeshua*—"Yahweh saves." An angel told Joseph to give this name to his son because "He will save His people from their sins" (Matthew 1:21). Jesus can be for you the opposite of what Dr. Steel was for me. He cares about your condition, your pain, and your future. *Jesus* was a common name in biblical times, but the power of this name is uncommon:

> God also has highly exalted Him and given Him the name which is above every name, that at the name of Jesus every knee should bow, of those in heaven, and of those on earth, and of those under the earth, and that every tongue should confess that Jesus Christ is Lord, to the glory of God the Father (Philippians 2:9-11).

In Jesus, we have the great I AM and everything that He is—gracious, merciful, patient, kind, truthful, just—coming down to our level, showing us who He is, and desiring a relationship with us.

The balance of His nature means we can't just be good for goodness' sake. His wants to help us, to fill our hearts with hope and our lives with purpose. But we have to receive Him, as He is, on His terms. All that God is, God will be to you. He won't always be what you want, but He will always be what you need. It's all there in His name.

Chapter 7

THE GOD WHO KNOWS IT ALL

God's Major Attributes, Part 1:
Omniscience

K*nowledge Is King.*
The statement seemed to jump off the kid's T-shirt. I liked
the design, color, and overall look of the shirt, but my mind immediately went into analyze mode. What was this statement really saying? Was it a message to would-be dropouts to stay in school? Did
it represent a sort of neo-gnostic pride in a special group of people
that possessed a special kind of knowledge that rest of us poor idi-
ots could never attain? The same statement has shown up in a number of places, including as the title of a 1989 album by popular rap
artist Kool Moe Dee.[1]

I now realize that the declaration "knowledge is king" probably hailed from the more widespread assertion that "knowledge is
power." We hear that phrase used in a wide variety of ways. Sir Francis Bacon, the seventeenth-century English statesman, first used this
aphorism to express how an education, which develops knowledge,
can, in turn, result in influence. Originally written in Latin as *scien-
tia potentia est*, the idea is that a person gains some kind of advantage when he or she possesses knowledge.

If knowledge is power, then what can be said of the One who has
all knowledge? A being who has all knowledge must likewise have
all power. Who better to appreciate the fact that knowledge is king
than the King of all knowledge? God created the universe, and one

way He proves His sovereignty is by His knowledge. In Scripture, God demonstrates this attribute in different ways—from knowing people's secret thoughts to predicting the minute details of events far in the future.

Knowing How We Know What We Know (and Don't Know)

The science of knowledge is called epistemology, which is a branch of philosophy that deals with the rationality of belief and how people come to believe things. Epistemology is concerned with giving an account of our knowledge. But knowledge ultimately has to do with the brain, which is amazingly fine-tuned to deal with the intake of information. In terms of raw memory, it is estimated that "the brain's memory storage capacity [is] something closer to around 2.5 petabytes"[2] (a petabyte is a million gigabytes). Conceivably, we could keep learning and storing information for centuries—if we lived that long.

Yet as humans, we're still limited. For example, attention helps preserve memory, but we can pay attention to only a few things at any one time. And even then, only certain types of information—like new experiences and unusual facts—tend to stay with us. Our brains are also sensitive to certain kinds of information at specific times of our lives. For instance, language is acquired early on, with sounds we've been exposed to becoming ingrained in the brain within the first year of life. Our brains are remarkable, yet also limited.

Is it any wonder, then, that we, as limited beings, cannot begin to fathom an unlimited being who knows absolutely everything? God is indeed the King of knowledge—not like the know-it-alls from your school days, but as someone who is always aware of every bit of knowledge there is, no matter how deep or arcane or far-flung. His breadth of His knowledge makes Google results look like a grocery list. The depth goes even further: He knows the thoughts, motives, agendas, feelings, and experiences of each and every person who has ever lived or will ever live. Trying to comprehend such infinite capacity will only blow our mental fuse. It's like trying to put the Pacific Ocean in a cup. When David tried to contemplate such horizons, he admitted, "Such knowledge is too wonderful for me...I cannot attain it" (Psalm 139:6).

What's the Most Important Thing to Know?

In that same psalm, David marveled at the God who knows it all and still loves us. Psalm 139 is like a highlight reel of four of God's most unique characteristics: His knowledge, presence, power, and holiness. Naturally, theologians have come up with fancy terms for three of these traits: omniscience (having all knowledge), omnipresence (always being everywhere), and omnipotence (having ultimately power). God is also holy—unlike any being who has ever existed or will ever exist.

The beauty and wonder of Psalm 139 is that David took theology off the top shelf and brought it down to a personal level. He used theology to inspire hymnology. He took a wide topic—God's nature—and narrowed it down, moving from the general to the specific and the theological to the personal, and then singing it out in a song. In this psalm, David described the extent of God's knowledge, studied it, and then responded with a fitting and necessary surrender. So let's begin where David did: by looking at just how much God knows—His omniscience.

The Value of Knowing It All

One Christmas, a befuddled husband wrote,

> Dear Abby,
>
> My wife insisted that I put the Christmas lights up this weekend. I went out of my way, taking valuable time away from watching football games to go out into the cold and put them up. Now rather than being appreciative of my efforts, she has stopped talking to me.

Signed,

Confused

His wife's response to his efforts would have remained confusing if this guy hadn't included a photo with his letter, which showed a snarled clump of lights hanging on a single nail.

To listen to his side of the story, you would think he had gone around the whole house, carefully stringing up the lights in the cold weather, and just happened to have the worst wife in the world. But having the whole truth makes a difference, doesn't it? As humans, we discover truth and accumulate knowledge bit by bit, through experience, research, and time. Then we have to sort through the reliability of the information, checking the sources and seeking confirmation or statistical support. Doing all this can be intimidating, frustrating, or just plain boring.

But that's not how God operates. He doesn't have to accumulate knowledge; He simply knows everything. We've all met know-it-alls (and some of us have *been* know-it-alls—by definition, you know who you are). They aren't much fun to be around, largely because they don't really know all there is to know; they just can't be told anything without acting like they do.

Again, God is different. He literally knows it all. Everything scientists and mathematicians discover, God already knows. Every insight philosophers and theologians gather, God already understands. And He knows the things no one else could possibly know—every thought in every mind, every possible outcome of every situation, every skeleton in every closet.

Genius Without Limits

If you've attended church for any length of time, David's description of God's all-encompassing knowledge in Psalm 139 will likely be familiar to you. But reading the familiar in a different translation (or in this case, a paraphrase) often freshens its impact, and I want these verses to surprise and rejuvenate you:

God, investigate my life; get all the facts firsthand. I'm an
open book to you; even from a distance, you know what
I'm thinking. You know when I leave and when I get back;
I'm never out of your sight. You know everything I'm going
to say before I start the first sentence. I look behind me and
you're there, then up ahead and you're there, too—your
reassuring presence, coming and going. This is too much,
too wonderful—I can't take it all in! (Psalm 139:1-6 MSG).

God is the ultimate knower in every field of knowledge. Without needing to learn anything, He knows everything—more stel-
lar astronomy than any astronomer, more algebraic geometry than
any mathematician, more quantum field theory than any physicist, more behavioral psychology than any therapist, more business
theory than any entrepreneur, more neurology than any brain sur-
geon, more theodicy than any theologian. Men and women often
fail to fully understand each other, but God gets them both. He even
understands teenagers! Now that's omniscience.

What's more, God fully knows Himself. Because no finite being
can ever know an infinite being, no human can ever fully know God.
Only God can fully know Himself in every detail. As Paul noted,
"The Spirit searches all things, even the deep things of God...No
one knows the thoughts of God except the Spirit of God" (1 Corinthians 2:10-11 NIV). Job's friend Elihu admitted that God is "perfect
in knowledge" (Job 37:16), and the apostle John affirmed that He
"knows all things" (1 John 3:20). God doesn't learn things in school,
on the streets, or by experience; He is totally and comprehensively
aware of everything.

How We Learn vs. What God Already Knows

Human knowledge is accumulated knowledge. It's the product
of tedious learning, research, and experience. And in this age of
exponentially increasing knowledge, information is especially susceptible to becoming obsolete. One researcher noted that "half of
what is known today was not known 10 years ago."[3] The impact this

has on education and employment is notable. There's a reason why the job of encyclopedia salesman no longer exists. A science textbook that is more than five years old might as well have been written in the nineteenth century. Information technology involves an ongoing battle against the half-life of knowledge. But does any of this knowledge truly matter?

> God's knowledge is immediate, instantaneous, comprehensive, and fully retained.

Human knowledge is found and lost. We explore the world around us, seen and unseen, trying to figure out what it all means—whether something matters or not, and if it does, why? We learn from both triumph and failure (ideally), but even then, our knowledge is always incomplete.

God's knowledge is immediate, instantaneous, comprehensive, and fully retained. What God knows He knows without any kind of painstaking research. What God knows did not have to be learned. He didn't have to move from one logical premise to another logical premise and so on to reach a conclusion. God never has to be informed about anything. Phrases common to human learning— "Huh?" or "Oh really?" or "Wow! I didn't know that"—don't exist in God's lexicon. And what He knows, He never forgets. He may choose not to remember certain things (like our sins, which are covered by the blood of Christ), but He doesn't lose recollection about things like where the keys are or how to say, "Where's the bathroom?" in Italian.

So, yes, that means that God knows who is going to win the Super Bowl next year and what the winning lottery numbers are. We might think those things would be fun to know, but what about when it comes to the hard things? Would you want to know the personal tragedies or evil intentions that reside in the hearts of those who passed by you at the store? Would you want everyone to know your most shameful moment or darkest secret? Mercifully, I believe, God has spared us that knowledge, leaving us to deal with the implications of all that He alone knows.

We All Hit Walls, but God Sees the Whole Maze

God's knowledge also has no limits. Doctors and science fiction writers alike have imagined what it would be like to access and utilize our entire brain, but even if we could, the resulting brilliance would be like a candle compared to the blazing sun of God's knowledge. The Bible makes sure we know who we're dealing with:

> The Lord searches all hearts and understands all the intent of the thoughts (1 Chronicles 28:9).

> Great is our Lord, and mighty in power; His understanding is infinite (Psalm 147:5).

> I am God, and there is none like Me, declaring the end from the beginning, and from ancient times things that are not yet done, saying, "My counsel shall stand, and I will do all My pleasure" (Isaiah 46:9-10).

> Oh, the depth of the riches both of the wisdom and knowledge of God! How unsearchable are His judgments and His ways past finding out! (Romans 11:33).

> Nothing in all creation is hidden from God. Everything is naked and exposed before his eyes, and he is the one to whom we are accountable (Hebrews 4:13 NLT).

> God is greater than our heart, and knows all things (1 John 3:20).

While we easily get tangled in the details and implications of knowing some of the things that are going on in and around our own lives, God doesn't struggle to balance each person's greatest good against the needs of the many and the needs of the few. There is no such thing as a puzzle to God, no such thing as a mystery or complexity or dilemma. We search, and we struggle, and we do our best. Sometimes we find and overcome, and circumstances work out. But God sees clearly, He knows all, and He does what He pleases, according to His good and perfect will.

The Limited Try to Limit the Unlimitable

Despite Scripture's clear stance on the issue, not everyone who calls themselves a Christian believes that God knows all. A teaching called *open theism* has infected a growing number of churches, including some whose ministry you know well. Open theism declares that God's knowledge has limits, that He created a world in which He doesn't know the future. Such a myopic view of God only strips Him of His deity and is surely proof that "the carnal mind is enmity against God" (Romans 8:7).

The argument advocating open theism hinges on the idea that, since God populated the earth with free agents who can choose their own futures, from daily decisions to eternal destiny, He must leave open the possibility of all those various choices. Thus, open theists get hung up on God's conditional promises—the ones where He says, "If you honor and obey Me, then I will bless you; if you don't, then things will go badly for you."

Open theists ask how a God who has all knowledge all the time could leave an open-ended option on the table. But they fail to reconcile God's knowledge with His methods. God does plenty of things that don't make sense to us, and they don't have to make sense to us for them to remain under His sovereign knowledge. He can know all possible outcomes and still leave a decision to us. And He may express disappointment when we choose poorly, even though He knew that was what we would choose. In the helpful words of Augustine, God has given us reasonable self-determination.[4]

God deals with us in terms we can understand. In fact, the Bible often describes Him as having human characteristics. In the last chapter, we talked about how God's longsuffering patience can be likened to Him having a long nose. It's goofy to picture God having a nose at all, since He is spirit, not flesh. But the Bible also speaks of His face, His strong arm, and His right hand. Such language is *anthropomorphic*—ascribing human characteristics to God for the sake of our understanding. The biblical authors employed this type of language not because God has any limitations but because of the limits that come from our own human shortcomings.

But open theists misstep at precisely this point. They ask questions like, "Why would God say He tests us unless He truly doesn't know how we're going to respond to the challenge He gives us?" I would say that God does know how we will respond; He uses the language of testing so that we understand that the test is not for His benefit but for ours. God tests us because He has prepared us for a challenge as part of our ongoing growth as His children. He knows it's a test, even if we don't (see Genesis 22). He is prepared for all possibilities. His knowledge isn't limited by our understanding of that knowledge (or the lack thereof).

Open theism is nothing more than an attempt to confine God to the same restrictions and limitations we have as finite, flawed beings. That would make God not omniscient but *semi*-omniscient, which is not what the Bible indicates (Psalm 147:5's "*infinite* understanding," anyone?). As God told His people, "I know the things that come into your mind" (Ezekiel 11:5). Sarah might have snickered to herself in her tent, but God heard her (Genesis 18:12-13). Achan might have stolen a wedge of gold and hidden it in the ground, but God knew where it was (Joshua 7:10-11, 18-22). David might have covered up his adultery for many months, but God dispatched His prophet to call him out on it (2 Samuel 12:1, 7).

Who's Your Father?

God's level of knowledge, wisdom, and understanding puts Him at a level well beyond our ability or right to question. Over and over, the Bible drives this truth home. The prophet Isaiah asked several rhetorical questions about God's knowledge:

> Who has directed the Spirit of the Lord, or as His counselor
> has taught Him? With whom did He take counsel, and
> who instructed Him, and taught Him in the path of jus-
> tice? Who taught Him knowledge, and showed Him the
> way of understanding? (Isaiah 40:13-14).

Clearly, the answer to each of these questions is *no one*. God asked similar questions of Job and his companions when they were trying to figure out why there is suffering in the world: "Who is this who darkens counsel by words without knowledge?...Where were you when I laid the foundations of the earth? Tell Me, if you have under-standing" (Job 38:2, 4). God didn't directly answer the question of suffering. "Well, you see, when I let people suffer, it's because..." Instead, God reminded them of who He is. He compared what they knew with what He knows.

We are limited not only in the amount of knowledge we have but also in our ability to comprehend. God won't answer all our ques-tions about the reach and extent of His knowledge because even the brightest human mind would be over-whelmed by His omniscience. Thus, God's response to Job is not the answer that we want to hear, but it's the one we need to hear. He took it back to basics, reminding Job that He, God, is the Creator. He gave a perspec-tive check—"Start here, and let the rest fall into place." The real question God was ask-ing Job was, "Even without all the answers you want, do you still me trust Me?"

> We might think
> mankind's
> greatest
> discoveries
> are impressive,
> but they are a
> preschooler's
> scrawlings
> compared
> to God's
> understanding.

I'm always floored when people think God owes them an answer to some ques-tion. Imagine an ant expecting a mountain to explain itself, or a jellyfish looking for answers from the ocean. Particularly when it comes to suffering, even if God chose to dis-till everything He knows into a single response—all the factors He takes into account, from each person's mind and make-up and background to the long view of all human history as well as the history of the spiritual realm—we wouldn't be able to receive it. Our minds would be blown.

The mind that conceived the universe and everything in it—with all its variety and complexity—is certainly beyond our human ability to comprehend. We might think mankind's greatest discoveries are impressive, but they are a preschooler's scrawlings compared to God's understanding. Fortunately, God likes to put our pictures on His fridge. He wants us to explore His creation, to seek understanding in every nook and cranny, because those paths lead us back to Him, the One who knows all.

Take It Personally

David humbly admitted that God's knowledge was overwhelming—"too wonderful for me, too great for me to understand!" (Psalm 139:6 NLT). But that didn't stop him from digging in and applying to his life the things he did understand. The truth of God's omniscience wasn't merely theological or philosophical for David; it was personal. Bible teacher J. Vernon McGee often said, "Every Bible should be bound in shoe leather." Scripture needs to be personal and practical for us for it to make a difference in our lives.

You can see how David brought this awareness home in his use of personal pronouns:

> Lord, You have searched *me* and known *me*. You know *my* sitting down and *my* rising up; You understand *my* thought afar off. You comprehend *my* path and *my* lying down, and are acquainted with all *my* ways. For there is not a word on *my* tongue, but behold, O Lord, You know it altogether. You have hedged *me* behind and before, and laid Your hand upon *me* (vv. 1-5, emphasis mine).

I count eleven personal pronouns. David didn't say, "Lord, You know all things and You've searched all things." He said, "Lord, You know me and have searched me." What David did here is what each of us must do with all truth. Making Scripture practical and personal means it's not enough to leave truth on the page of a book or talk about it with friends over coffee. When we want to get to know God in the Bible, we have to dig in and uncover the power of the living word for ourselves (see Hebrews 4:12).

How to Make Scripture Personal

Over the years, I've used a tried-and-true method of studying the Bible, a three-step process: observation, interpretation, and application. When you read a passage, first you observe what it's saying. That's just figuring out the basics—*who, what, when,* and *where.*

Then you interpret what the passage means—that's looking at the *why* or the *how.* Look at the verses in their immediate context— what's happening directly before and after them—and then in the context of the greater story of the Bible.

Finally, you look for how the passage applies to you personally. This is all about the *who*—God Himself. What could God be trying to say to you through this text? Studying the Bible has to be about more than just increasing your knowledge. If it's not about getting to know God better, you're missing the point. I've seen plenty of Christians—theologians, pastors, students—become intoxicated with *what* they know instead of *whom* they know.

If what you learn about God doesn't change you in some way, you're off target. If your marriage doesn't get better, if your attitude at work doesn't improve, if you don't manage your money more carefully, you're missing the point of Bible study. Knowing God Himself is the long game, but that won't happen without application. The goal isn't gaining more knowledge for its own sake, but putting into practice what you know about God. Only the Bible accurately tells us how to know Him—by doing His will—and that, when we do His will, His will for our lives will become clear.

J.I. Packer rightly cautions,

> We need to ask ourselves: What is my ultimate aim and
> object in occupying my mind with these things? What do
> I intend to *do* with my knowledge about God, once I have
> it? For the fact that we have to face is this: If we pursue
> theological knowledge for its own sake, it is bound to go
> bad on us.[5]

Knowing as David did that God can see right through you, it's ultimately futile to put on airs, to act super holy or oh-so-well-read. Jesus repeatedly called the Pharisees hypocrites for that very attitude. People can usually spot a fake, and God certainly can. That kind of behavior is something we all have to watch out for so we can resist the tendency to take part in it.

David resisted this tendency by holding nothing back from the Lord. To be searched by God is to realize that everything you think and feel is an open book to Him. To ask God to examine you is to invite exposure into your life, so you had better mean it when you say that. When we meet someone who's bad at hiding his agenda or motives, we say, "I can see right through him." David was telling God, "You know it all, so I'm not even going to try to hide anything from You, no matter how bad it makes me look; You can see right through me."

The Challenge and Joy of Being Known

To be known in that way and still loved is the rarest of gifts—and it just happens to be God's modus operandi. That's what David meant when he said, "You have searched me and known me." To be searched and known by God is to receive a thorough examination, much like when a doctor gives you every conceivable test before telling you what you need to do to get better. To be known in this way is like being transparent and pouring your heart out to a counselor or friend, who then has a real shot at being able to help you.

You may find it unsettling to imagine letting any one person know that much about you. It's human nature to fear having your most private thoughts and issues exposed. More than ever, information is power, and it's normal not to want to arm anyone who might use that power against you. But whereas you can hide certain types of information from most people (though privacy and technology issues are making that more and more difficult), there's nothing you can hide from God. That's what David comes to grips with in Psalm 139.

How do you relate to that kind of God? How do you deal with a God of whom it is said, "There is no creature hidden from His sight, but all things are naked and open to the eyes of Him to whom we must give account" (Hebrews 4:13)? Simply put, don't try to pull the wool over His eyes. You can't hide anything from Him, so don't try. Instead, be honest. "You can't whitewash your sins and get by with it; you find mercy by admitting and leaving them" (Proverbs 28:13 MSG).

David quickly balanced out the vulnerability he felt by looking to God's committed care: "How precious are your thoughts about me, O God. They cannot be numbered! I can't even count them; they outnumber the grains of sand! And when I wake up, you are still with me!" (Psalm 139:17-18 NLT).

I once heard the story about a rich elderly man who went to a doctor and got hearing aids. He came back two weeks later and said, "Doctor, these hearing aids are so good I can hear conversations in the next room." The doctor said, "That's great! I'll bet your family is really happy that you can hear." The old man smiled and said, "I haven't told any of them yet, Doc, but in the past two weeks, I've changed my will three times." *Busted!*

In a way, God has the ultimate hearing aid, one that picks up even our thoughts and emotions. But paired with His incomparable hearing is His matchless covenant love for His people. That love is what takes the hard edge off His omniscience. To realize that we're so utterly known yet completely loved removes any sense of anxiousness; it humbles us and comforts us at the same time.

Everything There Is to Understand

As a musician and poet, David was a wordsmith. Every word he wrote he chose with intention, using every nuance he could to shed light on God's greatness. And in Psalm 139, he described how detailed God's personal knowledge is of our lives, even down to unspoken thoughts. Nothing is hidden.

When I was a kid, I could've sworn my mom had a store of secret knowledge—or at least a real good *in* with God, who had been telling her all about me. I couldn't believe how much she knew about me, where I'd been, or who I'd been speaking to. I whispered, but she heard my secrets. I tried to hide, but she always knew where to look.

Of course, what I didn't realize then was that she was just an insightful and attentive mother. I was her fourth son, so she had already had plenty of experience with little boys and their ploys. She was simply paying attention to me and my habits, even when I thought I was getting away with something. As amazing as my mom's powers of observation were, her knowledge was still acquired. God's omniscience is on a much different level. When David wrote Psalm 139, he may have been remembering the words God told the prophet Samuel at David's boyhood home: "The Lord looks at the heart" (1 Samuel 16:7).

Good Thoughts About Bad Actors

Maybe at this point you're thinking, *It's pretty cool that God is aware of my slightest movements, but does He even really care about all that?* The answer is a resounding *yes*: "How precious are your thoughts about me, O God. They cannot be numbered! I can't even count them; they outnumber the grains of sand!" (Psalm 139:17-18 NLT). Have you ever had someone on your mind for some reason, and you're really glad when you see them? You want good things for them, to share some encouragement or wisdom, or to offer help or companionship. Well, God is thinking those kinds of thoughts about you right now—and the same goes for the rest of the almost eight billion people on earth.

What does that mean for you? It means God saw you yesterday when you were thinking about Him. He saw you digging into the Bible, saw you singing that worship song to Him (and really meaning it). He knew your thoughts when you wondered about His plans for your life, and He heard your encouraging words to that coworker. However, it also means He heard you criticize your kids again, heard you nag your husband or belittle your wife. He saw you checking out that person at the gym, and that gesture you made at the guy who cut you off on the freeway. He saw you check your social media feeds for the tenth time today, looking for likes in all the wrong places, and He saw what you were streaming in incognito mode. "Mark well that God doesn't miss a move you make; he's aware of every step you take" (Proverbs 5:21 MSG).

When a strange thought pops into your head and you wonder, *Where did that come from?*, God knows. He not only knows what you think before you even think it, but He also knows why—and He's probably the only one who truly does. Before those electrical and chemical signals were transmitted at the synapse between two neurons, He knew it.

God also knows how you really feel about Him. He is aware of any discrepancies between what you say and what you do. He knows whether you really hold to all the opinions you think you should hold. His awareness of you is complete. At every moment, He knows your walking out and your lying down, your spoken words and your buzzing thoughts, what's behind you and what's in front of you.

The Shot-Caller

But wait, there's more! Not only is God fully aware of all the details of the past and present, but He also knows everything about the future. God exists outside of temporal reality. Time is a construct

He invented, partly because of our limits as mortal, finite beings. In a way, creating a world that was never meant to last forever also created the moment in which time began. And at the end of this heaven and earth, time will also end. But God sees it all with the constraints of past, present, and future.

> We are right to be astonished at God's perfect prophetic record because it's one of the clearest evidences of His omniscience.

For God, everything is in a sort of eternal *now*. He sees the future and the past as clearly as if they were happening in this very moment. What we call prophecy is just God pointing out a moment that for Him is happening right now. But predictive prophecy isn't a parlor trick God breaks out to impress the rubes; it's one of His hallmarks (Isaiah 46:9-10; 42:8-9). We are right to be astonished at God's perfect prophetic record because it's one of the clearest evidences of His omniscience.

If God knows it all, then that must include knowing the future before it exists. The Bible is a record of this truth:

- Because God knows it all, He can announce 150 years before Cyrus was even born that he would release the Jews from their Babylonian captivity (see Isaiah 44:28–45:3).

- Because God knows it all, He can give Daniel a forecast of successive kingdoms that would rise to power following Babylon, from Medo-Persia to Greece to Rome, all while Babylon ruled the world (see Daniel 2:28-45).

- Because God knows it all, He can predict the Messiah riding into Jerusalem on a donkey 500 years before it happened (Zechariah 9:9-10).

- Because God knows it all, there is every reason to believe in the Bible's forecast of what will happen in the end times—the rapture, the tribulation, the second coming

of Christ, the millennial kingdom, the judgment, and
the creation of a new heaven and earth.

Contrary to the idea that God is learning the future as time goes
on (like we do), Scripture makes it clear that He knows exactly how
everything is going to turn out. "Because we are united with Christ,
we have received an inheritance from God, for he chose us in
advance, and he makes everything work out according to his plan"
(Ephesians 1:11 NLT). That's His sovereignty
and omniscience in a nutshell. God knows
the future because God controls the future.
Knowing that God calls the shots is meant to
bring us peace, unless we resist His sovereign
control of human affairs.

> God knows the future because God controls the future.

Living with the Ultimate Know-It-All

How should we respond to the limitless scope of God's knowledge? Anyone can say, "I believe God knows everything." But what
will you do with that belief? David, in utter honesty, wrote, "You
have hedged me behind and before, and laid Your hand upon me"
(Psalm 139:5). The word "hedged" can also be translated "enclosed,"
with the root word carrying the sense of laying siege to something.
Maybe David was saying, "Lord, the fact that You know everything
about me and the future makes me feel confined, even trapped."

God's sovereign omniscience can sometimes feel like a wet blanket thrown onto the fire of our relationship with Him. For instance,
people have asked me, "If God knows what I need before I even ask
Him, why bother asking?" But prayer is about a lot more than pre-
senting God with a list of requests; it's about cultivating a relationship that honors Him and satisfies you. So, while David may have
been implicitly acknowledging some tension he felt about God's
omniscience, he didn't get stuck there. He moved past the thought
of being a prisoner of fate by becoming a worshipper of God. He
looked at God's all-consuming, all-encompassing knowledge and

said, "Such knowledge is too wonderful for me, too great for me to understand!" (v. 6 NLT). He felt the tension of humanity rubbing up against divinity, and it brought him to his knees.

Search Me, Know Me, Guide Me, Direct Me

David approached God with humility, which is an essential part of responding to the God who knows it all. There's no place for pride, no wiggle room for self-assertiveness. A think tank of the most brilliant minds in the history of the world couldn't match wits with God. A collective of the most compassionate hearts couldn't out-love or out-serve Him. David himself was a dedicated shepherd, caring for and protecting otherwise defenseless animals. He was a talented musician, able to sooth tortured spirits and create songs of praise that Israel and the church have sung for centuries. He was a leader worth following, with a cadre of die-hard soldiers ready to lay down their lives for him. David was a king's king.

But when David looked at the God who knows and is in control of all things, he decided, "The best thing I can do is humbly let Him have full access to my heart, my thoughts, and my words." So he invited God to come even closer. "Search me, O God, and know my heart; try me, and know my anxieties; and see if there is any wicked way in me, and lead me in the way everlasting" (vv. 23-24). In other words, *Search me, know me, guide me, and direct me.*

Let me paraphrase David's thought process in this psalm: "God, I don't get it; I can't wrap my mind around it; I'll blow a fuse trying to figure this out, so I just surrender to it." David discovered that because God's ability transcends our reality, it's best for us to bow to His immensity. Put more simply: God's ability is always greater than our reality. We will never know all there is to know about God, and no PhD or ministry training can improve on that. We may grow in our knowledge of Him, but there is always more to know.

> If God was small enough for your brain, He wouldn't be big enough for your needs.

There's a mystery to our faith, however, that is precious. When you reach a saturation point beyond which you simply can't understand, you leave off. If God was small enough for your brain, He wouldn't be big enough for your needs. If you understood everything about God, you would be God. And to attempt to go down that path is both futile and dangerous—just ask Lucifer, Adam and Eve, and every other person who thought they knew better than God. Instead, we should end any exploration of God's nature in the same way David did—with worship.

The Liberating Effect of Letting God Be God

That attitude of worship—telling God (and reminding ourselves) how great He is—liberates us. How so? First, when you realize that God knows everything, you also realize that He knows the worst about you and still loves you anyway. The fear in almost any human relationship is that when the other person knows who I really am, they'll reject me. That's why we put on our best face and behavior—to win them over. And we hope that winning behavior will overshadow any skeletons that tumble out of the closet later on. But if you constantly live in that fear, you're never free to be real and you'll never know if you're loved for who you truly are, warts and all.

When I was dating my wife, I told her, "I'm a complicated person" (that was my flaky way of warning her about my flakiness). She married me anyway. That's how God's love works too. His love and grace free you from pretense, from having to put on some kind of holy show so that other people will see what a good Christian you are. God "knows our frame; He remembers that we are dust" (Psalm 103:14). What expectations would anybody have for dirt? God knows the worst about you and loves you anyway.

Then there's the flip side of that: Because God knows everything, He also knows the best about you. Like with Lenya—she didn't marry me because she loves flakiness, but because she saw more in me than that. She wanted to help me step up into being at my best as often as possible. That takes vision and commitment. Sometimes your best goes unnoticed. Other times, you do your best and fail. That can be like blood in the water for some folks. Without bothering to understand your motives or look at the whole picture, some people find it easier to criticize you or gossip about you. But God knows the whole truth. He can straighten you out when you're wrong and not love you a bit less. It can be hard for us to accept that kind of grace.

The apostle Peter had to learn to be content with that. He failed Jesus and denied Him three times, but after the resurrection, Jesus restored him—though it was a painful process. Jesus asked Peter three times if Peter loved Him, and by the third time, Peter's heart was stung. But he wisely answered, "Lord, You know all things; You know that I love You" (John 21:17). All pretense was cut away as Peter understood and trusted that God was looking for the best in him. *Lord, You know all things, including the love I have for You.* God has foreseen your every fall and foible, your every sin and stumble, but He also knows your heart of hearts to love and serve Him.

Finally, because God knows everything, He knows what He is going to make you into. This, for me, is the best part of God's omniscience. You're not done yet—you're still in the oven; you're still in process. God sees your imperfections, but He also sees the finished product. The Bible says this beautifully: "We are His workmanship" (Ephesians 2:10). You're a work of art in progress. All you see are the crooked lines and rough shapes, but the Artist sees the finished work. And that's where He is taking you.

How confident can you be about this? Extremely. Just let God be God. Most of us having a passing familiarity with Romans 8:28, which promises that God makes all things work together for good "to those who love God, to those who are the called according to His purpose." It's a powerful promise, especially when you put it in context with the next two verses:

> For whom He foreknew, He also predestined to be conformed to the image of His Son...Moreover whom He

predestined, these He also called; whom He called, these
He also justified; and whom He justified, these He also glorified (vv. 29-30).

God knows you, chose you, and called you. If you answer His
call, He will justify you and one day glorify you. You're not glorified
yet, and neither am I (just ask my wife). But God is so sure that one
day we will be that He wrote about it like it's a done deal. How can
He be so sure? Because He knows everything.

This single distinctive attribute of God turns conventional wisdom upside down. Knowledge isn't king; the God of all knowledge
is! New T-shirt idea, anyone?

Chapter 8

GODISNOWHERE

God's Major Attributes, Part 2:
Omnipresence

It seems two brothers, aged eight and ten, were always getting in trouble. If something went wrong in their town, people automatically assumed they were somehow involved. The boys' parents, aware of the brothers' reputation, got the local pastor involved. They had heard this man had a way with kids, and he agreed to come over and talk with the boys. He said, "First, I'd like to meet with the younger boy alone, and then afterward, I'll speak with the older one."

The preacher was a big man with a booming voice, which the parents hoped would have an effect on their sons. His plan was to get the kids to realize that God sees everything and is everywhere and was fully aware of all their activities. So he stood up, towering over the eight-year-old, and asked in a reverberating voice, "Where's God?"

His approach had the desired effect. The little boy's jaw dropped and his eyes were wide as saucers. He stared at the pastor and said nothing, so the pastor asked again, "Where's God?" No answer. The third time, the preacher stuck his finger in front of the boy's face, his voice thundering, "Where is God?" With that, the boy jumped up, ran to his bedroom, and hid in the closet. His older brother slipped in beside him and asked, "What's up?" The eight-year-old turned to him and said, "We're really in trouble this time, dude. God is missing, and they think we did it!"

Questions of juvenile delinquency aside, the preacher asked a good question—a question many of us have asked at one point or another: *Where is God?* The questions I asked as a twelve-year-old in my parents' backyard included this one. When I thought about God or prayed, I often looked upward. Why? Was God in the sky? Beyond the sky? Was He hiding behind a cloud? Did I expect Him to peek out? If I could look far enough into outer space, would I see heaven? Interestingly, even Jesus "looked up to heaven" when He prayed (John 11:41 NLT).

As for the title of this chapter, *Godisnowhere,* I confess I was having a little fun with the wordplay. Depending on your disposition toward God, you can read the title two different ways, depending on where you add spaces in between the letters. An atheist would look at it and see *God is nowhere.* But if you've been following our path thus far, soaking in the evidence for God's existence and goodness, you might see it as saying *God is now here.*

The Rhetorical Question: Where Is God?

That's David's take on the matter as we continue in Psalm 139. Where is God? He is everywhere. This facet of God is called omnipresence. The Bible sets forth God as One not having size or certain dimensions, but as One who is present at every point of space with His whole being.[1] As creator of the material world, He is Lord over time and space.

David unveiled this quality of God's character by asking a pair of rhetorical questions: "Where can I go from Your Spirit? Or where can I flee from Your presence?" (Psalm 139:7). Basically he was asking, "Is there a place where you are *not,* God?" His question implies the answer: There is no such place; God is everywhere. There is simply nowhere in the universe that one can run away from God.

When we were kids, many of us possessed a sense of mystery and wonder that allowed us to believe in God without concrete evidence. Even so, we still wanted to know where God was. We heard our parents talk about Him, but we never saw Him. He never showed up at our birthday parties. We also heard our parents talk about our grandparents who lived two states away, but even they show up for Thanksgiving.

Some kids, as they grow up, end up lumping their belief in God together with what they think about Santa Claus and leave the wonder to the next generation of kids. They think they know too much and have seen too much. They look at the messed-up world we live in and put a different edge on the question *Where is God?* They read about a tsunami or a mass shooting and demand, "Where were You, God?" They look at life's complexity, become overwhelmed, and project their concerns and fears onto what they believe about God's nature.

This is why some folks get mad when believers offer thoughts and prayers after a catastrophic event. "That's not doing any good," they say. "Invoking God at such a tragic time doesn't help us. If God were really present or if God really cared, He would do something about all these awful things." But such thinking reveals a shallow view of God.

As we'll soon see, God is both fully aware of and fully present in our concerns, and He cares very much about them. In fact, this broken world troubles Him more than it does us, because He is the only one who fully knows what He originally intended it to be. Our prayers seek the help of the only one who can do anything about the root cause of all the world's evil—and who promises He one day will.[2]

Nowhere Where God Is Not

David kept his question simple: "Where is God?" Then he answered simply as well, saying, "There, there, and there." David's creative use of questions is a clever poetic device that sets up a key observation: God is everywhere it is possible to be. A rhetorical question makes an indirect statement. In asking where he could go from God's presence, David wasn't saying, "I'm trying really hard to get away from God. Can anyone tell me a place where I can hide?"

When he asked, "Where can I flee?," there was only one answer: nowhere. And he knew it.

The real question implied is, Why would anyone *want* to run away from God? The answer depends on how you're living. If you're resisting God and fighting His supreme accountability, you won't want Him around. But if you've put your life in God's hands and you're aligning your thoughts, words, and deeds with what He says about Himself (and about you), then David's conclusion settles on you peacefully: There is nowhere you can go where God is not present.

And yet we still resist this truth from time to time, don't we? When Adam and Eve disobeyed God, what was the first thing they did? They tried to hide. "Hey, honey, get behind this bush so God can't see us!" Yet God formed them, the bush, and every atom filling the air around them. When God visited the garden that afternoon and asked, "Where are you?," He wasn't actually wondering, "Where on earth did those crazy kids go?" God was asking a rhetorical question, inviting His wayward children to step forward and face the music. Adam and Eve responded irrationally when they disobeyed God, which is standard operating procedure for people who know they're not right with Him.

> There is nowhere you can go where God is not present.

Jonah is another example. God called him to go to Nineveh, and based on Jonah's reaction, it seemed as if he imagined that God would never think to look in the exact opposite direction. "Jonah arose to flee to Tarshish [2,000 miles west of Nineveh] from the presence of the Lord" (Jonah 1:3). Any prophet should know you can't run away from God, but Jonah tried. Perhaps his attempted getaway was a symbolic act that he wasn't on board with the Lord's plans spiritually. He fled from God's "presence," which was like him resigning his office as prophet, saying, "I quit, Lord."

Jonah knew he couldn't escape God, so he deliberately disobeyed in protest. That reminds me of a springer spaniel I once had. Toby was a beautiful dog, but he was also either dumb or stubborn (likely the latter), because every time I told him to come, he would head in the opposite direction. One day his obstinacy almost got him killed when he bolted from me and ran toward a moving car. Fortunately for Toby, the car stopped at the same time as he did, and he just walked away dizzily. I should've renamed him Jonah.

Everywhere God Is—and Isn't

The omnipresence of God means that God is everywhere present in the totality—the wholeness—of His being at all times. God is fully God in all places at all times. Paul affirmed this truth at the Areopagus in Athens and noted that some Greek poets understood this too, saying, "'In him we live and move and have our being'; as even some of your own poets have said, 'For we are indeed his off-spring'"[3] (Acts 17:28 ESV).

As I've noted, that is either a great comfort to you or a great concern. However, your response to God doesn't change the facts about Him. You can stay away from church, or change the subject when others bring up God, or let your Bible gather dust on the shelf, but God will remain God. The reality of both His existence and His presence is inescapable, and you might be able to avoid account-ability to Him at least for now, but only for as long as you're draw-ing breath in this life. That's the truth that emerges from this part of Psalm 139.

God is God no matter where He is. That's what He told the prophet Jeremiah in what I would call a primary text on the pres-ence of God:

> "Am I a God near at hand," says the Lord, "and not a God afar off? Can anyone hide himself in secret places, so I shall not see him?" says the Lord; "Do I not fill heaven and earth?" (Jeremiah 23:23-24).

When God says He "[fills] heaven and earth," that's a way of saying He is present everywhere. But be careful not to confuse this biblical truth of God being everywhere with a false teaching known as pantheism. God is not equivalent to any part of His creation, nor to all of it. The biblical teaching of the omnipresence of God says that He is present in His creation while, at the same time, He is separate and distinct from it.

Wayne Grudem, in his fine volume *Systematic Theology*, helps us understand the matter by using the illustration of a sponge filled with water. Water is present everywhere in the sponge, but the water is still completely distinct from the sponge. The illustration fails when you consider that, on a smaller scale, there are certain points where there is only sponge and not water. But that's because the analogy is dealing with two materials that have spatial characteristics and dimensions while God does not.[4]

Pantheism says God *is* His creation, that they're one and the same, with no distinction between them. In other words, the sponge is the water and vice versa. Pantheists would say that God isn't just active *in* the world; God *is* the world. Let me illustrate the contrast: The Bible would affirm that right now, wherever you are sitting and reading this book, God is with you. He is not you or the chair you're sitting in or the tree that's providing shade for you. But pantheism would say, "The chair you're sitting in is God, the earth that holds it up is God, the trees and the bushes and the grass you see—all of those are God. They are all one and the same. No separation and no distinction."

Though pantheism is an ancient belief system, it's still around. Today we see neopantheism in movements like hyperenvironmentalism and in widespread references to the earth as our Mother. While we have a responsibility as God's children to take care of the planet, we mustn't cross over into worshipping what's been created rather than the Creator. Some people even say that God and Mother Nature are the same thing. That concept is inherent in the insurance policy terminology that refers to natural disasters as "acts of God."

Nature can be awe-inspiring in its beauty, majesty, and displays of overwhelming might. But to call it "God" is to undersell everything we've learned about God and rob Him of His glory. Unlike nature, God has no beginning and no end. This world, this universe, will wind down and pass from existence, but God never will. He exists outside of nature. And even though He is present in His creation, He is distinct from it and is not subject to the laws of nature in creation.

Faced with the truth of God's omnipresence, some might concede, "Yes, God is everywhere—He's big and He's out there." But God has made it more than clear that He also wants to be "in here," in our hearts and lives. That's why the Messiah is called Immanuel— *God with us.*[5] Jesus was physically present with us on earth for more than thirty-three years. And while He was here in time and space, He said that "he who has seen Me has seen the Father" (John 14:9).

Yes, Jesus left when He ascended to heaven, but then God sent the Holy Spirit to us to live in the hearts of everyone who claims God's Messiah as their personal Savior.[6] To be a follower of Christ is to live with His presence at all times. That gives us the answers to David's rhetorical questions: *Where is God?* Everywhere. *Where can you go to get away from God?* Nowhere.

Rational Conclusions: Three Responses to God's Presence

David followed his rhetorical questions with a trio of rational conclusions. Keep in mind that Psalm 139 was a worship song, so it seems David wanted to preserve these salient truths in the Israelites' musical memory banks (a good idea for modern songsters!). Look at these lyrics about God's omnipresence:

> If I ascend into heaven, You are there; if I make my bed in hell, behold, You are there. If I take the wings of the morning, and dwell in the uttermost parts of the sea, even there Your hand shall lead me (Psalm 139:8-10).

Wherever we could possibly be, God is there: heaven, hell, the horizons, and the ocean hollows—and everywhere in between. Wherever you may wander, you can't wander too far.

Death Can't Hide You from God

David investigated all the possible major options of where a person could hide from God, beginning with heaven. "If I ascend into heaven, You are there" (Psalm 139:8). Duh, right? That's God's unique dwelling place. Of course He's in heaven—and that's what David meant to say. He asserted that heaven is real and God is enthroned there, in His base of operations, so to speak.

But what about the next part of verse 8? "If I make my bed in hell, behold, You are there." The word "hell" is the Hebrew word *sheol*, used sixty-five times in the Old Testament. Typically this means the grave, the place of the dead—both the location where people get buried and the abode of those who have died. In biblical times, the thinking was that a person in Sheol was cut off from God. You die, you go down into the earth, and you hang up a sign that says, "God is nowhere." But David would say, "No, God is now here!" He is present on both sides of the grave.

Death is a transition, a threshold, and when we step across it, we step outside of time as we understand it. Death is not the end of our existence. When we say someone died, we might better say that he or she moved. The question is, to where? For the believer, as Paul said, "to be absent from the body" is "to be present with the Lord" (2 Corinthians 5:8). When a Christian dies, he or she experiences the immediate presence of God in a very special way—no longer by faith but face to face in glory.

But for the person who has tried to get away from God their whole life, death is not the final escape. Even in the grave you can't hide from God. "It is appointed for men to die once, but after this the judgment" (Hebrews 9:27). Not "after this, you float around," "after this, you just switch off like a light bulb," or "after this, you're eternally unconscious." Death opens the door to the hallways of judgment for how we've lived our lives.

It's easy—not to mention satisfying—to envision someone like Hitler coming face to face with Jesus Christ, a Jew who will decide his eternal fate. No political machinations, no war machine, and no inflamed rhetoric can deliver him from the staggering irony of God's righteous judgment. Hitler might have thought he escaped punishment by taking his life before being captured, only to find himself immediately in front of the ultimate Judge of all the earth.

Hitler's fate? "He himself shall also drink of the wine of the wrath of God, which is poured out full strength into the cup of His indignation. He shall be tormented with fire and brimstone in the presence of the holy angels and in the presence of the Lamb" (Revelation 14:10). That's a frightening reality, not just for the Hitlers of history but for the whosoevers—anyone who rejects Jesus as the Christ. You might think, *Hey, I may be a sinner, but I'm no Hitler*. Of course you're not. But because all of us have sinned and fallen short of God's glory (Romans 3:23), we all are destined to face the wrath of God unless we receive Christ as Savior. The reality of God's omnipresence is that death won't keep us from being held accountable for the lives we've lived. In fact, death is the gateway to ultimate accountability.

I have a book of the last words that numerous people, both believers and unbelievers, spoke near their deaths. Accordingly, these words are at times comforting, and at times terrifying. For instance, John Milton, the author of *Paradise Lost*, noted that "Death is the great key that opens the palace of Eternity." To him, death was a good thing to anticipate given that he had put his trust in Jesus.[7]

The sixteenth-century Italian scholar Olympia Fulvia Morata relied heavily on God to help her excel in a brief but challenging life. Her husband recorded her last words: "For the last seven years Satan has not ceased to use every means to induce me to relinquish my faith, but now it would appear that he has lost his darts, for I have no other sensation in this hour of my departure than of unperturbed repose and tranquility of soul in Jesus Christ."[8] Though she was only twenty-nine, her words are an inspiring reminder of the beauty of a life lived in God's presence.

Among the deathbed tragedies was an English nobleman named

Altamont, a charismatic and charming agnostic who lived during the 1800s. At his death, he said, "As for a Deity, nothing less than an Almighty could inflict what I now feel. Remorse for the past throws my thoughts on the future; worse dread of the future strikes them back on the past... My principles have poisoned my friends; my extravagance has beggared my boy; my unkindness has murdered my wife! And is there another hell? Thou blasphemed yet indulgent God, hell is a refuge if it hide me from Thy frown."[9] Can you imagine breathing those words and choking on your regrets as your time on earth ends?

> Death can't hide anyone, believer or unbeliever, from God.

Then there was Voltaire, the brilliant French writer and atheist, who at one point said of Jesus Christ, "Curse the wretch."[10] But when he died, he tried to bargain against the impending darkness he sensed, telling his doctor, "I am abandoned by God and man! I will give you half of what I am worth if you will give me six months' life. Then I shall go to hell; and you will go with me. O Christ! O Jesus Christ!"[11] What a shock for Voltaire to find that hell was no refuge from God's judgment. Death can't hide anyone, believer or unbeliever, from God.

David understood that people often live their lives without any real thought about death. Even today, especially in America, we struggle to face the certain prospect that we're going to die someday. We consume ourselves with the busyness with life, which we think excuses us from having to deal with death. And we use metaphors to describe death—passing away, kicking the bucket, or going to the great beyond—as if the cessation of life were part of some fairy tale and not our guaranteed end. Metaphorically, at least, we try to put distance between ourselves and death.

Of course, at some point, death will come knocking, striking close to home and often leaving us feeling vulnerable and unprepared. As David also wrote, speaking of man, "His spirit departs, he returns to his earth; in that very day his plans perish" (Psalm 146:4).

Distance Can't Hide You from God

For those who are unwilling to weigh their lives against death's reality, sticking instead to the safe immediacy of the cares of the everyday, David made it clear there is nowhere we can go in this world to get away from God:

> If I take the wings of the morning, and dwell in the utter-most parts of the sea, even there Your hand shall lead me, and Your right hand shall hold me (Psalm 139:9-10).

David was imagining traveling west, over the Mediterranean Sea, racing against the rays of the rising sun. But don't let his poetry distract from his point: Distance can't hide us from God. In modern terms, he might have been saying, "God, if I could travel at the speed of light, shooting across the universe at 186,000 miles per second, You're there too."

Back in 1968, I spent part of Christmas Eve gathered with my family in front of the TV, watching the flight of Apollo 8, the first manned spacecraft to orbit the moon and return. On December 24, the three astronauts aboard read the first ten verses of Genesis. I can still recall their voices crackling back through space into our living room, inspired by their view and reminding us that "in the beginning God created the heavens and the earth." Even as a thirteen-year-old I was moved by this statement.

What I didn't know at the time was that, as soon as the astronauts got back, the atheist Madalyn Murray O'Hair sued NASA over an alleged violation of the First Amendment. Whereas O'Hair would say, "God is nowhere," the astronauts responded to the wonder of what they saw by saying, in essence, "God is now here; in this groundbreaking moment, we know it, and we have to respond with praise." They weren't the only astronauts affected that way.

While Buzz Aldrin waited for NASA's go-ahead to take the second giant leap for mankind on the moon in 1969, he took communion in the lunar module.[12] He wanted the moment broadcast on television, but as a result of O'Hair's action a year earlier, NASA chose to avoid any potential religious distraction and told him to keep his observance discrete. Aldrin later noted that he represented "all mankind" when he stepped onto the moon's surface, regardless of creed. "But," he said, "at the time I could think of no better way to acknowledge the enormity of the Apollo 11 experience than by giving thanks to God."[13] His instincts in the moment were right on target. God was on the moon long before we were!

The Russian cosmonaut Yuri Gagarin became a national hero as the first man in space. Supposedly while in orbit he said, "I looked and looked but I didn't see God." One pastor heard that and quipped, "If he had stepped out of that spacesuit, he would have seen God!"[14] But there was more to the story. It turns out that the Russian premier Nikita Khrushchev, who considered faith in God to be outdated and superstitious and who predicted an end to Christianity in the Soviet Union, engineered Gagarin's comment.

According to a close colleague and friend of Gagarin, Khrushchev said at a Central Committee of the Communist Party meeting, "Why are you clinging to God? Here Gagarin went to space and he did not see God."[15] Khrushchev's agenda was to eliminate religion in the Soviet Union; in 1964, he famously promised that, by 1980, "I will show you the last priest."[16] Gagarin himself, according to his friend, in fact often got in trouble for his religious convictions.[17] Even though he was a Christian, he had to be careful in his role as a Soviet colonel.

Another story explains the quote's origin: Upon Gagarin's return from space, Khrushchev asked him, "Did you see God?" Gagarin replied, "Yes, I did," to which Khrushchev admonished, "Don't tell anyone." Shortly afterward, Gagarin spoke with the head of the Russian Orthodox Church, who asked him, "Did you see God up there?" The cosmonaut hesitated, then said, "No, I did not." The clergyman replied, "Don't tell anyone."[18] Despite having to lie under pressing circumstances, Gagarin was better remembered by a biographer who wrote, "I always remember that Yuri Gagarin said: 'An astronaut cannot be suspended in space and not have God in his mind and his heart.'"[19]

My point in sharing this story is twofold: one, the battle between those who acknowledge God's presence and those who don't plays out across time and space, even in the least expected places. And two, we can't compromise a search for the truth because we don't like a certain outcome of that search. We must be willing to apply the truth to our situation and see if it will change us. If it's God's truth, it will change us for the better.

> God is always near because there is no such thing as a place where He is not.

That's why you have to ask, "What does all this mean to me?" If death and distance can't hide you from God, what's the upshot? Just this: You don't have to go to a special place to meet with Him. You don't have to visit a certain shrine or make a pilgrimage on your knees to a "holy site." God is where you are. You can make contact with Him in your apartment, your car, at work, or in your hospital bed. God is always near because there is no such thing as a place where He is not.

Old Testament worship, on the other hand, centered on the temple in Jerusalem. The Jewish people brought their animals for sacrifice there because that's where God was. No matter where they were in Israel, they knew they could find God in the temple. As Israeli tour guides like to joke when they take you to the Western Wall, where the ancient temple enclosure still stands, "You can pray to God anywhere on earth, but here it's a local call." Of course, that's not the truth. When Solomon built the temple, he said, "Behold, heaven and the heaven of heavens cannot contain You. How much less this temple which I have built!" (1 Kings 8:27). If you want to talk to God, it's always a local call.

Paul told the Athenians that God "does not dwell in temples made with hands" (Acts 17:24). Where, then, does He hang out? Is there any special place He is willing to reside? To demonstrate His unceasing, unlimited presence, God has made the human heart

His dwelling place, mobilized and multiplied throughout the world. "We are God's fellow workers; you are God's field, you are God's building" (1 Corinthians 3:9). Peter wrote that Christians are "living stones that God is building into his spiritual temple" (1 Peter 2:5 NLT). We live our lives in the constant presence of God. Will you choose to become a vessel of that presence?

Darkness Doesn't Hide You from God

Every one of us, from childhood on, is aware of the darkness of night. From a kid's perspective, darkness can hide monsters and other unseen terrors. I myself used to be terrified of the dark. It was too unknown, too filled with potential risks. There was a season during which I was plagued by night terrors and was even afraid to fall asleep. As we grow older, however, we learn to appreciate the beauty of the stars and the deep quiet of midnight. But some people use the night as a cover for things they know they shouldn't be doing, deeds they think no one can see. Yet darkness doesn't hide us from God's presence, as David made clear.

> If I say, "Surely the darkness shall fall on me," even the night shall be light about me; indeed, the darkness shall not hide from You, but the night shines as the day; the darkness and the light are both alike to You (Psalm 139:11-12).

There's a reason why bars and nightclubs are dimly lit. Darkness obscures details, hides those who don't want to be seen, and provides cover for things we wouldn't do in daylight. King Saul went to the witch of Endor in disguise at night (1 Samuel 28:7-8). When Judas, satanically inspired, went out to arrange Jesus's betrayal, "it was night" (John 13:30). Night reflects the darkness in the human soul. Jesus said as much: "This is the condemnation, that the light has come into the world, and men loved darkness rather than light, because their deeds were evil" (John 3:19).

When David wrote Psalm 139, however, he wasn't trying to cover anything up (though he had personal experience doing that). The

Hebrew word he used for the darkness *falling* on him in verse 11 literally means "to bruise" or "to crush." Darkness, whether literal or figurative, can be oppressive. When it's too dark to see, we lose our frame of reference even in familiar settings. It's unsettling to stumble or bump into an object that you wouldn't give a moment's thought in daylight. In the dark, our thoughts tend to go wild, even if we suspect we've only run into a chair or a shoe.

Darkness can also refer to the irrational behavior of people who deliberately disobey God. The Bible calls this having a darkened understanding (Ephesians 4:17-18) or having one's heart darkened (Romans 1:21). Beyond that, we all go through dark seasons in life spiritually and emotionally. We all have to deal with darkness.

But, according to David, darkness and light are the same to God. Whether we're talking about nighttime or a dark night of the soul, He is present in both. "Even the night shall be light about me; indeed, the darkness shall not hide from You" (Psalm 139:11-12). It's as if David was saying, "Even if the darkness starts to mess with my mind, You're there with me." Whether darkness manifests as a simple fear of what you can't see, financial hard times or work-related stress, or something more personal and complex, like depression, illness, or anxiety, God is present; He is right there with you (Matthew 28:20).[20]

Some people believe that the presence of evil in the world means that God doesn't exist, He's not present, or He doesn't care. But I would say that the very existence of darkness points to the existence of God. Because there is darkness, light means something. C.S. Lewis argued, "If the whole universe has no meaning, we should never have found out that it has no meaning: just as, if there were no light in the universe and therefore no creatures with eyes, we should never know it was dark. *Dark* would be a word without meaning."[21]

When we recognize contrasts—good and evil, light and dark, right and wrong—we are acknowledging that the universe means something. We are sensing that one way is better than the other.

That takes us back to the argument for God's existence from moral law. To concede that evil exists is to say that good exists too.

Follow that chain of reasoning back, as we did in chapter 3, and you arrive at the conclusion that God exists. And if God exists and good exists, it must be because God is good. If God is good, that means He cares. And if He is going to care like a good God should, He will always be present in your darkness, bearing witness to your life and offering comfort, hope, and strength. God's omnipresence, then, means that your presence has purpose. The problem isn't on the transmission end of God's presence but rather in our reception of it. Perhaps we need a frequency adjustment.

God's light cuts through the darkness, giving meaning to your life today. Whatever you have done in the darkness is known to God, so there's no point in trying to hide it. Whatever web you weave to try to cover up wrongdoing will only exhaust your energy and your sense of purpose. Maybe the idea of God being present in the mess you've made irritates you, and you think, *Why didn't He keep me from getting into this in the first place?* But it's often those very messes—as well as pain and guilt—that God uses to get your attention.

Guilt is like a pebble in your shoe that won't go away no matter how many times you change shoes. Eventually, you have to consider that this metaphorical pebble might have a purpose: It's God's way of telling you that you're off-course—His way of saying, "This problem is rubbing you the wrong way because it's pointing you to something better."

And that problem, in this case, is accepting God's omnipresence. To believe that God exists is to accept Him as He describes Himself. Otherwise, He isn't God. If God exists, He knows everything. If God exists, He is everywhere. You tip that first domino and the others must fall. God's presence can be a liberating force for you if you let it be.

But if God's omnipresence feels more like a pebble in your shoe right now, it could be His way of telling you that you're farther from

His heart than you realize. Remember, however, that you are never too far away from Him no matter how lost you may—or may not—feel. You don't have to be at the end of your rope to turn to God and seek His presence. In fact, it's more dangerous to think you're good enough to stand on your own without Him. The people Jesus took the greatest issue with were the super-religious, those who thought their obedience to custom and tradition outweighed God's own goodness, justice, and holiness. The Lord seeks the lost, not those who assume all is well.

One of the most compelling aspects of God's omnipresence is His pursuit. When you're lost, He comes to find you. This was God's very first move after Adam and Eve fell in the garden (Genesis 3:9). When you run from Him because of fear or shame or guilt, He pursues you to bring you home. His pursuit and presence remind you that you matter, that you're worth something, and that whatever comes your way, you're not alone.

What a comfort God's presence has been to His people throughout the ages. When God called Moses to take a message to Pharaoh, at first Moses didn't want any part of that. He felt that he couldn't speak well enough on his own to confront Egypt's ruler and that he didn't deserve the chance to represent God among his fellow Hebrews. But God told him, "Don't worry, I'm going with you. I'll tell you what to say and do."[22] When Joshua took over for Moses years later, what a comfort it must have been to hear God say, "As I was with Moses, so I will be with you" (Joshua 1:5).

Gideon was the runt of the family litter, and his tribe the runt of Israel, but God promised him, "Surely I will be with you, and you shall defeat the Midianites as [if they were] one man" (Judges 6:16). Because Gideon trusted God's promise and presence, he and a tiny squad of 300 men wiped out an army of 120,000 (Judges 8:10-12). When Paul experienced frustration along the way from Athens to Corinth, God encouraged him, saying, "Do not be afraid, but speak, and do not keep silent; for I am with you" (Acts 18:9-10).

Surely those days of God declaring His presence to people are long over. It seems that in the West, we no longer hear Him speak audibly in words we know aren't our own. But we have the astonishing record of the Bible as a precedent. Scripture tells us repeatedly that not only is God present everywhere at all times—He also wants to be personally involved in our lives.

But we must accept God's offer of friendship. We will by no means get away with doing otherwise. In biblical times, there was a saying in the Roman Empire that "the whole world was one great prison to a malefactor."[23] Roman law had such a hold on everyday life that to commit a crime was to practically guarantee eventual—if not swift and immediate—punishment. That's what it's like to reject God in this life. You may build yourself Jericho-like walls of intellectual might, mortared with disdain for the poor fools who rely on faith in a God that can't be seen. But reliance on science or philosophy is like every other veil we put between us and our Maker; eventually, it will all be torn away. That may not happen on this side of eternity, but be assured, there is nowhere you can go to escape coming face to face with God one day. Will it be as friend or foe?

You have everything to gain from choosing His friendship: You'll inherit His presence and His promises in this life and an eternity enjoying Him in the next. "He Himself has said, 'I will never leave you nor forsake you'" (Hebrews 13:5). As one translation puts it, emphasizing the literal meaning of the original Greek text,

> I will never [under any circumstances] desert you [nor give you up nor leave you without support, nor will I in any degree leave you helpless], nor will I forsake or let you down or relax My hold on you [assuredly not]! (AMP).

God uniquely dwells with and in His children. If you've accepted His friendship, you can filter everything through this great truth: God is now here.

Chapter 9

MY GOD IS BIGGER
THAN YOUR GOD

God's Major Attributes, Part 3:
Omnipotence

My dad was more than six feet tall, so he was bigger than a lot of kids' dads. That came in handy when my brothers and I would get into those classic arguments with other kids—the ones about whose bike is faster or who can throw a ball farther. Sometimes these battles of one-upmanship could only be decided by the dreaded bottom-line words: "My dad is bigger than your dad." The implication that my dad could beat up their dad was hard to top.

King David, throughout his life, was never shy about recognizing God's bigness. He didn't hesitate to talk trash about other powers, kings, and gods as they compared to Yahweh. His confidence was bolstered knowing that other gods were just made up and there was only one real One. When Goliath cursed David by his gods, David famously replied, "You come to me with sword, spear, and javelin, but I come to you in the name of the Lord of Heaven's Armies" (1 Samuel 17:45 NLT). In Psalm 115, David asked his countrymen,

> Why let the nations say, "Where is their God?" Our God is in the heavens, and he does as he wishes. Their idols are merely things of silver and gold, shaped by human hands. They have mouths but cannot speak, and eyes but cannot see. They have ears but cannot hear, and noses but cannot smell. They have hands but cannot feel, and feet but

cannot walk, and throats but cannot make a sound. And those who make idols are just like them, as are all who trust in them. O Israel, trust the Lord! (vv. 2-9 NLT).

This was David saying, in essence, "My God is bigger than your gods!" Of course, trash talk means nothing unless you can back it up, but God never falls short on that account. Throughout the psalms, David frequently affirmed God's vastness and strength. "Power, O God," he wrote in Psalm 62, "belongs to you" (v. 11 NLT).

How big is God? Big enough to create everything in the universe—and big enough to care for every detail in your life. God not only knows everything (omniscience) and is everywhere (omnipresence), but He has all power—what we call omnipotence. This attribute is proclaimed by the hosts of heaven in Revelation: "Alleluia! For the Lord God Omnipotent reigns!" (19:6).

> God's power never weakens. It doesn't have a shelf life, nor does He ever need to be recharged.

God's omnipotence means that He has all power and ultimate control over everything. This includes His absolute rule and authority over His creation. And just as His knowledge never gets added to and His presence never diminishes no matter where we go, so God's power never weakens. It doesn't have a shelf life, nor does He ever need to be recharged.

That level of power is hard for us to wrap our minds around. Sometimes I think kids have an easier time understanding and articulating how great God is. I have a wonderful book of letters children have written to God, some of which wrestle with issues we've been looking at. For instance, Lucy wrote, "Dear God, are you really invisible or is that just a trick?" Jeff said, "Dear God, it is great the way you always get the stars in the right places." And Donna said, "Dear God, we read that Thomas Edison made light. But in Sunday school they said you did it. So I bet he stole your idea."[1]

In Psalm 139, David wrote:

You formed my inward parts; You covered me in my mother's womb. I will praise You, for I am fearfully and wonderfully made; marvelous are Your works, and that my soul knows very well. My frame was not hidden from You, when I was made in secret, and skillfully wrought in the lowest parts of the earth. Your eyes saw my substance, being yet unformed. And in Your book they all were written, the days fashioned for me, when as yet there were none of them.

How precious also are Your thoughts to me, O God! How great is the sum of them! If I should count them, they would be more in number than the sand; when I awake, I am still with You (Psalm 139:13-18).

David clearly just scratched the surface of God's might in these six verses. As he mentioned earlier in the psalm, the scope of God's knowledge and power were too much for him to fully take in. So he kept things basic here. But that's a good place to begin.

David framed God's omnipotence in the most personal terms, bringing home a concept that could otherwise easily go cosmic on us. When we're talking about a being who holds the universe together, from the smallest quark to the largest galaxy, it's easy to think in impersonal terms. But one of the more amazing facts about God's unique traits is that He puts them to work for our benefit. God scales down and displays His immense power in ways we can grasp, and that's what David touched on here.

God's Work Is Marvelous

In the first part of Psalm 139, David basically told God, "Marvelous is Your knowledge." In the second section, he said, "Marvelous is Your presence." Here, David marveled at God's ability. His key point in this passage appears in verse 14, which you just can't beat in the King James translation: "Marvellous are thy works; and that my soul knoweth right well." It's like David picked up where Job left off, standing in awe of God's power and saying, "I know that

You can do everything, and that no purpose of Yours can be withheld from You" (Job 42:2).

How do you acknowledge God's marvelous works? Often, you just have to keep your eyes and heart open to what's around you in nature. Living in New Mexico, I admit that's easy for me to do. God operates at full power, but often in what we might call everyday ways. Once I was driving west toward Arizona in the snow. Watching the distant mountains and mesas fall gently under a white blanket was stunning—and then the storm cleared just in time for a glorious sunset to break through the clouds.

The sheer wonder of this spectacular scene put me in mind of David's words: "Marvellous are thy works." When we get in the habit of not only looking for evidence of God's wonders but acknowledging them out loud, it keeps our hearts soft. It helps us resist all the ways the world hardens us. While the world's power puts us on the defensive, God's power opens us up with gratitude.

What Can't God Do?

Few have defined God's power as well as Paul did when he wrote about "the purpose of Him who works all things according to the counsel of His will" (Ephesians 1:11). God's omnipotence means that He is able to do anything that is according to His will. The Bible is full of amazing works that God did to bless people and further His overall plans—things that only He could do. God waited until a ninety-nine-year-old man named Abraham and his ninety-year-old wife Sarah were as good as dead—reproductively speaking— before keeping His promise to give them a son of their own. Sarah laughed at God when He predicted this baby was coming, and God called her on it, asking a simple question: "Is anything too hard for the Lord?" (Genesis 18:14).

God opened up a body of water so that three million Hebrews plus their livestock could escape their enemies on dry land—and then He buried the Egyptian army in that same body of water. God dropped bread from the heavens for His people every day as they crossed the desert, and He kept their clothes and shoes from wearing out for decades. He kept a wayward prophet alive in the belly of a big fish, brought down the walls of a city with a marching band, and prevented a pack of lions from dismembering an old man.

Then, in the second act of the great biblical story, God divinely conceived the Savior of the world in the womb of a virgin, for, as the angel said, "With God nothing will be impossible" (Luke 1:37). The child who was born then grew up, turned water into wine, healed people of everything from paralysis to blindness to leprosy, fed huge crowds with a few loaves and fishes, walked on water, came back to life after being dead for three days, and declared to His disciples, "With God all things are possible" (Matthew 19:26).

And God still works powerfully today. Families, physicians, and missionaries of every generation are able to share about how the impossible has occurred—a lifesaving mercy while traveling, a healing against all odds, an opportunity to share faith under hostile circumstances. This is one of God's calling cards—that He can do the impossible. When something happens that can't be naturally explained, the people involved are suddenly confronted with the opportunity to see how comfortable they are with the idea of an unlimited divine power moving in and around them.

What God Can't Do

Sometimes these miraculous interventions get chalked up to unexplained phenomenon or coincidence, both of which serve as a flimsy cover for not acknowledging the existence, presence, and power of God. People will even argue against the idea that God could be all-powerful, asking self-canceling questions like "Can God make a square circle?," or "Can God make a rock so big He can't lift it?"

Rather than dignify such questions with an answer, I would make a simple distinction: God can do anything He pleases that is in harmony with His nature. That's what all the biblical teaching about God's power comes down to: God does what is in accord with His nature. That means there are some things God can't do. For instance, God can't lie (Hebrews 6:18). God can't wink at evil or even stand it in His presence (Habakkuk 1:13). God also can't be unfaithful (2 Timothy 2:13). Those things, and many others, are in opposition to His nature. Sometimes we learn about God via contrast with what we would call His positive characteristics—love, goodness, kindness, patience, and so on. So even the things God *can't* do are still defined by their ultimate outcomes—His glory and our good. "Marvellous are Thy works."

God's Workmanship Is Meticulous

In Psalm 139, David also pointed out that God's workmanship is meticulous. Notice that he didn't go big here as he did in other psalms, where he turned to the cosmos for evidence of God's power: "When I consider Your heavens, the work of Your fingers, the moon and the stars, which You have ordained" (Psalm 8:3), or "The heavens declare the glory of God" (Psalm 19:1). Rather, David went small—he looked into the womb to consider human gestation.

When the Bible speaks of the supernatural origins of the universe and human life, some folks squirm. "Why do you have to bring God into everything?" they say. "Anyone with any intelligence knows we evolved. It's a closed case." Some even insist that science and God shouldn't mix. But if we maintain that an all-powerful God created the universe, what are we to do with science?

Remember, the task of science is to learn about the physical world. Using observable phenomena, scientists come up with testable hypotheses that tell us something about the world around us. But there are limits to what hypotheses and testing can prove, and one of those limits is when the evidence points to an intelligent designer. Science can't prove there is a God—and that's not the goal of science, anyway. But science can look at the effects of a foundational cause and follow it back to a designer. Of course, that designer can't be tested, replicated, or verified in the same way physical causes and effects can.

Most scientists don't like this one bit. But there are a number of scientists who are willing to follow the evidence where it leads and are more open to the idea of God and His role in creation. As for the whole evolution versus creation debate, I'll stand by the comments of molecular biologist Michael Denton: "[Darwin's] general theory...is still, as it was in Darwin's time, a highly speculative hypothesis entirely without direct factual support and very far from the self-evident axiom some...would have us believe."[2]

When David wanted to demonstrate God's meticulous workmanship, he got much more personal. Speaking to God, he said, "You formed my inward parts; You covered me in my mother's womb. I will praise You, for I am fearfully and wonderfully made" (Psalm 139:13-14). The implication is that God crafted us from conception and was fully aware of us in our mother's womb:

> My frame was not hidden from You, when I was made
> in secret, and skillfully wrought in the lowest parts of the
> earth. Your eyes saw my substance, being yet unformed.
> And in Your book they all were written, the days fashioned
> for me, when as yet there were none of them (vv. 15-16).

One translation even puts it, "Like an open book, you watched me grow from conception to birth; all the stages of my life were spread out before you, the days of my life all prepared before I'd even lived one day" (MSG).

What's evident here and in other Bible passages is that we humans are the crowning jewel of God's creative genius, the crescendo of His astonishing inventive work.[3] Perhaps this is why, rather than pointing to the stars, David turned the spotlight on the womb. Instead of celestial heights, David went to terrestrial depths, ignoring planet-scale glory for the atom-sized wonder of cellular development—tiny factories working the coded messages of DNA into a living being.

> You are God's marvelous work! You are made in His image, He loves you, and you are a jewel in the crown of His creation.

The universe is full of astonishing wonders, but God wants His glory to shine most brightly through us. Mind-boggling, right?

Now, a lot of people might look at the wonders of the human body in general and say, "Marvelous are Your works, God." But those same people would be reticent to look at their own bodies and say, "Marvelous is this work." Being content with our bodies is never-ending struggle as we fight against age and grapple with societal standards. But hold any negative thoughts you might have about your body for a minute and let the implications of David's words wash over you: You are God's marvelous work! You are made in His image, He loves you, and you are a jewel in the crown of His creation.

No wonder David used *in utero* development as his example of God's workmanship. When he said, "My frame was not hidden from You" (v. 15), he spoke of the formation of the skeletal, nervous, and vascular systems—the development of which he said is "skillfully wrought" (v. 15). To be wrought means to be knit or embroidered together. David was poetically describing the networks of veins, arteries, and nerves—the fractal root system by which we live and feel.

God works out all the details of the human body in the darkness of the womb—"the lowest parts of the earth" (v. 15)—seeing the final product while our "substance [is] yet unformed" (v. 16). During the embryonic and fetal stages of human development, God's cellular programming unfolds, even as He fully sees you, in all your stages of life, in His mind.

We all start out humbly—as a speck called a zygote. As you grow and develop from embryo to fetus and then infant, 100 trillion cells, 100,000 miles of nerve fiber, 60,000 miles of veins and arteries, 206 bones, and dozens of specialized organs all carry out God's plan for the creation and functioning of your life.

Beyond the sheer wonder of the human body itself, David's point is this: God has superintended your development from the moment you were conceived. He has watched over you from the beginning in your mother's womb, and He won't stop now. This was David's theme from the start of the psalm: "O Lord, You have searched me and known me" (v. 1).

The culture around us continues to debate what this passage makes so clear. The Bible acknowledges personhood from the moment of conception. A fetus is not a nuisance. A baby is a gamechanger, for sure, and can be a disrupter of plans, but that's true whether a pregnancy is planned or not. From a standpoint of faith, new life is always to be celebrated—whether it's a brand-new baby or a life redeemed by Christ. Nowhere else do we see such a marvelous result of all God's attributes: His omniscience means He knows who you are. His omnipresence means He is always with you. And His omnipotence means He can help you live a meaningful, satisfying life.

To recognize God's attributes is to see the value of human life. That's why abortion is problematic to the believer, to say the least. Since Roe v. Wade in 1973, there have been more than 61 million abortions in America.[4] That's roughly the 2018 population of Italy, Tanzania, or South Africa—or the combined populations of Australia, Taiwan, and South Sudan. It's six times the population of Portugal, Jordan, or Sweden.[5] When you don't see the value of life the way God does, the result is devastating.

> To recognize
> God's attributes
> is to see
> the value of
> human life.

David's view of God's omnipotence was tied closely to his view of the sacredness of human life. Perhaps this is why people with the highest view of God are those who also have the highest view of human life. God is bigger than the gods of reproductive rights, eugenics, and inconvenience. A big God means He has big plans for His crowning creation. Even when David was in the earliest stages of development in his mother's womb, God knew his entire future. "In Your book they all were written, the days fashioned for me, when as yet there were none of them" (v. 16). This is a beautiful, poetic way of saying, "God, You know every detail of my life as if it were written in a book." But it's also a glimpse into the all-inclusive nature of God's handiwork.

I can't help but think of all that has been discovered about human DNA, the unlocking of the genetic code. Earlier in this book I mentioned Dr. Francis Collins, head of the Human Genome Project. What he discovered as he worked on human DNA convinced him of something he hadn't believed before—that God exists. I don't agree with everything he writes in his book *The Language of God*, but the information he gives about DNA itself is compelling. "The human genome...[is] three billion letters long, and written in a strange and cryptographic four-letter code."[6]

You have 100 trillion cells in your body, and every cell has forty-six chromosomes—matching pairs of twenty-three segments from your mom and twenty-three from your dad. These molecules contain densely coded information that tells every cell of your body how it's going to function and act from the moment of conception to the moment of demise. Your DNA determines your body type; the color of your skin, hair, and eyes; how your body will respond to the aging process; diseases you're prone to getting; and even how tall you'll be.

It's all part of a program so detailed and complex that "a live reading of that code at a rate of one letter per second would take thirty-one years...Printing those letters out in regular font on normal bond paper and binding them all together would result in a tower the height of the Washington Monument."[7] And that's just the DNA for one human being. God's power is evident in the magnificent complexity and diversity of every person, each of us examples of His meticulous workmanship.

God's Wisdom Is Matchless

Even though the Bible says God formed the first man from the dust of the ground, the last thing He will ever do is treat you like dirt. David reveled in this great truth: "How precious also are Your thoughts to me, O God! How great is the sum of them! If I should count them, they would be more in number than the sand; when I awake, I am still with You" (Psalm 139:17-18).

What stirred David more than his knowledge of God was God's knowledge and care of him. David wasn't rereading his work, thinking, *You know, I'm a pretty good poet. I've managed to articulate three essential doctrines of truth in just a few verses.* Instead, the more he wrote about God, the more God blew him away. What astonished David was that this omniscient, omnipresent, omnipotent God even knew he existed, much less cared deeply about him. He understood that God's wisdom is matchless.

"How precious also," David wrote, "are Your thoughts to me." Before God created the universe, He had you in mind. This great truth produces a sense of purpose, especially when life gets heavy. Can you imagine walking through the trials of life not believing that God exists, that an all-powerful divine being who superintended your development from before you were conceived is watching over you now? It's the difference between seeing your life as a fortuitous occurrence of accidental circumstances—and waiting for your luck to run out at any given moment—and getting up every morning with the knowledge that you belong to a God of power and purpose. It's the difference between being a victim and a victor.

Recognizing that God thinks about you also fuels your faith. If everything David said about God is true, it makes sense to entrust everything in your life to Him. If God is that big, that knowing, that powerful, and that careful, then He knows what you need, and you can trust Him with your present and future.

In the end, knowing all this about God should fill you with a sense of responsibility. If God has a purpose and plan for your life, and you're willing to trust Him with all of you, then you should make sure you understand what He wants for you and live your life as close to His will as you possibly can. Paul desired this for the Colossian believers, praying that they might "be filled with the knowledge of His will in all wisdom and spiritual understanding" (Colossians 1:9). God lovingly and painstakingly crafted you from the moment you came into being, and He has a specific purpose for your life.

One of my favorite authors is Donald Grey Barnhouse, the peerless expositor who taught at the Tenth Presbyterian Church in Philadelphia and was an early pioneer of Christian radio preaching. He was trained at Princeton Theological Seminary. A dozen years after he graduated, he went back to Princeton to speak at Miller Chapel. In the front row was his former Hebrew professor, Dr. Robert Dick Wilson. After Barnhouse spoke, Wilson came up to greet him and told his former student, "If you come back again, I will not come to hear you preach. I only come once. I am glad that you are a big-godder. When my boys come back, I come to see if they are big-godders or little-godders, and then I know what their ministry will be."

Barnhouse asked Wilson to explain. He said,

> Well, some men have a little god, and they are always in trouble with him. He can't do any miracles. He can't take care of the inspiration of the Scriptures and their preservation and transmission to us. They have a little god and I call them little-godders. Then there are those who have a great God. He speaks, and it is done. He commands, and it stands fast. He knows how to show himself strong on behalf of those that fear him. You have a great God, and he will bless your ministry.[8]

Which are you—a little godder or a big godder? What do your fingernails say about your view of the Lord? Are they constantly bitten away from anxiety? Or have you put your trust in the God who is bigger and more powerful than any other gods?

Chapter 10

GOD'S MOST UNPOPULAR ATTRIBUTE: HOLINESS

The Problem of Evil, Part 1

Yousuf Karsh was an Armenian-Canadian artist, world-famous for his large-format film photography. One of his most famous published collections is called *Portraits of Greatness*. It features ninety renowned figures, including Winston Churchill, Ernest Hemingway, Georgia O'Keeffe, Albert Einstein, and Robert Frost.[1] His goal was to capture the common traits of greatness—and he succeeded. But greatness isn't always what people expect.

Seventy of Karsh's ninety portraits feature people who could be considered physically unattractive. The high detail and resolution of the large-format 8 x 10-inch film camera he used reveal a host of imperfections: thirty-five of his subjects have moles, thirteen show liver spots, twenty have acne, and two sport visible scars. In a way, Karsh showed these famous people for who they really were—no pretenses, and certainly no smartphone filters. And yet many of his photographs are considered the most iconic shots ever taken of these people.

Holiness Challenges Self-Sufficiency

Some of God's characteristics have broad appeal. Who doesn't want to hear about His love, grace, or compassion? Who isn't drawn in by accounts of God's faithfulness or providence? But what about His holiness? It seems that one of the least-discussed attributes of

God is, to many, one of His least attractive. That's because this attribute accounts for some of God's unappealing actions. It's because of God's holiness that He is a God of judgment. It's because of God's holiness that He is a God of wrath and even, at times, vengeance. God's holiness led Him to create hell.

But God's holiness is not a flaw. In fact, it's His most-noted characteristic throughout the Bible. God is called holy in the Scriptures more than He is called loving, mighty, or gracious—or anything else. Isaiah alone referred to God as "the Holy One" thirty times. But God's holiness still makes a lot of people squirm.

This isn't a new development. Rather, it's simple human nature—we shy away from hard truth, especially when that truth is so *unlike* our character. Paul warned the young pastor Timothy about this trend: "A time is coming when people will no longer listen to sound and wholesome teaching. They will follow their own desires and will look for teachers who will tell them whatever their itching ears want to hear" (2 Timothy 4:3 NLT). This sounds like it's describing modern times, but it was written in the first century!

Certain teachers today play to this tendency, giving crowds the parts of Scripture that make them feel good but not the parts that challenge them with their shortcomings. But the good news of the gospel isn't that God is a really nice guy who's there for you when times are tough. While it's true that He is good and that He is there for you through thick and thin, that's only the secondary good news. The primary good news is that God has met the requirements of His holiness by giving His Son as a sacrifice to pay the cost of our sin.

I understand that *sin* is an ugly word; it ought to be. Not only is it a catch-all for all the evil things that people do—murder, rape, fraud, oppression—it describes a fundamental flaw in human nature. Sin most often results when we determine that we have more love, more grace, or more mercy than God does. In short, we put ourselves in His place, but we do so without His character or qualities. When we do, we hurt ourselves and others. And yet we seldom give thought to our lack of holiness—those perfect, unstained, undiluted qualities that make God who He is. Instead we downplay our sin and focus on the attributes that make us feel better about ourselves. We center our lives on our versions of mercy or grace or love and then create a version of God where those are the only things He cares about.

Could it be, perhaps, that we have been so conditioned by this hyperpositive environment that we overestimate God's love and kindness and underestimate His other characteristics like justice, wrath, and holiness? We have to ignore a lot of valuable real estate in the Bible to make such an approach stick. Over and over, the Scriptures speak of God's holiness. It's the one word that best describes Him—the frequency that resonates at the core of His being.

God is loving, gracious, merciful, and patient, but are those characteristics the entire essence of His being? If love was, I suppose God would just let everyone into heaven—"Come on in and we'll sort it out later." After all, if anyone could love a tyrant or a wicked person, it would be God, right? So why not let Hitler and Mao into heaven? Surely they'll behave with God hanging around. That would be the loving thing to do, wouldn't it?

But because God is holy, that doesn't happen. Yes, 1 John 4:16 says that "God is love," and He certainly is. But don't misunderstand John's meaning in writing that. He didn't mean that love defines God, but rather, God defines love. Whenever we see a demonstration of love, that doesn't necessarily mean that such love embodies God's heart. Rather, who God is defines what real love is.

And when it comes to His attributes, God doesn't compartmentalize. You have to take Him as He says He is—loving, yes, and merciful and gracious, but also holy and wrathful and just. These attributes are all interrelated, all part of the unique, undivided being of God. And holiness drives the bus. It is the engine of His character.

A god who is not holy is a god who is not worth loving or following, much less living for. A piece of clothing is clean when it is free from spots. Precious metals like silver and gold are pure only if the dross has been burned away. Likewise, to say that God is holy is more than acknowledging His uniqueness as the Supreme Being

of the universe without rival or competition. It is also to acknowledge that no part of Him is evil. "God is light," wrote the apostle
John, "and in Him is no darkness at all" (1 John 1:5). As God, He is
free from any spot of moral evil or impurity.

When I looked into the subject of God's holiness, one of the first
books I turned to was *The Great Doctrines of the Bible*, by William
Evans. Light reading, right? But Dr. Evans hit the nail on the head
when he wrote, "If there is any difference in importance in the attributes of God, that of his holiness seems to occupy the first place. It
is, to say the least, the one attribute which God would have His people remember Him by more than any other."[2]

You might be thinking, *I've heard all this stuff before—but holiness
is just an Old Testament concept, isn't it?* While the Old Testament certainly touches on the theme repeatedly, holiness is important in the
New Testament too. After all, Jesus taught us to pray, "Our Father
in heaven, hallowed be Your name" (Matthew 6:9). To hallow is to
revere and set apart in our hearts, minds, and habits that which is
holy. And when Jesus went back up to heaven at His ascension, His
task of salvation complete, He sent the third person of the Trinity,
the Holy Spirit. Notice He isn't called the Loving Spirit, the Merciful Spirit, or the Gracious Spirit—though, being God, He is all
those things. Rather, above all, He is holy.

All of this to say that you can't pick and choose the characteristics
of God you prefer and toss the rest or relegate them to nonessential
status. You can accept or reject the true God as He reveals Himself,
but you're off base if you say, "I worship a God of love, not a God
of holiness or wrath."

Years ago, I visited a temple in Kyoto, Japan, called
Sanjūsangen-Dō. It's a national landmark, known for its 1,001 stat-
ues of the Buddhist goddess of compassion, Kannon. Each statue
has a slightly different facial expression, and tradition has it that
each worshipper may find a face that either resembles their own or
that of "the person you long to meet."[3] That is the approach many
people take to God—we create God in our image and then worship

what we've created. And yet the Bible clearly indicates that God never changes. He is always who He is, regardless of the way people view Him.

Jerry Bridges, in his book *The Pursuit of Holiness*, gives excellent insight into the extraordinary holiness of God:

> The absolute holiness of God should be of great comfort and assurance to us. If God is perfectly holy, then we can be confident that His actions towards us are always perfect and just. We are often tempted to question God's actions and complain that He is unfair in His treatment of us. [It is] impossible in the very nature of God that He should ever be unfair. Because He is holy, all His actions are holy.[4]

If you're going to truly encounter God, you must accept that He is holy. If you can wrap your mind around His holiness and how it affects you, you can draw close to Him in the most satisfying way.

Holiness Describes Separation

A friend of mine once said, "God rules the universe with his feet up." We get worn down managing the ins and outs of our busy everyday lives, so imagine what it would be like to run the entire universe. That's what God does. But even if He had to superintend a billion other universes like this one, the job wouldn't tax Him in the least. That's the upshot of what we looked at in the previous three chapters: God is in charge, and He is ruling the universe without working up a sweat.

Simply put, that means God is not like us. He is perfect, absolutely pure and good and just—and He is that way all the time. We are not so consistent in anything we do, good or evil. Our best efforts, however impressive they may be among our own kind, are just a child's macaroni sculptures on God's desk. That difference creates separation between us and Him.

In fact, God's holiness means we can't approach Him on our terms. Our sin creates a barrier between us and Him—a buffer zone that we can't penetrate. And yet God calls us to be holy just as He is holy—to be separated from the ways of our flesh and the world around us. This is a key theme of the New Testament, and it echoes God's Old Testament command, which is repeated several times in the law.[5]

God definitely wants a relationship with you. That's the very reason you were created. But this relationship has to be on His terms—namely, you have to come to Him through Jesus Christ. In essence, the New Testament writers were saying, "You know how God told you to be holy because He is holy? Look! He made a way to do that in Jesus Christ!" Jesus made it possible to break through the previously impenetrable wall of holiness, to move from being separated from God to being sold out for God.

To get a better sense of the wonder and necessity of being holy, it's helpful to get an idea of just how separated God is from us. The prophet Isaiah had a vision that enables us do just that.

> In the year that King Uzziah died, I saw the Lord sitting on a throne, high and lifted up, and the train of His robe filled the temple. Above it stood seraphim; each one had six wings: with two he covered his face, with two he covered his feet, and with two he flew. And one cried to another and said: 'Holy, holy, holy is the Lord of hosts; the whole earth is full of His glory!' And the posts of the door were shaken by the voice of him who cried out, and the house was filled with smoke (Isaiah 6:1-4).

The first thing to notice in this passage is that God is seated—He is in charge, calmly settled and running the world. He's ruling with a steady and just hand, not wringing His hands and saying, "Oh no! Uzziah was one of the good ones. What do I do now?"

Before Uzziah came on the scene, Judah had had a centuries-long shortage of good kings. But Uzziah was a reformer who stabilized the nation after his father's bloody, militaristic reign. Most importantly, he trusted God on a remarkably steady basis, especially for a politician. As a result, God blessed him and helped him build up Judah's military forces, which were used primarily for defensive purposes and not to oppress his subjects.

In the end, Uzziah's pride got the better of him, which led to a chastening disease, but he was miles better than most of the kings who came before or after him. When Uzziah died in 739 BC, fifty-two years of relatively great leadership came to an end. At his death, the people were shaken, making it clear that they had put their hope primarily in their earthly king rather than in God. The lesson of Uzziah's life, however, is that God is in charge, and when we—and our leaders—trust Him, good things happen.

But apparently even Isaiah, God's own prophet, needed to be reminded of this. So God gave him this vision. And the key of this vision is God's holiness. Remember, holiness describes separation. Isaiah saw God, large and in charge, calmly enthroned and surrounded by worshipping angels—and the angels were crying out these words: *Holy, holy, holy.*

Now, God's splendor was filling the temple. The doorposts were shaking with the cries of His praise, and the room was filled with the smoky mystery and wonder of His majesty. And yet the angels' words of worship were not about God's might or mercy, but rather were a threefold proclamation of His holiness. This expression is called the *trihagion* (Greek for "thrice holy"). In Hebrew, the triple usage emphasizes the ultimate nature of something. This is significant. The Bible never says that God is *merciful, merciful, merciful,* or *loving, loving, loving,* or *just, just, just,* but it does call Him *holy, holy, holy.*

Think about it this way: If we heard about a strident battle among politicians over an issue, we might say, "There's a war going on in Congress." If we then watched a TV special about World War II, we would say, "Now that's a *war* war." But if we looked ahead to the ultimate gathering of earth's armies against God Himself at

Armageddon, we could describe that as a *war war war*. There's a war of words, then there's a real war between nations, but then there's the war to end all wars. That's how it is with God's holiness. He is not just holy; He is thrice holy to emphasize that holiness is central to His nature and to express the triune nature of God as Father, Son, and Holy Spirit.

What does holiness actually mean? It sounds so churchy and ancient, like stained glass and clean fingernails, barren deserts and long, flowing robes with sandals, like fasting and praying on your knees for hours. It sounds like something meant only for a chosen few, something beyond our reach and about as much fun as a week's worth of casseroles.

In some ways, that's not totally off the mark. Holiness doesn't have high entertainment value (and it's not supposed to). It's pretty straightforward. In Exodus 40, God commanded Moses to apply a little bit of oil to each of the utensils and objects that would be used to worship Him in the tabernacle (vv. 9-15). That anointing oil set apart each object as special, something to be used *only* in the worship of God. It's not that the oil was magical or that the utensils, altar, or priests had special properties. It's that all those things were set apart for God's purposes, to be used solely for worship. They were made holy because He is holy.

God is not the Man Upstairs or the Big Guy in the Sky. He's not your pal, the grandfather you never had, or an old codger with a flowing white beard. God is unique, unprecedented, and unparalleled. In the church we often mistake God's desire to draw near to us as chumminess. But the Bible tells us differently: God dwells in indescribable glory, in unapproachable light. He is a consuming fire. Yes, Jesus broke down the sin barrier and invited us into an intimate friendship with Himself and His Father (John 15:15; 17:3), but that's because He paid the ultimate price to bring His Father and us together. To have a relationship with God, you have to start by recognizing the separation between you and Him, between His holiness and your sinfulness.

Holiness Deepens Conviction

Isaiah immediately recognized this separation. Look at his response:

> Woe is me, for I am undone! Because I am a man of unclean lips, and I dwell in the midst of a people of unclean lips; for my eyes have seen the King, the Lord of hosts (Isaiah 6:5).

Isaiah didn't say, "Hah! I saw God and you didn't." He didn't say, "Great! I'm going to get me some answers now that I have an audience with God." No, he said, "I'm undone!" *I'm ruined; I'm doomed; I am lost!* Why would he, a prophet of God, say that? After all, his vision was a special moment that few, if any in his generation, would ever experience. These days, someone might be tempted to write a book about it—*The Day I Saw God*—and then go on a speaking tour, make TV appearances, and maybe even get a YouTube channel going. Instead, Isaiah responded with profound conviction of his own sinfulness.

"Woe is me, for I am undone!"

Upon seeing the holy God, Isaiah saw himself in comparison as unholy and unclean. God's light reveals our darkness, His perfection, our imperfection. Any illusions of self-importance, accomplishment, or pride are put in check. Pride and holiness are like oil and water, or paper and fire. Pride is for those who have never encountered God. It's for shower-singers who have never crooned next to Pavarotti. It's for those who paint by numbers who have never worked next to Van Gogh. It's for the garage rocker who has never strummed next to Clapton. Isaiah, an educated poet of royal descent who prophesied about the coming of Messiah, stood in God's presence and said, "I'm dirt." And he was right.

Even such a prophet standing next to a holy God must confess his utter spiritual bankruptcy. Jesus called it being "poor in spirit" (Matthew 5:3). As Max Lucado said, "You don't impress the officials at NASA with a paper airplane...And you don't boast about your goodness in the presence of the Perfect."[6] If holiness is a central characteristic of God, and if the uniqueness of God's holiness brings out a sense of conviction when people truly experience it, it makes sense that we would see reactions like that of Isaiah's throughout the Bible.

And so we do. Take Job, for example. By human standards, Job was just about perfect. God Himself said as much: "There is none like him on the earth, a blameless and upright man, one who fears God and shuns evil" (Job 1:8). Perhaps that was why God allowed Satan to test Job, giving the devil permission to strike him in every major area of his life—family, livelihood, and health. Job lost it all.

There were times during his suffering when Job asked God, "What's up with all this? What have I done wrong?" But when all was said and done, and God finally spoke to Job of His greatness and holiness, notice how Job responded: "I have heard of You by the hearing of the ear, but now my eye sees You. Therefore I abhor myself, and repent in dust and ashes" (Job 42:5-6). His encounter with God gave him perspective. All his concerns—and they were many—burned away before God's holiness.

This happened to Peter too. Instinctively boastful and even aggressive in asserting himself, Peter was a natural-born leader. He first encountered Jesus after a long, fruitless night of fishing. At that time, Jesus promptly told Peter, the expert fisherman, to let down his nets one more time. Peter was probably thinking something like, *I'm the fisherman here, but sure, preacher man, I'll go out again*. But when the nets filled to bursting and he had to call in reinforcements to unload the massive catch, Peter fell to his knees before Jesus and said, "Depart from me, for I am a sinful man, O Lord!" (Luke 5:8).

In John's great vision of heaven, he saw Jesus Christ in His glory: snow-white hair, eyes aflame, face like the noonday sun. His response? "I fell at His feet as dead" (Revelation 1:17). Like Isaiah before him, John was undone—unraveled before the presence of God. And like Isaiah, when John saw God enthroned in majesty, he heard the angels saying, "Holy, holy, holy, Lord God Almighty, who was and is and is to come!" (Revelation 4:8). Then he saw the response of the twenty-four elders, who threw their crowns before God's throne and said, "You are worthy, O Lord, to receive glory and honor and power" (v. 11).

Why all this falling down, groveling, and self-abasement? Don't any of these people have any sense of self-assurance or self-esteem? Not in God's presence! It's as if they are all saying, "In Your presence, Lord, no honor can come to me. It must all go to You—all my power, authority, and honor are merely offerings at Your feet." No one rightly viewing God wants any honor at all—no recognition for deeds done in His service, no pat on the back for a life faithfully lived, no acknowledgement of suffering. Faced with God's holiness, all the things that we think truly matter in this life fall away like autumn leaves in a strong breeze.

God's power astonishes us, His knowledge amazes us, and His kindness wins our hearts. But His holiness convicts us of our greatest need: His forgiveness. Jesus said we would be blessed if we mourned our sin, lamented our errors, and grieved our pride. When we experience God's holiness, we feel the depth of those transgressions, and we know there is only one right thing for us to do: recognize that God alone is holy.

In fact, acknowledging God's holiness is one of the ways we are to praise Him. Moses sang the first recorded song about God's holiness back in the desert after seeing the powerful and humbling display of God's power at the Red Sea. Some of the lyrics included, "Who is like you, O Lord, among the gods? Who is like You, glorious in holiness, fearful in praises, doing wonders?" (Exodus 15:11).

> God's holiness convicts us so He can begin to heal us.

Of course, acknowledging God's holiness also means facing our own darkness, and that's not easy to do. But what's wonderful about God's holiness is that it doesn't just leave us exposed and feeling guilty. It moves us through the debris of our hearts and lives toward a peaceful, satisfying way of living. God's holiness convicts us so He can begin to heal us.

Holiness Demands Purification

That healing begins with our purification. Isaiah witnessed God's holiness and saw for himself that God is separate from His creation. That awareness overwhelmed him with his own inadequacy. But that sense of conviction led him to want to be near God. To do that, he had to be made pure. He couldn't do that for himself, though, so God arranged for it to happen:

> Then one of the seraphim flew to me, having in his hand a live coal which he had taken with the tongs from the altar. And he touched my mouth with it, and said: "Behold, this has touched your lips; your iniquity is taken away, and your sin purged" (Isaiah 6:6-7).

What would you think if you saw an angel, already terrifying with his six wings, perhaps with two covering his face and two covering his feet, moving toward you with a red-hot coal held out by a pair of tongs? *What is he going to do with* that? *Touch my mouth?*

In New Mexico, where I live, the state vegetable is the green chile. Folks here put it on just about everything, from eggs to burgers to enchiladas to just eating a bowl of the stuff with some tortillas. Green chile comes in varying degrees of hotness, the lowest of which can be mild, and the highest of which is not quite like having a burning coal touch your lips. The first time I tried the hottest, I thought, *Oh, come on! Who can do this to themselves?* But before long I got hooked. Now it's like, "Bring the fire!"

It's noteworthy that Isaiah didn't describe feeling any pain at this point. In his vision, the coal purified his unclean lips and heart, but not through physical pain. In fact, it actually gave him relief from the anguish he felt moments before when he realized his unworthiness to stand before a holy God. The coal symbolically purged him of his sin.

How? The text says the angel took the coal from the altar—presumably the altar in the outer court of the temple, the setting for Isaiah's vision. This altar was where sacrifices were offered and blood was spilled to pay for the people's sin. When the angel touched the coal to Isaiah's lips, he cleansed the prophet from his sin. There was no blood involved, but the true power of forgiveness comes not from an animal's blood or a burning ember but from God accepting His Son's blood as payment for sin's price and saying to those who receive Christ, "I forgive you. You are clean."

Why did God have to symbolically cleanse His prophet here? Because holiness cannot exist with unholiness. God must first destroy what is unholy so He can truthfully declare that something has been made holy. That's true throughout the Bible.

Consider the tabernacle and the temple. If God ever sent a message that He is untouchable and set apart from His sin-stained creation, it's built into the foundations of the places where He was formerly worshipped. Only the high priest could enter the Holy of Holies, the central place where God's presence dwelled. And even then, he could enter only once a year—and if he wanted to exit alive, he had to be ceremonially purified before he went in.

> Spiritually speaking, trusting in Jesus's sacrifice on the cross is like going from being bankrupt to being a gazillionaire.

The tabernacle and temple showed us that there is a huge gap between people and God: His holiness demands perfection, which we can never attain. But these places of worship also demonstrated that the gulf could be bridged by sacrifice. A person would bring an animal, the priest blessed it and killed it on the altar, and its life counted in place of the person who made the offering. The concept is the same in the New Testament, except the altar was the cross. Jesus, the perfect Lamb of God, became the ultimate sacrifice, paying for the sin of anyone who would believe in Him— thus bridging the gap between man and God once and for all. His purity paid for our impurity, meeting the demand of God's holiness while fulfilling God's great heart of love and mercy toward us.

Spiritually speaking, trusting in Jesus's sacrifice on the cross is like going from being bankrupt to being a gazillionaire. All of God's perfection and holiness, found in Jesus Christ, gets transferred—or "imputed" (Romans 4:22-24)—to your account with God.

On the cross, Jesus purchased us an unlimited supply of God's favor, which is why we should be stoked about God's holiness. Peter said that we are not redeemed by gold or silver, which maintain their value for only as long as you live, or by the inconsistent conduct of religion, "but with the precious blood of Christ, as of a lamb without blemish and without spot" (1 Peter 1:19). In other words, a perfectly holy lamb. Only the one who is perfectly holy could cleanse those who are perfectly unholy. Now an infinite stream of God's generosity can flow in our direction.

But before you can become a recipient of God's favor, you must first open your eyes to the gulf that exists between you and God. Many good churchgoing folk haven't taken this step, which is how they can continue to attend services every week while remaining unchanged between Sundays. They don't see the great distance between unholy people and holy God, so they stay closed off to life-changing truth.

We see this attitude show up when someone prays, "Lord, if I have sinned, forgive me." *If?* Is there any uncertainty in that prospect? How about, "*Because* I have sinned, forgive me"? After all, why bother talking to God unless you're sure that you have sinned and that He is the only one who can do something about it? Unless you experience the conviction of God's holiness, you won't see the need for your purification. That's why religious people so often reject God's cleansing—they don't see their need for it. They figure they're good enough, even holy enough, before God based on their good deeds and proper behavior. But as Isaiah later noted, "Our best efforts are grease-stained rags" (Isaiah 64:6 MSG).

But if, like Isaiah, you recognize your need for cleansing, God's got you covered: "If we confess our sins, He is faithful and just to forgive us our sins and to cleanse us from all unrighteousness" (1 John 1:9). Admitting that your so-called goodness is nothing before God's holiness makes getting cleaned up possible. The whole concept of purification suggests that God's holiness heals us, helping us become who God made us to be: His people in heart, word, and deed.

Holiness Develops Commission

Once you've seen where you stand before God, and you've responded by saying, "God, I can't be made clean without You," then God's holiness at work in you will result in service, a sense of mission. That's what happened to Isaiah. After his purification, he heard God ask, "Whom shall I send, and who will go for Us?" (Isaiah 6:8). Isaiah immediately responded, "Here am I! Send me" (v. 8).

The plural pronoun "Us" that God used probably refers to the Trinity—the Father, Son, and Holy Spirit (Genesis 1:26). God wasn't asking who would go for Him and the angels. The very name *angel* means "messenger," and that's what angels do—they serve God in heaven and do special jobs on earth, including delivering God's messages. Rather, this was the royal "Us" here—a reference to the triune, eternal community of God. It's a hint that God, who always lives in perfect, harmonious community within Himself—needing nothing—desires community with His creation.

But God is looking for volunteers to commune with and participate in His plans, not draftees. He doesn't force a person into service. He doesn't do guilt trips. You have to want to serve Him. And holiness is the very thing that develops purpose and commission. That's always the pattern. Once I, an unholy person, am declared holy by holy God through the sacrifice of Christ, and once the weight of my sin has been lifted off of me, my gratitude and love inspire me to say, "Here I am, God—send me!" I want Him to get ahold of all of me, to do what He wants with me, to make me a part of the work He is doing through His people in the world.

I see this pattern play out over and over in the lives of the pastors I work with, the people I serve with, and the people I serve. I see it in missionaries across the globe. I observe it in volunteers at our church who work full-time jobs during the week yet pour themselves out in service to God and others in their remaining hours. The way in which these people have surrendered to the Lord has been brought about by God's holiness, driven by a deep sense of conviction and a desire to be holy like God is holy.

Becoming Holy (or At Least Holier)

When God declares you holy, the Holy Spirit sets up shop and begins to work in your heart to make holiness possible in everyday life. As Leighton Ford notably said, "God loves us the way we are, but He loves us too much to leave us that way."[7] Holiness is a process, and the goal is always to match our practice to our position.

> Pursue holiness, and you will get happiness thrown in.

Holiness is not optional for the Christian. "Pursue peace with all people, and holiness, without which no one will see the Lord" (Hebrews 12:14). In fact, holiness is the answer to a question I hear as often as any other: *What is God's will for my life?* Simple: To be holy like He is holy. If you were perhaps hoping that God's will is for you to be happy, I'll let you in on a surprise: Pursue holiness, and you will get happiness thrown in. Happiness is never obtained by direct pursuit; it's a byproduct of chasing after holiness. That's because to pursue holiness is to aim for the essence of God. You can't help but become more like Him, and that will make you happier.

We all want to be better people than we are. We all want to understand and move toward fulfilling our purpose in life. We all want to be healed from regret and brokenness. But true, abiding satisfaction comes from knowing the Lord and seeking to become more like Him—more holy.

How can you know whether you're growing in holiness? It's pretty easy, actually: When you love what God loves and you hate what God hates, you're on a holy path. Becoming holy isn't something you do by striving to be a better person; it's something you let the Holy Spirit do inside you that then comes out in your words and actions. Holiness is something that affects your daily life, manifesting itself in God-imitating and God-pleasing qualities—kindness, grace, purity, moral integrity, mercy.

C.S. Lewis said, "How little people know who think that holiness is dull. When one meets the real thing...it's irresistible. Even if 10% of the world's population had it, would not the whole world be converted and happy before a year's end?"[8] Imagine the impact even a small group of people could have if they said, "I will live to become more holy, to please God in all areas of my life"—and then they let the Holy Spirit do just that in and through them!

That's the challenge of my own life—that, by God's grace and through the help of the Holy Spirit, my practice would increasingly match what I read, study, and preach. My earnest hope and honest prayer is that God's holiness would no longer be His most unpopular attribute, but His most popular. To tap into God's holiness is to access the core of His being, to know beyond any doubt what pleases and displeases Him, and to let that fuel our lives.

Chapter 11

THE DARK SIDE OF GOD: JUSTICE

The Problem of Evil, Part 2

During a recent flight I found myself flipping through one of those catalogs where you can buy unique items like a life-sized Bigfoot statue or a mother-of-pearl hand razor—you know, the essentials. And I came to a section that featured motivational posters and plaques that extolled the virtues of success, determination, achievement, greatness, and imagination. As I looked over them, a thought occurred to me: *I've never seen a poster or plaque extolling pain. Or suffering.* Have you?

I can recall a lot of songs expressing personal pain and suffering, but I can't think of a song that celebrates them, that speaks of how great they are and what wonders they accomplish in us. There are days where we commemorate shared suffering, like Pearl Harbor or 9/11, but there's no national Day of Pain (though, for some, April Fools' Day comes close). Philip Yancey said, "If pinned against the wall at a dark, secret moment, many Christians would confess that pain was God's one mistake. Really, he should have worked a little harder to devise a better way for us to cope with danger."[1]

Thus far in this book, we have moved from the general to the specific concerning God. We've seen that God definitely exists. We've learned that He reveals Himself to us as holy, perfect, just, all-knowing, all-powerful, and everywhere present. But when we think about what all that looks like in everyday life, an unpleasant question rears its head: If God is so perfect and so loving and so knowing and so powerful, then why is His world so messed up? If all the things we've uncovered about God's character and nature are true, why does He allow evil and pain to continue? If He can stop them, why doesn't He?

A Rock in the Windshield

One day I was driving a 1967 truck that had a flat windshield. When a pebble suddenly shot up and struck it, the entire windshield fractured immediately. What had been clear and clean and whole was now fragmented and distorted, right across my line of vision. Everything I viewed from the driver's seat was now warped by a spider-webbed panorama. That can also happen to your view of God. You can be cruising along with a clear, bright view of Him, with no big questions and everything going just as you think it should for a follower of Christ. You've got this Christian life down pat. And then a pebble hits the glass.

Maybe the pebble is more of a boulder—a death, a diagnosis, a devastating loss. A rock like that struck my theological windshield when I was 22. I had been a Christian for four years by that time, getting firmly established in my faith. I had been reaching out to my family with the gospel and trying to explain to them, especially to my next-oldest brother, why they should commit their lives to Christ. My brother and I had a long conversation about the brevity of life and the certainty of a future judgment for choices and actions made in this life.

And then, a week and a half later, it happened. My father called and told me my brother had been killed instantly in a motorcycle accident. To say it caught me off-guard is a massive understatement. Predictably, my first response was denial. This couldn't be so. I had just been with him. He rejected what I had to say, but maybe, I thought, just maybe he would change his mind. God can do anything, right? Now any change of heart would be impossible. My mouth went dry. Shock, disbelief, anger, and extreme sadness became my roommates. The pebble of pain struck and my view of God became fractured.

Another rock would strike some time later when my wife, Lenya, was in the second trimester of pregnancy with our second child. One morning, she felt something wasn't quite right inside her and went in for a routine obstetrics visit. The doctor's grim countenance and somber tone revealed the miscarriage. Our baby, now the size of an adult hand, complete with fingers, toes, eyelids, eyebrows, nails, and hair, was gone.

I was with an evangelical delegation that day planning for an upcoming event, so Lenya and I wept over the phone together, completely unaware that round two was about to hit. Just hours later, my mother called from California to let us know that my dad had suffered a fatal event due to congestive heart failure. He died just hours after his own grandchild had expired in the womb.

It felt like a meteor shower had battered my windshield. It wasn't that I didn't believe in God or that I trusted Him less, but my view of life wasn't the same. I would be changed forever. I knew God was there, but it was harder for me to see Him—harder to make sense of His purposes and will in these gut-wrenching events. I'm guessing that you or someone you know has had a similar experience. Looking back, I think of what C.S. Lewis famously (and wisely) said: "God whispers to us in our pleasures, speaks in our conscience, but shouts in our pain; it is his megaphone to rouse a deaf world."[2] If that's true, then what is He saying, exactly? How are we to interpret episodes of pain, suffering, and evil in the world? Does God have a dark side to Him to allow all the hardship we see around us?

Does God Have a Dark Side?

As we've seen in previous chapters, there is no darkness whatsoever in God's character. So when I talk about the "dark side of God," what I mean is that, from our limited human perspective, we see certain dark things in the world and have no clear explanation for them. In this chapter we'll consider why that is, but we'll also see that because God is who He is, those dark things always have a bright side for those who love and follow Him (Romans 8:28).

Evil is a fact of life in this world. I trust I don't have to break out a philosophical argument or a theological treatise to prove this. Evil has its testimony in every broken home, hungry child, display of greed, and act of senseless violence we see on a daily basis. It's human nature to look for someone to blame all the bad things on, and a lot of people look up when they do. They say, "If God exists, if He is truly all-knowing, all-good, and all-loving, why does evil still exist? Why does it exist at all?" As Peter Kreeft noted, atheists jump on this dilemma because the "problem of evil is the most serious problem in the world. It is also the one most serious objection to the existence of God."[3]

Particularly appealing to atheists is the argument posed by the Greek philosophical sage Epicurus 2,300 years ago:

> God either wishes to take away evil, and is unable; or He is able and unwilling; or He is neither willing nor able; or He is both willing and able. If He is willing but unable, He is feeble, which is not in accordance with the character of God. If He is able and unwilling, He is envious, which is equally at variance with God. If He is neither willing nor able, He is both envious and feeble, and therefore not God. If He is both willing and able, which alone is suitable for God, from what source then are evils? Or why does He not remove them?[4]

These are valid questions, and people have grappled with them for ages, probably since the fall itself. It's a natural response to a world gone awry. Like Epicurus twenty-three centuries ago, theologians and philosophers continue trying to wrestle these sticky issues to the ground. There's even a whole branch of philosophy dedicated to these issues: theodicy, which comes from two Greek words, *theos* ("God") and *diké* ("justice" or "righteousness"). Theodicy attempts to deal with the problem of evil in light of the existence of God.

For many people, however, the issue is more personal than just a philosophical debate. Job, who experienced some of the worst suffering possible, said, "What I always feared has happened to me. What I dreaded has come true. I have no peace, no quietness. I have no rest; only trouble comes" (Job 3:25-26 NLT). How do we reconcile God's righteousness with all the trouble we experience in the world? The pollster George Barna asked people, "If you could ask God only one question and you knew he would give you an answer, what would you ask?" The largest percentage in the poll—17 percent—responded, "Why is there pain and suffering in the world?"[5]

Who Do We Blame?

This question was probably also one of the big questions in Jesus's day, as we learn from an encounter He had with a man born blind. Jesus's disciples figured the man's blindness was the consequence of sin. They just wanted to know whose sin it was that caused it—the man's or his parents'—because, in their minds, it had to be somebody's fault. But Jesus took the discussion in a different direction.

"It was not because of his sins or his parents' sins...This happened so the power of God could be seen in him" (John 9:3 NLT). Then, just in case the disciples weren't already thinking, *Wait—what?!*, Jesus spat on the ground, made some mud, and rubbed it on the blind guy's eyes. "Go wash that off," He told him, and when the man did, he could see for the first time in his life.

Now, the disciples had brought this guy to Jesus's attention because he was suffering for no apparent reason. *Jesus seems to have all kinds of answers for hard things like this—let's ask Him!* There could have been a number of reasons the man couldn't see. Given that he was born blind, he could have contracted neonatal conjunctivitis, an infection that would have been transmitted as he passed through the birth canal. In that day, the condition was untreatable, leading to lifelong blindness. Whatever the case, it's interesting that Jesus's disciples equated suffering with sin. They understood that sin separates us from God, and they saw suffering as the primary consequence of that.

Human suffering is one of the great roadblocks to people believing in God. It would be one thing if only criminals got cancer, if only thieves contracted dementia, if only murderers suffered heart attacks. We could see some sort of celestial justice in that. Instead, we see some of the best people we know going through tragedy and tribulation. And it's not just generically *good* people who suffer—it's also *God's* people. Where is God in *that*?

The peerless expositor Dr. G. Campbell Morgan noted,

> Men of faith are always the men who have to confront problems. Blot God out, and all your problems are ended. If there is no God in heaven, then we have no problem about sin and suffering...But the moment that you admit the existence of an all-powerful governing God, you are face-to-face with your problems. If you say that you have none, I question the strength of your faith.[6]

So then, as people of faith we wonder, *Where is God in the pain?*

It's worth mentioning that this question is far more typically asked in first-world nations like America. In places where society has moved past the struggle to survive, where the pursuit of happiness has morphed into the quest for pleasure, suffering is the enemy. People in developing countries seem far less preoccupied with the issue; suffering is just a fact of life—part of the grind of everyone's existence. But where there is opportunity not just to survive but to thrive, pleasure soon becomes the highest good. Freedom turns to hedonism so easily, and then suffering becomes a constant concern, something to be avoided at all costs. We're typically the ones asking, "Why is there suffering?" So let's be the ones to look for an explanation too.

The Sin Explanation

One common explanation for suffering in Jesus's day was that it was caused primarily by sin. As the disciples asked Jesus, "Rabbi, who sinned—this guy or his parents—that he was born blind?" Now, when would this guy have sinned to be born blind? In the womb? It sounds a little silly, but that is exactly what many religious Jews believed back then. Some rabbis taught that the impulses for evil developed in the embryonic stages. They took a baby's kicking as a sign of rebellion, of prenatal sin. Weird, right?

Another strong influence in Jesus's time was Plato, who believed that the soul was immortal. He held that all souls pre-existed before their birth, waiting around for bodies to inhabit. Some Hellenistic Jews who had been swayed by Greek philosophy believed those who suffered in this life were being punished for sins committed in their previous existence. This ideology of pre-incarnate sin was prevalent in the ancient world, much as it still is in the Hindu and Buddhist concept of karma.

Then there was a mistaken view of Scripture. God had told Moses, "I, the Lord your God, am a jealous God, visiting the iniquity of the fathers upon the children to the third and fourth generations of those who hate Me" (Exodus 20:5). Some Jewish folk took this to mean that if your great-grandpa sinned, he began a curse that would pass down through the generations and blindside you even if you hadn't committed that same sin. So you had to go through a process of casting out a generational curse. There was even a Jewish Targum (an interpretive Aramaic paraphrase of the Scriptures from the first century AD) that used this text to refer to "ungodly fathers" and "rebellious children." Many Jews believed that sin was perpetuated by subsequent generations.

This kind of thinking continues in some churches today that want to blame every sin and problem on a generational curse. This is an extremely dangerous and grossly misleading practice. God's words about visiting iniquity on future generations is part of Old Testament law as a specific consequence to Israel for the particular sin of idolatry. And Jesus's reply to the disciples' question—"Neither this man nor his parents sinned"—plainly shows that there is not always a direct link between personal suffering and sin.

Ultimately, sin is the root cause of all misfortune in the world. However, not all suffering is caused directly by personal acts of sin. Yet a false theology exists today that says if you're a Christian and you have enough faith, you won't be susceptible to sin's effects on the body. You'll never experience illness, only perfect health. So if you do get sick or go through hardship, it's either the result of your lack of faith—you sinned and now you're suffering for your faith-lessness—or it's the devil. So-called believers look at illness and ask the question from the old *Saturday Night Live* skit, "Could it be...*Satan?!*"

But we can't ignore the story of Job. God Himself said of Job, "There is none like him on the earth, a blameless and upright man, one who fears God and shuns evil" (Job 1:8). And yet, Job suffered immensely. When his friends came along to offer their version of support, they all basically ended up asking the same thing: "What did you do, Job, that God punished you like this? How did you sin?" God came along and set the record straight, but He never directly explained why Job suffered. He just made it clear that Job's suffer-ing was not the result of any sin he had committed. That tells us that God doesn't automatically remove pain, instantly heal diseases, or prohibit suffering if you're His child.

> Sometimes God will calm the storm for His child, but more often He will calm His child in the storm.

Well, why not? you might be wonder-ing. *If God is who He says He is, He could do something about my pain in a heartbeat. Why doesn't God step in and put a stop to all this?* That question makes sense on the surface, but underneath it is the dangerous assump-tion that God should prevent all suffering in the lives of His kids, no questions asked, because even God in His sovereign knowledge and goodness couldn't possibly bring anything good out of suffering.

But Chuck Colson refuted this point very clearly: "It is absurd for Christians to constantly seek new demonstrations of God's power, to expect a miraculous answer to every need, from curing ingrown toenails to finding parking places: this only leads to faith in miracles rather than the Maker."[7] The truth of the matter is that sometimes God will calm the storm for His child, but more often He will calm His child in the storm.

The No-God Explanation

Another explanation for evil and suffering, common among atheists and agnostics, is that suffering and evil exist because there is no God. After all, goes their reasoning, how could a God who is all-powerful, all-loving, and all-knowing allow evil to exist? First posed by Epicurus, this argument still rattles around the halls of academia in the form of a syllogism (a series of logical statements that build on each other):

1. The biblical God is loving, perfect, all-knowing, and all-powerful.
2. Such a God could destroy all evil.
3. Yet massive evil and suffering exists.
4. Therefore, the biblical God does not exist.

Christians won't find a problem with the first statement. That's what the Bible teaches, after all. Even the second and third statements resonate as true. But how do atheists and agnostics get away with using the word *evil*? To call something evil assumes that there must be a standard of goodness. Without goodness, how would we even know what evil is?

C.S. Lewis wrote, "If the universe is so bad, or even half so bad, how on earth did human beings ever come to attribute it to the activity of a wise and good Creator?"[8] It's been a fairly recent development in human history to question God's existence. And that could be traced back to societies and cultures that, as I mentioned earlier, got bored when they stopped having to fight for survival and started digging into questions about pain and pleasure. They turned the focus from seeking God (or choosing not to) to seeking to put themselves in God's place as controllers of fate and judges of righteousness.

But the very fact that we still talk about good and evil, right and wrong, and darkness and light points to a standard of good, right, and light that goes way above our pay grade. God is that standard. One-third of the world's population claims to be Christian—about 2.2 billion souls—a number that has stayed the same for the past century.[9] That's the largest single religious group on the planet, which is remarkable when you consider it started with 120 people gathered in a room in first-century Jerusalem (Acts 1:15). Even if the current numbers of serious, practicing believers is smaller than the figure given, they are following a faith that has survived in the face of tremendous adversity—dissension, persecution, false teachers, executions, and defections. The only plausible explanation is 2,000 years of trust in an all-good, all-perfect God. I suggest that it takes more faith to believe God *doesn't* exist than to rest on the evidence that He does.

The Give-God-a-Break-He's-Trying Explanation

A third explanation for evil and suffering draws on the belief that God Himself is still a work in progress. We touched on this idea in chapter 7 of this book; it's called open theism. In a nutshell, this view says, "God would love to help stop evil, but He's not powerful enough yet." Open theism sees God as someone who learns the way we learn, studying and making mistakes and increasing in knowledge as He goes along. Accordingly, God is not the same today as He was yesterday, and He'll be different tomorrow. Even though this view is completely counter to biblical theology, it's out there making the rounds.

As Harold Kushner, a rabbi who believes in a finite God, wrote in his book *When Good Things Happen to Bad People*, "God would like people to get what they deserve in life, but He cannot always arrange it...Even God has a hard time keeping chaos in check and limiting the damage evil can do."[10] He went on to tell his reader to forgive God and pray for Him.[11] I just have to ask: When you pray for God, to whom are you praying? A God who is as equally victimized by evil as we are may empathize with us, but He certainly won't inspire us. A God like that is certainly not a God worth believing in. He would be impotent, like a big brother who can't stand up for you when a bully comes around.

Out of Darkness and Onto Higher Ground

None of these explanations provide a truly satisfactory answer to the problem of evil in view of the complexities of everyday life, and especially in light of all we've learned about God. So let's go back to the response Jesus gave His disciples when they asked why the blind man was born blind: "Neither this man nor his parents sinned, but that the works of God should be revealed in him" (John 9:3).

Jesus wasn't saying that the man and his parents were sinless, just that their sin didn't cause this malady. Jesus wasn't in the habit of giving tidy, pat answers, especially to such a complex question. Instead, He offered here a needful clarification. As another translation puts His reply: "You're asking the wrong question. You're looking for someone to blame. There is no such cause-effect here. Look instead for what God can do" (MSG).

> Beneath, beyond, and behind your suffering, God is working for your good and His glory. To see that, you must move to the higher ground of His sovereignty.

Jesus elevated the whole discussion. He took it from a dirt-level issue of pain and difficulty to heaven's throne room and the wide-sweeping sovereignty of God. He reached down into this man's darkness, into the mud of hardship, and gave him not only physical sight but a vision of God's greater work that was in play. Beneath, beyond, and behind your suffering, God is working for your good and His glory. To see that, you must move to the higher ground of His sovereignty.

Higher Ground Shows Us God Didn't Create Evil

What does it mean to move to that higher ground? How does taking that perspective change our view of the problem of evil? First, it shows us that God did not create evil. When God made creation, He called all of it good (Genesis 1:31). But He also gave human beings the privilege of free will. That means He allowed for the possibility of evil to exist. Why? Because if we are to be truly free in our choices, we must be free to choose other than what God has called good. As the twentieth-century Bible translator J.B. Phillips noted, "Evil is inherent in the risky gift of free will."[12]

Now, good existed first, as part of God's creation. Evil is only a corruption of the good things God made. God could have made robots that loved Him on command and never sinned because He didn't write that option into their programming. But robots don't have free will, and God wants us to freely choose to love Him. To force us to love Him wouldn't be love on His part. Part of giving us the freedom to choose to love Him is giving us the freedom not to. Love is a risk, and God took that risk.

God, being all-knowing, knew that we would choose to do evil. But that doesn't mean He created evil. Our choices did. And God cannot totally destroy all evil without simultaneously destroying free will.[13] If He did that, He would then by necessity destroy the possibility of all moral good. We can't have it both ways. We can't enjoy freedom of choice and then turn around and blame God because we don't choose to believe in Him.

Higher Ground Shows Us God Can Produce Good Out of Evil

According to the Bible, suffering is caused by the world, the flesh, and the devil. In this context, the "world" doesn't refer to the planet (which we are to steward) or its people (who we are to love), but the system of thinking, being, and doing that opposes God.[14] The "flesh" is the sinful nature every person is born with. Even if we are born again spiritually, we will continue to fight against the selfish impulses of our old nature for the rest of our lives.[15] Fortunately, with God's Spirit inside us as believers, we can overcome the flesh's temptations.[16] And finally, the devil is a real being whose objective is to destroy what God loves—namely, people. He is the personal, avowed enemy of every person who has ever lived.[17] But Jesus came to "destroy the works of the devil" (1 John 3:8). This triad of evil—the world, the flesh, and the devil—works in concert to oppose everything the Bible calls good.

That's quite the trio of doom, right? But a key theme of the Bible is that suffering in the hands of a loving God can produce great good. We've all suffered from those three troublemakers, but the great hope of God is that He brings light into our darkness, life into our death, hope into our fear, and strength into our weakness. David said, "Before I was afflicted I went astray, but now I keep Your word" (Psalm 119:67). Even the worst things we go through have purpose—even if we don't yet know what that purpose is.

Oswald Chambers offered an illustration of what that looks like. If you've ever had to pull a thorn out of a pet dog's paw or clean its wound, you might remember the patient trust with which it waited for you to finish what you were doing. He looked at you, and you knew what you were doing was hurting him, but you also knew it would help him get better. The look in his eyes said, "I don't understand what you're doing, and it hurts, but go ahead."[18] That's a good illustration of suffering "according to the will of God" (1 Peter 4:19).

I read an observation that really helped this make sense to me. Dr. A.E. Wilder-Smith, an organic chemist and strong believer, tells of how before World War II, he often visited a gothic cathedral in Cologne, Germany. He was inspired by its magnificent architecture—buttresses and domed roof and stained glass, the architects' vision and the builders' skills perfectly blended. The cathedral's beauty revealed the excellence of the minds and hands behind it.

Cologne was bombed repeatedly during the war, and the cathedral, being near the center of town, suffered heavy damage. The roof was blasted away, the organ was incinerated, and knee-deep piles of rubble lay everywhere. Its two famous towers still stood, but even they now had massive holes in the masonry. The contrast of this chaos with the cathedral's former beauty left a deep impression on Wilder-Smith. The destruction didn't make him doubt the work of the architects and masons; in fact, it reinforced his respect for the work they had done. The fact that even that much of the cathedral was left standing demonstrated that they had done their work very well. "In some ways, the ruined structure showed even better than the intact one the perfection of the architects' plans and construction."[19]

Looking at the ruins, no logical mind could conclude that the architects and masons hadn't designed and built the cathedral well. Similarly, creation today shows evidence of order and design even in the midst of disarray. Though ugliness and decay and destruction have left their marks, we can still see in creation a good plan and design. In other words, just because we have messed up creation doesn't mean that God must not have made it.

Some atheists claim that the contradiction of a good God and a world damaged by evil must mean that God is either not good or doesn't exist. But any evidence of goodness and order in the midst of a sea of chaos still points to a good and orderly God. And sometimes, as with the cathedral, the ruin of what was good can bring out the quality of the mind behind it better than order can.

> In God's hands, what looks bad to us can be used to bring about a higher good than we can imagine.

That's why we have to be careful when we call something good or bad, because we might just be wrong about it. When we ask, "Why would God let that bad thing happen?," we are assuming that thing can serve no possible good purpose. In and of itself, perhaps it can't, but in God's hands, what looks bad to us can be used to bring about a higher good than we can imagine. We see this in chemistry, where sodium and chlorine—two substances that are harmful by themselves—combined properly become salt, a chemical compound that is helpful and necessary to our health (in the right amounts).

Think of the terrible circumstances, one after the other, that fell on Joseph because of the jealousy and hatred of his brothers. Yet after being sold into slavery, going to prison, and suffering false accusations and neglect, he ended up as the second-most-powerful ruler of ancient Egypt. Because of this, he was able to save his father and brothers during a severe famine. Keep in mind that jealousy and hatred are evil. Selling another human being into slavery is repulsive. Yet the string of avarice, accusation, and abandonment that Joseph experienced worked out for great good. As Joseph told his brothers, "As for you, you meant evil against me; but God meant it for good, in order to bring it about as it is this day, to save many people alive" (Genesis 50:20).

God took this principle from theory to practice at the cross. Playing by His own rulebook, God took the worst event in human history—the brutal betrayal, abandonment, and execution of a truly innocent man—and turned it into the best possible outcome that could have happened to the human race: the opportunity for salvation and relationship with our Maker. All of history hinges on this unmitigated act of evil. Yet the killing of the Son of God became the very thing we are continually grateful for, and will be forever (Revelation 5:9).

Remember that when the atheist argues that the existence of evil proves that the God of the Bible doesn't exist, the burden of proof is on the atheist. We claim that God does exist, and have accordingly looked at proof after proof of His existence. So when someone says, "Evil proves God doesn't exist," he must likewise support that claim. As we've seen in this chapter, the typical unbeliever's arguments don't hold up well. No one can claim to understand beyond a doubt that God can't use suffering to work out some good.

But if God could bring about ultimate good from the very worst evil at the cross, don't you think He can do this on a smaller, more personal scale—like in your life? What if God is actually behind the scenes of our suffering and pain, working something good through them? Maybe you're wondering, *What good could come from my suffering?* How about character development? I can almost guarantee that the people you know who have the most integrity have suffered in some significant way.

If you were to ask Corrie ten Boom during her time in Ravensbrück "Where is God?," she might have answered at first, "I don't know." But she came to know. And she looked back on her time in the German concentration camp as a good part of God's plan for her and all those she helped. If you asked Joni Eareckson Tada how she felt right after the diving accident that made her a quadriplegic, she might have said, "Oh God, *this* is now my life? You actually expect me to *do* this?"[20] But now, after more than fifty years of helping others learn to cope with disabilities, she admitted, "I really would rather be in this wheelchair knowing Jesus as I do than be on my feet without him."[21]

Several years ago, I had the privilege of visiting the grave of Samuel Rutherford at St. Andrews in Scotland. In the 1600s, Rutherford pastored and preached faithfully to his congregation in Anwoth but was exiled by the church of England for his strong, biblical sermons. As I read his gravestone on that blustery Scottish afternoon, a simple but powerful statement he made about his own suffering came to mind: "Why should I tremble at the plow of my Lord, that maketh deep furrows in my soul? I know He is no idle husbandman. He purposeth a crop." I have always loved that little quip and recall it frequently. Suffering can fertilize the one who God intends to make fruitful.

Suffering can also produce repentance. I've met so many people over the years who have been drawn to Christ through divorce, imprisonment, illness, or the death of a loved one. I recall one man I met who seemed like the guy you'd vote "Least Likely to Give Jesus a Shot." In fact, he had been saving his shots for his work as a leader in a drug cartel in another country. I went to visit him at his home in Albuquerque because Ruth Graham, the wife of evangelist Billy

Graham, had called and asked that I pay him a visit. She had been close friends with his mother for years and told her, "I know someone who lives in Albuquerque. I'll bet he will go see your son."

When I first met this soft-spoken man, he explained that he had been involved in an assassination attempt on his country's president decades before and had to flee to the States. As I began to present the gospel to him, it was obvious he didn't want to hear it. He had heard it all before from Billy and Ruth's son, Franklin, and was quite dismissive. I politely left his home after a few cordial remarks.

But then, one day, out of the blue, I heard that this same man had become afflicted by a very aggressive form of cancer. I immediately went to see him in the hospital, but he politely refused to discuss the gospel any further. When I visited him a few weeks later, his condition had dramatically weakened him. I told him about the thief who was crucified next to Jesus and how, in the last moments of his life, he placed faith in Christ as Savior. I then explained how Jesus welcomed this criminal, saying, "Today you will be with me in Paradise" (Luke 23:43).

At this, tears welled up in his eyes, and he whispered, "That's the most beautiful thing I've ever heard." Hours before he left this world, he, too, like the thief on the cross, placed his life in the Savior's care. He finally realized what his mother knew all along: that all the power, wealth, and political advancement you can grab for yourself in this world means nothing before the God who made you. But it took pain and suffering to bring him to that realization.

Are you willing to embrace your suffering if it drives you to God? And if your pain does spur you toward a deeper relationship with the Lord, then is it really bad? My mind goes back to receiving Christmas gifts as a kid. Some gifts I loved, and others I didn't. Bicycles and trains, yes; gloves and socks, not so much. Though I didn't think this way as a kid, I realize now that I needed both kinds of presents. Bikes and trains helped me develop my imagination and dream of bigger things, and gloves and socks kept me warm and clean so I could grow up and pursue those dreams. Both kinds of gifts were good. And the older I've gotten, the more I understand how God has used both blessings and suffering to carry out His will in my life. This kind of perspective is how Job was able to say, "The Lord gave, and the Lord has taken away; blessed be the name of the Lord" (Job 1:21).

Higher Ground Shows Us God Makes Our Pain Useful

The problem of evil and the gift of free will are complex subjects, and I won't pretend to have said all there is to say about them. But I do want to go back to the story of Jesus and the blind man one more time because it illustrates a valuable point: If God can work our pain and suffering into good, then we have a spiritual obligation to Him. That means the best thing we can do in response to our pain is lean into a God worth trusting.

Picture Jesus kneeling down in front of the blind man. The man, his ears attuned to compensate for a lifetime of sightlessness, heard the rabbi spit, heard Him rubbing His hands together. What was He doing? Then a strong hand gently rubbed something cool and moist on his eyes, which probably closed reflexively. "Go to the pool and wash," said the rabbi. The man knew the way, so he went. And when he washed the mud away, the darkness was gone as well.

Jesus wants us to see past the darkness as well. Wrestling with the problem of suffering and evil and sin is not an academic exercise, reserved for philosophy classes or seminary students. The disciples looked at the blind man and saw a case study in sin's consequences. But Jesus saw a soul in need of compassion. He healed the man so that "the power of God could be seen in him" (John 9:3 NLT).

That power was miraculous, to be sure, but it was also practical. Jesus said as much to the disciples: "We need to be energetically at work for the One who sent me here, working while the sun shines. When night falls, the workday is over. For as long as I am in the world, there is plenty of light. I am the world's Light" (vv. 4-5 MSG). Jesus didn't allow Himself to be pulled down into the mire of a philosophical discussion about why this man was suffering. He attended to more pressing needs.

Sometimes God will intervene in suffering through a miracle—that is, He will supersede the natural laws He has put in place to bring about a healing or blessing. More often, He uses us to model the compassion He feels for those in pain. Through our natural gifts and honed skills, but mostly through open hearts, we can help alleviate pain and bring healing. And God often uses what we've suffered to develop empathy in us so we can be useful to others who are going through the same hardship. Paul wrote of God as one "who comforts us in all our tribulation, that we may be able to comfort those who are in any trouble, with the comfort with which we ourselves are comforted by God" (2 Corinthians 1:4).

For the Christian, this life is our one opportunity to watch God work in and through our pain, for one day God will give each of us a perfect, glorified body in which we will spend eternity with Him in heaven. This is the only chance we will have to pray for and bring practical relief to those who suffer, to offer counsel or simply sit beside them in their pain or grief. So if you call yourself a follower of Christ, you have a spiritual obligation.

I saw a cartoon in which one turtle said to another, "I'd like to ask God why He allows poverty and disease and famine and injustice when He could do something about it." The other turtle responded, "I'm afraid God might ask me the same question."

Historically speaking, the people who have led the charge to alleviate suffering and hardship in this world have been followers of Jesus. Many hospitals, orphanages, and universities were started by people who believed that God cares deeply about human suffering and wants us to do something to make life better for others. Ultimately, Christians deal with suffering by putting it into perspective. We lean into what the Bible says is true about God: He is all-knowing, all-loving, all-powerful, and all-good. One day, He will judge evil and eradicate injustice. In the meantime, God works with incredible patience, over lifetimes and even centuries, to relieve the suffering we have chosen. He wants to do so in your life, if you'll let Him put the pain to work for you.

I have long loved a parable used by Charles Spurgeon to illustrate the principle of growing through pain (I've paraphrased it so you won't be inconvenienced by nineteenth-century English):

> A little plant, small and stunted, grew beneath the shade of a broad, spreading oak. It enjoyed the covering and the companionship of its noble friend. One day, a woodsman came and cut down the great oak with his axe. The tiny plant wept and cried, "My shelter is gone! Now the rough winds will blow upon me and the storms will uproot me." But the woodsman replied, "Nonsense. Now the sunshine will reach you. The rain will feed your roots like never before, and you will spring up, tall and strong."[22]

I'm so grateful that God looks on my stunted spiritual growth and says, "I've got just what it takes to shape you into a strong, persevering, well-rounded person." Evil isn't God's fault, but it still falls under His sovereignty. That's why Romans 8:28 resonates with so many believers: "All things work together for good to those who love God, to those who are the called according to His purpose." That promise would be easier to believe if it said, "God works some things together for good," or "God works a few things together for good." Instead, we are told that God works *all* things together for good—our suffering included.

The next time a pebble cracks your theological windshield, use it as an opportunity to seek higher ground, to view yourself and your circumstances through the eyes of a sovereign God who loves you and is able to use your suffering for your good, the good of others, and His glory. He is committed to your growth, and no pain or suffering can ever separate you from His love.

Chapter 12

HOW CAN THREE BE ONE?

The Trinity, Part 1

I read about a prisoner in solitary confinement whose cell was pitch-black. The complete lack of light would drive anyone to the edge of sanity, but the man held on to his by means of his one possession—a marble. To relieve the tension, he would throw the marble against the side of the cell, then listen for the impact and gravelly rolling of the little sphere. When it stopped, he would search in the darkness until he found it. Then he'd do it all over again, hour after hour, day after day.

One day, he resolved to try something new: He would throw the marble up and then try to catch it. He tossed the marble up, held out his hands, and waited. He felt nothing, heard nothing. Dropping to his knees, he crawled across the floor, then along the walls, searching for the marble with his hands. But he couldn't find it. Worse than the loss of the marble was the mystery of its disappearance. He made a quick descent into madness that ended with his death.

When a guard came to remove the man's body, he turned on a light. A glint in an upper corner caught his eye—a marble caught in a spider's web. The guard squinted, then scratched his head. "How on earth," he said, "did that spider manage to take that marble all the way up there?"

All of us have marbles that we wonder about—mysteries we can't make heads or tails of, no matter how much we struggle or search for the answers in the dark. One such mystery—and perhaps the greatest theological marble of all time—is the Trinity. How can three be one?

There's a Mystery to It

In previous chapters, we've wrestled with how to relate to someone who is all-knowing, all-powerful, everywhere present, and perfectly holy. The more we've learned about our Maker, the more we've realized that He simply isn't like us. But perhaps nowhere else is that truth more apparent than in the doctrine of the Trinity: God is one being in three persons. The math of that doesn't even line up—how does 1 + 1 + 1 = 1?

And it only gets more difficult from there. As Christians, we have a lot of questions: Who do I address my prayers to—the Father, the Son, or the Holy Spirit? All three at once? Does it depend on the situation? What if I get it wrong and address the wrong person? How does this Trinity situation work, anyway? Are the terms *Father*, *Son*, and *Holy Spirit* really just different names for the same person? How are they different from each other?

> The triune nature of God is a mystery to be approached with great humility.

Many people have tried to describe how the Trinity works, but we must be careful not to trivialize the transcendent. Whether you say God is like an egg (which comprises the shell, the white, and the yolk), an apple (core, peel, and flesh), or the three states of water (liquid, solid, and gas), no comparison fully gets the job done. We can only use finite illustrations to describe an infinite reality. They make for useful starting points as long as we recognize they don't fully explain the concept. The last thing we want to do is diminish God's majesty by comparing Him to water, an egg, or an apple.

Even so, Christians as far back as the early church used symbols as a starting point for understanding the basics of the Trinity. For example, the church in Ireland used a symbol called the triquetra, three interlaced leaf shapes symmetrically arranged around a circle. And in medieval times, there was the *Scutum Fidei* ("shield of faith"), shown here.[1] It communicates that none of three persons in the Trinity are each other, but all are God. That lays out some basic truths nicely, but it still doesn't explain how these truths are possible.

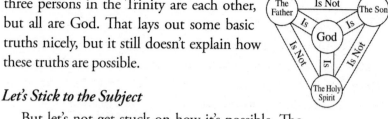

Let's Stick to the Subject

But let's not get stuck on how it's possible. The truth is that not only is the Trinity possible, but it is also the reality. At some point we have to accept that the mystery of the triune God is too big for us. I'll be the first to say I don't completely understand the Trinity. I can't fully explain it, and I don't fully trust anyone who says they can. The triune nature of God is a mystery to be approached with great humility, and we should lean into it relationally.

When my wife and I were married, we entered into a covenant for life. We became the Heitzigs. Vows were said, rings were exchanged, and two people became one. Our friend who presided over the service even used the first book in the Bible to explain the process, saying, "Therefore a man shall leave his father and mother and be joined to his wife, and they shall become one flesh" (Genesis 2:24). Lenya and I have been married now for decades, and yet we've never lost our individuality. We are unique and different persons, but in a mystical way we've become a unified entity, sharing a relational oneness.

That illustration may be helpful, but the Trinity remains a difficult concept for even advanced theologians to comprehend. It's hard to wrap our minds around this. Even so, it's possible for us to know and trust the biblical truth that God is three in one. Let's look at two principles that will help us find the balance between knowing what we can know and having humility about what we can't.

The Natural Resists the Supernatural

The first principle is that the natural resists the supernatural. Attacks on the doctrine of the Trinity are nothing new. But whether they happened in the second century or the twentieth, many of them boil down to semantics—word games. The standard criticism is that "you never read the word *Trinity* in the Bible"—the idea being that, if the Bible doesn't use the word specifically, the entire concept has no biblical basis.

But there are several key biblical concepts that aren't named in the Bible. The Bible doesn't use the term *second coming*, but it leaves no doubt that Jesus will return. It doesn't use the word *rapture*, but Paul describes the event in detail. And though the word *millennium* isn't to be found in Scripture, we clearly read that Jesus will establish a thousand-year-long reign after He returns. The word *Bible* isn't even in the Bible. So the argument that a certain concept isn't biblical because the Bible doesn't mention it by a specific term holds about as much water as a broken mug.

The Struggle Is Real

Still, it's human nature to doubt concepts that don't make sense to us. We see that even among Jesus's own disciples. Jesus plainly told them He was going to Jerusalem to be executed and that He would be raised on the third day. Peter, perhaps figuring that Jesus was giving them a loyalty test, jumped in and said, "Far be it from You, Lord; this shall not happen to You!" (Matthew 16:22). Peter didn't get it; he wasn't connecting the dots; he didn't understand the concepts of vicarious atonement and bodily resurrection, even after hanging out with Jesus on a daily basis for three-and-a-half years.

On the night of the Last Supper, Peter asked Jesus why he couldn't follow Him to where He was going (John 13:36-38). Soon afterward, Jesus said, "If I go and prepare a place for you, I will come again and receive you to Myself; that where I am, there you may be also. And where I go you know, and the way you know" (John

14:3-4). Thomas responded, "Lord, we do not know where You are going, and how can we know the way?" (v. 5). Hadn't he been listening?

The incredible, unexpected, supernatural events Jesus was describing overwhelmed the disciples in the midst of their everyday, natural circumstances. This is a biblical principle; as Paul noted, "The natural man does not receive the things of the Spirit of God, for they are foolishness to him; nor can he know them, because they are spiritually discerned" (1 Corinthians 2:14). This explains why we struggle with the concept of the Trinity without the help of the Holy Spirit. Yet even with His help, our understanding will still be limited.

Even after the resurrection, when the disciples gathered in Galilee and actually saw Jesus for themselves, "they worshiped Him; but some doubted" (Matthew 28:17). It's hard to imagine where the doubt came from—*Is it really Him? Did He really die? But there He is!*—but that's the point: to be confined to the natural in terms of perspective, experience, and outlook is to struggle with the supernatural. We might look for the supernatural as proof that there's more to this life, but so often if it doesn't look or work the way we expect it to, we resist it.

So if you've ever struggled with the concept of three being one, you're in good company. Modern theologians still struggle with this. R.T. Kendall admitted, "The Trinity is the most difficult subject in Christian theology. By the end of the day in studying this, you will still feel like you're out to sea."[2] Billy Graham said, "The Bible teaches us that God is in three Persons. God is one, but He is manifested in three Persons. God the Father, God the Son and God the Holy Spirit. Don't ask me to explain it—I can't. It's impossible for me to explain to you the Holy Trinity. I accept it by faith."[3]

A legend says Saint Augustine was walking along the beach, struggling to wrap his mind around the mystery of the Trinity, when he saw a boy with a spoon. The boy was walking back and forth between the sea and a small pit he had dug in the sand, dumping a spoonful of seawater at a time into the hole. Augustine asked him,

"What are you doing?" The boy said, "I am putting that ocean in this hole." And Augustine realized, "That's what I've been trying to do. I've been trying to take this vast ocean of God's transcendent truth and stuff it in this hole called my brain, and it can't contain it."[4] There's a point at which we have to choose to live with the mystery of the Trinity, believing it to be true even though no one can explain it completely.

Don't Give Up!

That doesn't mean we can't know anything about the Trinity, or we shouldn't try to understand all we can. Over the years I've visited a lot of American churches, listened to their pastors, and sometimes taught from their pulpits, and unfortunately, it seems like a lot of people who profess unwavering belief in God really struggle with what the Bible says about His triune nature. Partly, that's due to a lack of teaching on the Trinity in general. In many Western denominational churches, the liturgical calendar features a day called Trinity Sunday, the first Sunday after Pentecost. In many of those churches, that's the only time the Trinity gets mentioned throughout the year. And even then, the general thought among congregants seems to be, *The Trinity is for pastors to wrestle with; ordinary people don't have to deal with it.*

That attitude is dangerous because the truth only has to go untaught for a single generation for it be lost. A Gallup Poll in 1965 revealed that 98 percent of Americans believed in God, and that 83 percent of that group believed the Godhead consists of one being in three persons, Father, Son, and Holy Spirit. A 2002 Barna poll showed that 79 percent believed the same—not much of a dip but still a slight decline.[5] More recently, however, a LifeWay Research survey from 2016 revealed that about 69 percent now hold to that view.[6] Doubt and disbelief arise when truth is put on the shelf.

The survey also indicated startling numbers of people who call themselves evangelical Christians being way off the mark theologically. While seven in ten still said that the Trinity consists of

Father, Son, and Holy Spirit—and that they are three persons but one God—more than half agreed that Jesus "is the first and greatest being created by God" (which is a first-century heresy called Arianism). Another 56 percent agreed that the Holy Spirit is a "divine force," not a personal being, and 28 percent indicated that the Holy Spirit is not equal with God or Jesus.[7]

Not only do many Christians not know what's in the Bible, but that lack of knowledge is leading them down the path of heresy.[8] A lifelong, active member of a large fundamentalist church said she had never heard an entire sermon or Sunday school teaching on the Trinity.[9] The church will continue to lose members to anti-Trinitarian groups unless it teaches people how to handle the Scriptures correctly.

Don't Leave the Door Open, Either

If, as Jesus claimed, the truth sets us free (John 8:32), then lies (even in the form of half-truths and good intentions) enslave us. Too many people in the church are settling for an uninformed reverence of God and the Bible, as opposed to committing to know a God who makes Himself known best in His Word. To understand God, you have to know what He says about Himself. You also have to wrestle with the aspects of God that aren't easy to understand.

Some would rather spend their energy attacking the teaching of the Trinity. There is the semantic argument I mentioned earlier—the attempt to invalidate biblical concepts because certain words that describe them aren't found in the Bible (*Trinity, millennium,* and so on). But there is also the religious argument. The protest is that there are a lot of religious groups that don't believe in the Trinity and have argued against its existence. The implication is that if a lot of people are protesting something, there must be something wrong with the object of their protest.

But for me, this kind of attack is like a bug ramming into a porch light—drawn to the light without really knowing why, the bug ends up banging against it and fizzling out. Whenever you turn on the light of biblical truth, the attacks will come. That's been true since the first days of the early church. And the early church had no doubts at all about the Trinity. They believed, held to, and taught that God is one being in three persons. The disciples asked Jesus a lot of questions, but never in the Bible do you see them questioning the concept of Father, Son, and Holy Spirit as God. When Jesus said, "I will ask the Father, and he will give you another Advocate [the Holy Spirit], who will never leave you" (John 14:16 NLT), they didn't say, "Hold on, time out—what's this bit about Father, Son, and Holy Spirit?" The Trinity didn't seem to be an issue with them.

When Paul said his goodbyes to the elders at Ephesus, he spoke of the work of each member of the Trinity as the foundation of the church: "I have not shunned to declare to you the whole counsel of God. Therefore take heed to yourselves and to all the flock, among which the Holy Spirit has made you overseers, to shepherd the church of God which He purchased with His own blood" (Acts 20:27-28). Paul mentioned the Holy Spirit, who had made them overseers, and God, who purchased the church with His blood, which refers to the work the Son did on the cross. It's all right there, the Trinity in a nutshell.

Making an Old Truth Official

The historic Christian church—including most early fathers, medieval theologians, Reformers, and evangelicals—has maintained that God is a unitary essence consisting of three coequal persons: Father, Son, and Holy Spirit. The early church found it important to clarify that the Godhead was not three gods in a kind of tritheistic committee, but only one.[10] The consistent view has been that the Father is unbegotten, the Son was begotten from the eternal essence of the Father, and the Spirit proceeds from the Father and the Son.[11] This Trinitarian formula is found in the first-century document *The Didache*; Irenaeus argued it in the second century, Tertullian discussed it in the third century, and the Council of Nicaea nailed it down in the fourth century.

Whenever the truth of the Trinity has been challenged throughout history, councils like Nicaea have developed official creeds that affirmed what the Bible said and, therefore, what the church believed. These statements of truth have upheld the biblical understanding of the Trinity against various attacks again and again. For example, in the second century, Monarchianism and modalism wrongly argued that the different names of the Trinity actually referred to the same person. The false teaching of Arianism in the fourth century taught that the Spirit is an impersonal force and that Jesus isn't really divine, so there's no Trinity. And in the sixteenth century, another group claimed that believing in the Trinity was a form of polytheism—worshipping multiple gods—and was therefore blasphemous (Socinianism).

Some people today mistakenly assume that it was the various creeds that developed in response to these heresies that actually invented the concept of the Trinity. However, these creeds weren't teaching something new but were simply responding to historical attacks on an already-established understanding of Scripture. The Nicene Creed, for example, affirmed the doctrine of the Trinity in the face of fourth-century Arianism. And the Apostles' Creed was developed as a "symbol of the faith" as early as AD 150.[12]

The historical record tells us that the teaching of the Trinity was well-known and widely accepted among orthodox Christians very early on. As Justo L. González writes, "The original purpose of most ancient creeds was to affirm faith in the Trinity—Father, Son, and Holy Spirit—and to bolster believers against those views that at the time seemed the greatest threats to Christian faith."[13] Creeds didn't become necessary until attacks came.

Rooted in History

There is, in fact, a long record of theologians and Bible teachers throughout history affirming the Bible's teaching. The teaching of the Trinity has historical roots in the early church.

In AD 96, Clement of Rome formulated an oath using all three members of the Trinity: "As God lives, and as the Lord Jesus Christ lives and the Holy Spirit (on whom the elect believe and hope)."[14] Clement also said, "Do we not have one God, one Christ, one Spirit of grace which was poured out on us?"[15] Just to give you a bit of perspective, AD 96 is right around the time the apostle John likely wrote the book of Revelation. In other words, there were still people around who had known Jesus, seen Him in person, and listened to Him teach. In historical terms, that makes Clement a primary source.

In AD 107, Ignatius used the formula of the Father, Son, and Holy Spirit to call for unity of faith in the church. Also in the second century, Justin Martyr defended the veneration and worship of all three members of the Trinity.[16] A few decades later, Athenagoras declared to Roman emperors Marcus Aurelius and Lucius Aurelius, "The Son is in the Father and the Father in the Son by the unity and power of the Spirit."[17] He also wrote, "We speak of God, of the Son, his Word, and of the Holy Spirit; and we say that the Father, Son, and the Spirit are united in power."[18]

Another second-century theologian, Irenaeus, defended the gospel against the Gnostics and spoke of the Holy Spirit as the one "through whom the prophets prophesied, and our forebears learned of God and the righteous were led in the paths of justice, and who, in the fullness of time, was poured out in a new way on our human nature in order to renew humanity throughout the entire world in the sight of God."[19] Irenaeus studied under Polycarp, who studied under the apostle John himself. So he had a direct link not only to John's eyewitness account of Jesus but to a historically reliable and doctrinally correct primary source.

> Believing in the triune God is necessary to believing in the gospel.

The theologian Tertullian first coined the term *trinitos*, Latin for *Trinity*, in the early third century, although some church historians believe the term was in use even earlier. For example, in AD 180, Theophilus of Antioch compared the first three days of creation to the Trinity: "In like manner also the three days which were before the luminaries, are types of the Trinity, of God, and His Word, and His wisdom."[20] Theophilus was clearly using a familiar term; he didn't take time to define it or develop the concept, so it must have been in regular use by that time. The Trinity was at the heart of early Christianity.

Moths to the Flame

Belief in the Trinity is one of the key points of difference between Christianity and any cult (along with the identity, nature, and mission of Jesus Christ). But believing in the triune God is necessary to believing in the gospel. As Charles Spurgeon passionately said,

> A Gospel without a Trinity? It is a pyramid built on its apex!...It is a rope of sand that cannot hold together! A Gospel without a Trinity? Then, indeed Satan can overturn it. But, give me a Gospel with a Trinity and the might of Hell cannot prevail against it. No man can anymore overthrow it than a bubble could split a rock, or a feather break in halves a mountain.[21]

And yet, the same anti-Trinitarian arguments keep popping up not just in philosophy and liberal theology but in the beliefs of religious cults like the Jehovah's Witnesses, Mormons, Christian Scientists, Unitarians, and so on. These groups aren't shy about being anti-Trinitarian, either. In fact, they are among the most aggressive anti-Trinitarian opponents. Mormons are infamous for historical revisionism of their own scriptures, yet they say that their understanding of the Trinity is actually the truth and that the church had it wrong for 1,800 years before Joseph Smith came along. These kinds of claims are just an old tactic in a new generation.

Another major example of anti-Trinitarian teaching comes from Islam, the second-fastest growing religion in the world.[22] The Qur'an teaches that believing in a triune God is not only illogical but a serious sin against Allah.

> O People of the Book [a common phrase used to address
> Jews and Christians]!...Christ Jesus the son of Mary was
> (no more than) a messenger of Allah, and His Word, which
> He bestowed on Mary, and a spirit proceeding from Him:
> so believe in Allah and His messengers. Say not "Trinity":
> desist: it will be better for you: for Allah is one Allah: Glory
> be to Him: (far exalted is He) above having a son.[23]

This passage denies Christ's divinity and His identity as the Son of
God, and warns its readers not to use the term "Trinity" (or "Three"
in other translations) to talk about God.

Other verses in the Qur'an make it clear that God will show
mercy to adulterers and liars[24] but never to Trinitarians: "Indeed,
he who associates others with Allah—Allah has forbidden him Paradise, and his refuge is the Fire. And there are not for the wrong-
doers any helpers. They have certainly disbelieved who say, 'Allah is
the third of three.'"[25] In Muslim theology, Trinitarians deserve hell.

Part of the reason beliefs like this gain traction is because many
Christians aren't even sure what they believe about the Trinity. We
can see the impact of that uncertainty as cults and heretical beliefs
make inroads into the church in record numbers. A failure among
churches to address the biblical and historical basis for the Trinity
leaves people feeling unequipped to respond to the knock at the
door and the subsequent well-versed assaults on the triune God. As
one veteran Jehovah's Witness said, "I have never before met a Trinitarian who actually seemed to believe the doctrine!"[26] Jehovah's Witnesses are always prepared to go to the Scriptures—or at least their
erroneous version of the Scriptures—to support their beliefs. Bible-
believing Christians should be prepared to do the same.

Paul said of the gospel, "How then shall they call on Him in
whom they have not believed? And how shall they believe in Him
of whom they have not heard? And how shall they hear without a
preacher? And how shall they preach unless they are sent?" (Romans
10:14-15). Pastors are called to preach the entire word of God, but
many have fallen short when it comes to the Trinity. Because of that,

many Christians revert to their default setting and let natural reasoning resist God's supernatural truth. Fortunately, by God's grace, we have the Bible to set us on a better, more trustworthy path. His message of truth resets our way of thinking.

The Scriptural Remedies the Natural

When the Bible is our source of truth, it corrects our natural view of things, upgrading us to a broader, supernatural view of the world that is centered on God rather than man. Matthew 28:17, which I mentioned earlier in this chapter, shows us the conflict between these two views—between doubt and belief, between the natural mindset and the supernatural one. When Jesus's eleven disciples saw the risen Christ, "they worshiped Him; but some doubted." We recognize and understand their turmoil, how their belief in the resurrection debated their common sense: *Jesus must really be God; we saw Him die but here He is, more alive than ever! But dead men don't come back to life.*

Jesus responded by giving them an anchor to hold onto. "Jesus came and spoke to them, saying, 'All authority has been given to Me in heaven and on earth'" (v. 18). That's the umbrella under which we should shelter our concerns about the Trinity. Let God's authority—His Word—be the final word on your questions. Even if it doesn't provide every detail you would like to have, you can still trust that you have what you need to move on.

And we have our marching orders: "Go therefore and make disciples of all the nations, baptizing them in the name of the Father and of the Son and of the Holy Spirit" (v. 19). This verse is pregnant with Trinitarian truth. It teaches that the Father, Son, and Holy Spirit are all on the same level as God. We cooperate with them as partners in sharing the gospel, but there is no other name that can be added to theirs. It's not "Father, Son, Holy Spirit, and Frank," or "Father, Son, Holy Spirit, and (insert denomination)." The Trinity is an exclusive club, and only the Father, Son, and Holy Spirit enjoy that unique unity. But what's amazing is that God calls us to share in that oneness with Him—that's the baptism Jesus mentioned. First we must seek to understand what the Scriptures say about the Trinity.

Because the Bible Tells Us So

So what does the Bible say about the Trinity? For starters, it teaches that Jesus is God. Every now and then, I run into someone who claims that Jesus never said He was God and I think, *What Bible are you reading?* Jesus's claims to deity are evident all through the Gospels. When Thomas saw the risen Lord and said, "My Lord and my God!" (John 20:28), Jesus didn't rebuke him or say, "Hey, don't go there." He received Thomas's worship because Thomas was right on target.[27]

Jesus was clear about His identity throughout His ministry. He once healed a paralyzed man and told him, "Be of good cheer; your sins are forgiven you" (Matthew 9:2). Some of the scribes (Jewish experts on the Bible) accused Jesus of blasphemy, saying that only God can forgive sins. But that was exactly the point Jesus was making—"the Son of Man has power on earth to forgive sins" (v. 6). He had the authority of God because He is God.

Jesus couldn't have been clearer about His identity than when He told the Jews, "Before Abraham was, I AM" (John 8:58). He deliberately used the name with which God introduced Himself to Moses in Exodus 3:14 to make it clear that He is God—and Jesus's opponents immediately tried to stone Him for blasphemy. They later asked Jesus directly, "How long do You keep us in doubt? If You are the Christ, tell us plainly" (John 10:24). When Jesus answered, "I and My Father are one" (v. 30), they picked up their rocks again. They knew who He was claiming to be. Jesus said, "'I have shown you many good works from the Father. For which of these do you stone me?' 'We are not stoning you for any good work,' they replied, 'but for blasphemy, because you, a mere man, claim to be God'" (vv. 32-33 NIV). Doesn't leave much room for interpretation, does it?

Scripture also teaches that the Holy Spirit is God. The most well-known example is in Acts 5, where Peter accused Ananias of lying to the Holy Spirit (v. 3) and said, "You have not lied to men but to God" (v. 4), equating the Holy Spirit with God.

Regarding God's plan of salvation, Paul wrote, "It was to us that God revealed these things by his Spirit. For his Spirit searches out everything and shows us God's deep secrets. No one can know a person's thoughts except that person's own spirit, and no one can know God's thoughts except God's own Spirit" (1 Corinthians 2:10-11 NLT). Throughout the Bible the Holy Spirit is repeatedly described as a person who has knowledge (John 14:26), a mission (John 15:26), will and purpose (Acts 15:28; 1 Corinthians 12:11), and a desire to help us know God better (Romans 8:26).

Jesus called the Holy Spirit "another Helper" (John 14:16) whom He would send to be with us when Jesus returned to the Father in heaven. The original Greek word for "another" here means "another of the same kind." The idea is that Jesus was our first Helper and the Holy Spirit is our second Helper, but they are the same in nature and character. In other words, Jesus and the Holy Spirit are both God—and they both advocate for believers (see 1 John 2:1).

The Beauty of Unity

But how can the three persons of the Trinity—Father, Son, and Holy Spirit—be one? How can there be unity and yet diversity within God? After all, Judaism in the Old Testament was fiercely monotheistic, asserting the truth that God is one in the midst of the polytheism that surrounded Israel. To this day, the Shema remains the most important prayer for Jews: "Hear, O Israel: The Lord our God, the Lord is one!" (Deuteronomy 6:4). This prayer is mainly about God's unique position as Israel's one and only God, but even so, the Hebrew word used for "one," *echad*, carries some hints about His nature.

Echad doesn't refer to singularity or isolation. In fact, the Bible uses the term to describe unity. In Genesis 2, we read about God's pattern for marriage: "A man shall leave his father and mother and be joined to his wife, and they shall become one flesh" (v. 24). That one-flesh relationship is *echad*. Do husband and wife morph into a single being after they say, "I do"? Of course not. They don't lose their individuality or personhood, but they do become one unit, a family, united in spirit. We see that same unity in the Trinity, three persons in one being—one unit.

Another example of this oneness is found in the description of the tabernacle. God told Moses, "You shall make fifty clasps of gold, and couple the curtains [of the tabernacle] together with the clasps, so that it may be one tabernacle" (Exodus 26:6)—*echad*, one unit. The tabernacle was made up of many different parts, but it was one center of worship. Similarly, after the Jews returned from Babylonian captivity, we read that "the people assembled together as one in Jerusalem" (Ezra 3:1 NIV). That's *echad* again, this time indicating that the people were unified in their purpose to seek God. This is how we can say there is multiplicity in unity in one God.

The very first verse of the Bible tells us, "In the beginning God created the heavens and the earth" (Genesis 1:1). The word used for "God" here is *Elohim*, which is a masculine plural noun. A few verses later, we read that God said, "Let Us make man in Our image, according to Our likeness" (v. 26). That's not a "royal we" used by monarchs, nor was this God speaking to the angels (they didn't help with creation). It's a statement of plurality in will and purpose—the voice of the Trinity. *Elohim* does the creating again in verse 27: "God created man in His own image; in the image of God He created him; male and female He created them."

Isaiah the prophet heard God ask, "Whom shall I send, and who will go for Us?" (Isaiah 6:8). Again, God wasn't speaking to the angels, for they are the ones God sends on various missions, but to the Son and the Holy Spirit, the triune God in conference. Many other passages throughout the Bible describe Christophanies (pre-incarnate appearances of Jesus in the Old Testament) and the actions of the Holy Spirit (coming upon people to give them God's power).

Isaiah famously prophesied that the Messiah would be called "Wonderful, Counselor, Mighty God, Everlasting Father, Prince of Peace" (Isaiah 9:6). Some anti-Trinitarians, especially those in the Oneness movement, claim that the name "Everlasting Father" means that Jesus actually is the Father. But that's not the case at all. This list of characteristics simply indicates that Jesus shares these qualities with God the Father and God the Holy Spirit. Jesus isn't the Father in the administrative order of the Trinity, but He does share the Father's characteristic of eternality. There is also certainly a *fatherhood* role in the ministry of Christ. Just as George Washington is considered the father of America and Abraham is referred to as the father of the Jewish race, Jesus as King of the Jews will be the protector, provider, and thus the father of the Messianic kingdom.

By the time we get to the New Testament, the evidence for the Trinity becomes more overt. As we saw earlier, Jesus commissioned His followers to "go therefore and make disciples of all the nations, baptizing them in the name of the Father and of the Son and of the Holy Spirit" (Matthew 28:19). Paul even offered the Corinthians a benediction based on the Trinity: "The grace of the Lord Jesus Christ, and the love of God, and the fellowship of the Holy Spirit be with you all" (2 Corinthians 13:14 NIV). The reality of the Trinity is well supported throughout Scripture.

A Little Tension Is Healthy

Like the Holy Spirit hovering over the waters at creation, we've covered a lot of ground in this chapter. And whether you're wrestling with all of this for the first time or for the dozenth, there will always be tension when it comes to the Trinity. Any progress you make from buckling down and saying, "Okay, I'm really going to try to understand this" will inevitably come up short. But my encouragement to you is to let the tension remain.

J.I. Packer used a philosophical term to describe this tension: antinomy. Antinomy is simply when two contradictory principles are both true. For example, light exists in two forms: waves and particles. It's not clear how light can be both waves and particles, but because the evidence points to it, you have to treat both facts as true.

Packer noted that you can't argue away antinomy, but you can't fully understand it, either. "It is not deliberately manufactured; it is forced on us by the facts themselves. It is unavoidable, and it is insoluble. We do not invent it, and we cannot explain it. Nor is there any way to get rid of it, save by falsifying the very facts that led us to it."[28]

A suspension bridge functions because of the tension pulling in opposite directions. Remove that tension and the bridge collapses. Because we are finite creatures, there are some things we don't get and never will—especially the deep mysteries of God. Don't believe anyone who says, "I've got this Trinity thing down." The Bible tells us we will one day see God face to face, and then we will know everything we need to know. Until then, we trust what Scripture teaches and worship God the Father, the Son, and the Holy Spirit.

Chapter 13

TWO-THIRDS IS NOT ENOUGH

The Trinity, Part 2

I have a confession to make: My primary aim in writing this chapter is to make you dissatisfied.

Whether you have been a Christian all your life, have been for just a little while, used to be but now aren't, never have been, or think you never will be, my hope is that, as you read, you won't say, "That's enough. I don't need to know any more about God. I'm good where I am spiritually." In fact, I am hoping for the exact opposite, because the more you learn about God, the more you should want to know. And the more you know about God, the better you'll understand what relationship with Him requires. There's no coasting with God, no settling for vague spirituality or keeping Him at arm's length.

This should especially hold true for the child of God. There is a sort of *holy discontentment* that is built into our relationship with God, a perpetually unsatisfied hunger. A.W. Tozer said that those who are caught up in pursuit of the Lord "will not be satisfied till they have drunk deep at the Fountain of Living Water."[1] Moses wasn't content in his own relationship with God even after seeing many of His miracles firsthand in Egypt and the wilderness. He heard God's audible voice and saw the phenomena of the plagues, the Red Sea opening and closing, manna falling from heaven, and water flowing from a rock, yet he still told God, "Please, show me Your glory" (Exodus 33:18). He wanted more. Thomas Edison once said, "Show me a thoroughly satisfied man and I'll show you a failure."[2]

Even Paul the apostle, after thirty years of walking with Christ, said, "Not that I have already attained, or am already perfected; but I press on, that I may lay hold of that for which Christ Jesus has also laid hold of me" (Philippians 3:12). The more we learn about God and His attributes, His grandeur, and His desire for relationship with us, the more we'll long to know Him better.

But when we come to the teaching of the Trinity, we tend to falter a bit. As if God's omnipotence, omniscience, and omnipresence weren't large enough waves washing over our minds, we stop short at the Trinity, like we would at the base camp of a towering peak. This is particularly true when it comes to understanding the Holy Spirit. As Lloyd John Ogilvie, who was once chaplain for the United States Senate, wrote,

> Sadly, many Christians settle for two-thirds of God...God the Father is way up there somewhere, aloof and apart from their daily lives. Christ is out there somewhere between them and the Father. The Holy Spirit is some kind of vague force or impersonal power that they hear about but do not know intimately...We overlook the clear biblical assertion that "no one can say that Jesus is Lord except by the Holy Spirit" (1 Corinthians 12:3).[3]

In the last chapter, we considered how three could be one and saw that the Scriptures clearly teach the doctrine of the Trinity. But we were still left with the tension of not being able to fully grasp the mystery of it. In this chapter, I want to help us get unstuck, to clear away the haze of misunderstanding by explaining some of the ways in which the three persons of the Trinity work together. Though we will never totally comprehend the Trinity (and we need to be okay with that), having a deeper understanding of how the Godhead works in our lives will cultivate in us a heart of awe and worship toward the God who longs for us to know Him.

When I was a boy, our church recited a creed that included Father, Son, and Holy Ghost. That word *Ghost* didn't make a great impression on my young mind, because every Saturday morning, I would watch *Casper the Friendly Ghost*. He didn't scare me, but I carried that whole backdrop of otherworldly spirits and haunt- ings into Sunday mornings. The idea that God was somehow associated with a ghost, even if it was a holy one, unsettled me. That kind of mystery thrilled me in a cartoon but pushed me away from God. I didn't under- stand then that there's a big difference between an unsolved murder kind of mys- tery and the mystery of a truth so wonderful and deep that it can't be fully grasped. Even so, part of me understood that I was missing out on something—that two-thirds of God was not enough.

> Though we can't unravel the mystery of the Trinity, we can appreciate the ministry the Trinity has in our lives.

That's why, in this chapter, I also want to show you how to enjoy the Trinity. I want to explore the Father, Son, and Holy Spirit from the relational point of view—how they work together and what their work means in your daily life. Though we can't unravel the mystery of the Trinity, we can appreciate the ministry the Trinity has in our lives through three great truths.

First Great Truth: All Three Work Together

Each member of the Trinity is engaged in certain works, certain acts, every day. Those works are distinct for each member but are also done in concert with the acts of the other members. Jesus made that clear when He spoke to His disciples the night before He was crucified. Let's break down John 14:10-18 for a closer look:

> *Jesus's words and miracles demonstrated the special relation- ship that God the Father has with Jesus, God the Son:* "Do you not believe that I am in the Father, and the Father in Me? The words that I speak to you I do not speak on My

own authority; but the Father who dwells in Me does the works. Believe Me that I am in the Father and the Father in Me, or else believe Me for the sake of the works themselves" (vv. 10-11).

Jesus had worldwide plans for the gospel message, but this required Him to return to the Father so the work could continue through Spirit-indwelt followers: "Most assuredly, I say to you, he who believes in Me, the works that I do he will do also; and greater works than these he will do, because I go to My Father" (v. 12).

Jesus's followers would have all the means necessary to finish the task of the gospel even without His immediate presence: "Whatever you ask in My name, that I will do, that the Father may be glorified in the Son. If you ask anything in My name, I will do it. If you love Me, keep My commandments" (vv. 13-15).

The Father, responding to the request of the Son, would send the Holy Spirit to take up residence in His followers: "I will pray the Father, and He will give you another Helper, that He may abide with you forever—the Spirit of truth, whom the world cannot receive, because it neither sees Him nor knows Him; but you know Him, for He dwells with you and will be in you. I will not leave you orphans; I will come to you" (vv. 16-18).

Jesus also assigned personality to each member of the Trinity. We're used to seeing the pronouns *He* and *Him* applied to God the Father and God the Son. But Jesus also used those pronouns in reference to the Holy Spirit. He didn't say, "I will pray to the Father, and He will send you that impersonal force to help you." He said, "I'm sending you another Helper, and *He* will stay with you forever—the Spirit of truth." Jesus promised His followers the personal, harmonious help of Father, Son, and Holy Spirit.

Do you think the disciples understood any of this at the time—that God is one being but three coequal, coeternal persons? Not even. These guys grew up Jewish; they were fiercely monotheistic. That fact was hammered into their hearts and minds. This threefold description of God was new to them and difficult to grasp. But they still wrote in the Gospels what Jesus said, and they came to believe it.

Beyond the theological truth that the Trinity exists, there is something far more practical and personal at work here. The Father, Son, and Holy Spirit are each doing certain things in the world and in our lives—and the Bible tells us what those things are.

The Provider: The Father

God the Father's actions are often focused on taking care of what we need. And what we need is help. Jesus, our first Helper, came because God sent Him: "He who did not spare His own Son, but delivered Him up for us all, how shall He not with Him also freely give us all things?" (Romans 8:32). Jesus then told His disciples that the Father would send another Helper, the Holy Spirit, to enable an ongoing connection between us and Him.

God the Father is also the sovereign architect of creation. The first line in the Bible tells us that: "In the beginning God created the heavens and the earth" (Genesis 1:1). God the Father spoke the creative words to bring the universe into being. He is the provider of life itself and of the wisdom to live it well.[4] The Father gives us the ability to work, to produce what we need to survive physically, and He also set in motion the plan to provide for our spiritual survival.[5]

The Builder: The Son

If God the Father was the architect of creation, then Jesus was the builder. "There is one God, the Father, by whom all things were created, and for whom we live. And there is one Lord, Jesus Christ, through whom all things were created, and through whom we live" (1 Corinthians 8:6 NLT). Creation was the Father's idea, and the Son executed His plan. John described Jesus as the Word, the *Logos*, the principal player who established creation and maintains its existence: "All things were made through Him, and without Him nothing was made that was made" (John 1:3).

Fast forward to Bethlehem circa 5 BC or so, and we see the Son step into everyday life. Now, the Bible tells us that God the Father is spirit (John 4:24)—not some wispy ghost-like apparition, but rather, a being completely unbound by the physical constraints of His creation. In other words, God doesn't have a body—but the Son does. "No one has ever seen God, but the one and only Son, who is himself God and is in closest relationship with the Father, has made him known" (John 1:18 NIV). Jesus made the most personal of introductions. When "the Word became flesh and dwelt among us" (John 1:14)—what we call the incarnation—God the Son let Himself be constrained by a mortal human body. He did so because the Father wanted to draw us back into relationship with Himself. And in doing so, the Son circled back to achieve the Father's plan to save us. Jesus came to buy back from sin's grip the creation He built.

The Helper: The Holy Spirit

As the Son built creation, the Holy Spirit acted as the project manager. He insured the security of the project, as Genesis 1:2 tells us: "The Spirit of God was hovering over the face of the waters." The Hebrew word used for "hovering" can also be translated as "brooding" or "moving," like "a bird above the watery abyss" (MSG), implying a sense of invested care in creation's progress.

That set the tone for the Holy Spirit's work in the world and in human hearts—to oversee and help bring to fruition the Father's plan and the Son's rescue mission. While Jesus did all the work in making salvation possible, you've probably heard it said that living the Christian life is a two-step process: first you receive Christ as Lord and Savior, and then you spend every moment afterward becoming more like Him. The Holy Spirit helps you do both. Jesus called Him "the Helper" (in other translations, "the Friend" or "the

Advocate") and provided a job description of the Spirit's work (if a phrase so mundane can be applied to such an amazing task):

> When he comes, he will convict the world of its sin, and of God's righteousness, and of the coming judgment...When the Spirit of truth comes, he will guide you into all truth. He will not speak on his own but will tell you what he has heard. He will tell you about the future. He will bring me glory by telling you whatever he receives from me. All that belongs to the Father is mine; this is why I said, "The Spirit will tell you whatever he receives from me" (John 16:8, 13-15 NLT).

The verbs Jesus used in this passage are significant: *convict, guide, tell, reveal.* When the Holy Spirit first does His work in your heart, it won't feel like help. That's because conviction chafes. It stings when you begin to realize that your life doesn't measure up to God's standards—and that He will hold you accountable for that. But you'll never realize you need Jesus until the Holy Spirit convicts you that you need to be forgiven by the Father.

Far more powerful than preaching or pleading is the work of the Spirit in a heart. He convinces you of the bad news so you can grasp how good the good news is. And once you're saved, He points you to Jesus, and Jesus points you to the Father in heaven, who loves you dearly. That Christians exist at all testifies to the presence of the triune God. Jude wrote about the ongoing work of the Trinity in the life of the believer:

> You, beloved, building yourselves up in your most holy faith and praying in the Holy Spirit, keep yourselves in the love of God, waiting for the mercy of our Lord Jesus Christ that leads to eternal life (Jude 20-21 ESV).

How the Work Gets Done

Once we see the roles of each member of the Trinity, we can look at the work they do together. For starters, the incarnation involved all three members of the Trinity: the Father sent, Jesus went, and the Holy Spirit lent His power and presence to make it happen (Matthew 1:20). All three members also played a role at Jesus's baptism: Jesus allowed John to baptize Him so that the Father would be honored, and the Father voiced His approval, claiming Jesus as "My beloved Son; in You I am well pleased" (Luke 3:22). The Holy Spirit also appeared in the form of a dove resting on Jesus (John 1:32)—that is, making it clear He would be present with Jesus throughout His ministry on earth.

Fast-forward again to the moment of salvation in someone's life—say, yours or mine. Being saved is a lot more than saying, "I accept Jesus Christ as my Lord and Savior," though that profession of faith is crucial. Salvation was actually set in motion long ago by the Father. "Long before [God] laid down earth's foundations, he had us in mind, had settled on us as the focus of his love, to be made whole and holy by his love. Long, long ago he decided to adopt us into his family through Jesus Christ" (Ephesians 1:4-5 MSG). And, in order to bring you to salvation, the Holy Spirit convicted you of your sin and God's righteousness and judgment (John 16:8).

Here's how it all happened: The Father chose you, the Holy Spirit drew you to Christ, the Son redeemed you, and the Holy Spirit now works in you to make you more like Jesus. If you'll permit me a fishing analogy, the Father made the plan to reel you in, the Spirit baited the hook, Jesus caught you, and then the Spirit went to work on cleaning you. Here's how Peter summarized salvation and sanctification: "God the Father knew you and chose you long ago, and his Spirit has made you holy. As a result, you have obeyed him and have been cleansed by the blood of Jesus Christ" (1 Peter 1:2 NLT).

The Revelation: The Bible Is a Work of Three Hands

The way we can even know about the works of the Trinity is because the Bible tells us about them. The Bible is a major source of

God's special revelation—an account of His historical interactions with humankind. It speaks of things that have happened, things that have yet to happen, and God's modus operandi for things that are currently happening in this age of grace.

Where did the Bible come from? Simply put, "All Scripture is given by inspiration of God" (2 Timothy 3:16). Another translation of that verse gets at the nuance of the Holy Spirit's contribution: "All Scripture is God-breathed" (NIV). "God-breathed" is one word in the original Greek text, *theopneustos*. This is reminiscent of the Hebrew phrase for "Spirit of God" in Genesis 1:2, *ruwach Elohim*, which literally means "breath of God." The idea is that the Holy Spirit moved in the hearts and minds of the authors of Scripture, leading them to record the truth. J.I. Packer's commentary is helpful here:

> *Spirit* is a picture-word with a vivid, precise, and colorful meaning. It pictures breath breathed or panted out, as when you blow out the candles on your birthday cake or blow up balloons or puff and blow as you run. *Spirit* in this sense was what the big bad wolf was threatening the little pigs with when he told them, "I'll huff, and I'll puff, and I'll blow your house down!" The picture of air made to move vigorously, even violently, and the thought that the picture expresses is of energy let loose, executive force invading, power in exercise, life demonstrated by activity.[6]

All three members of the Trinity played a crucial role in getting the Bible recorded and passed down intact through the generations. Generally speaking, when it comes to scriptural truth, God the Father is the source of revelation, God the Son is the subject of revelation, and God the Holy Spirit is the supervisor of revelation.

What this means in a practical sense is that Isaiah the prophet didn't sharpen his pencil one morning and think, *What cool ideas could I write down about God?* Nor did he take word-for-word dictation from God. But the Holy Spirit enabled Isaiah and the other authors of Scripture, through their own personalities and styles of writing, to record exactly what God wanted to record.

As Peter put it, "No prophecy of Scripture is of any private interpretation, for prophecy never came by the will of man, but holy men of God spoke as they were moved by the Holy Spirit" (2 Peter 1:20-21). In other words, the Spirit carried along the biblical writers to their final literary destination, much like a prevailing wind carries a sailboat in the direction that wind is blowing.

> One of God's primary purposes in providing the Bible is to draw us deeper into relationship with Him.

Beyond having inspired the writing of Scripture, the Holy Spirit also unlocks the power of God's Word for believers in their daily lives. The Bible isn't just another book of thoughts that are relevant only for certain people in certain times and situations. The Bible is a living document in the sense that it is God's living Word (Hebrews 4:12). It says what God wanted to say to all of us. It tells us He is holy and that He loves us, and that Jesus is the bridge between our lack of holiness and His great love.

In fact, one of God's primary purposes in providing the Bible is to draw us deeper into relationship with Him. That is both a supernatural work and a practical one. Practically, we draw closer to God by trusting Him—taking Him at His Word, so to speak. And what we trust are the promises He gives in the Bible, and the good news He offers. But we don't do that blindly; we have to read God's words, pay attention to them, and apply them to ourselves and our lives. Then, supernaturally, the Holy Spirit helps us do all of that—He makes the Bible come alive for us through our attention to it and our action based on it.

That's why the Bible is a book for all people, all times, and all situations. That's why even the most familiar verse can take on added importance and new life. For, we are told, "the Spirit searches all things, yes, the deep things of God" (1 Corinthians 2:10). The Spirit works to unveil an aspect of a passage to give it fresh application to your life now.

We wouldn't grasp the fullness of God's plan without understanding the work of the Trinity as revealed in the Bible: The Father purposes that all these good works should happen, Jesus sacrificed Himself to make them possible, and the Spirit works inside those who believe to continue the globetrotting scale of the work.

Second Great Truth: All Three Deserve Honor

In light of the first great truth, the proper response is the second great truth: We should honor God. When Jesus was on earth, He clearly indicated that all three members of the Trinity deserve our attention, praise, and honor. More to the point, we relate to and communicate with the triune God through worship and prayer. For example, we baptize in the name of the Father, Son, and Holy Spirit (Matthew 28:19). Paul asked that the Father might give His people "the Spirit of wisdom and revelation, so that you may know him better" (Ephesians 1:17 NIV). And Jude instructed believers to "pray in the power of the Holy Spirit" (Jude 1:20 NLT).

Prayer is probably the Christian's least-used resource. Even when you know how much of a privilege it is to talk to the Maker of heaven and earth, the Author and Perfecter of your faith, the heavenly Father who loves you with an everlasting love, praying can be a challenge. There are many reasons to pray, and yet sometimes all we can think of are the reasons why it's hard—we're busy or overwhelmed, we have compassion fatigue, or we simply don't really know how to pray.

That's why it's good to keep prayer simple. For instance, we should avoid the reductionist tendency to pray to the Father, Jesus, or the Holy Spirit only. Jesus did teach us to pray to "Our Father in heaven" (Matthew 6:9). But that's not to say we can't pray to Jesus, for He also said, "You may ask me for anything in my name, and I will do it" (John 14:14 NIV). Furthermore, the Holy Spirit is involved in prayer. Paul wrote that the Spirit helps us when we pray because we don't know how to pray like we should, He intercedes for us in harmony with God's will (Romans 8:26-27).

As children of God, we can practice the presence of the triune God by acknowledging each member of the Godhead without fear of insulting the others. We can often find reason to praise all three. I love the classic hymn that encourages us to

> Praise God, from whom all blessings flow;
> Praise Him, all creatures here below;
> Praise Him above, ye heav'nly host;
> Praise Father, Son, and Holy Ghost.[7]

Addressing the entire Trinity in prayer and worship cultivates in us a deeper sense of God's presence. Reading your Bible regularly can also bring an awareness of how all three persons are at work in your life. When you read a passage of Scripture, note who is at work—is it Father, Son, Holy Spirit, two members, or all three? What is revealed about them, both individually and collectively? Notice who is saying or doing what, and how He is (or they are) doing it. Then take a moment to pray to God about what you've discovered. The Bible says that, if you're a believer, the Spirit will open the eyes of your heart—your deepest understanding—to rejuvenate you and restore your hope (Ephesians 1:18).

What's in a Name?

Jesus was big on prayer. The Bible makes mention of Jesus praying about thirty times. His disciples saw Him praying regularly, and finally one of them asked Him, "How should we pray?" Jesus's response became known as the Lord's Prayer (Matthew 6:9-13; Luke 11:1-4). Then, the night before Jesus's crucifixion, the Lord let His disciples in on some very good news: They would soon have direct access to God the Father through prayer:

> This is what I want you to do: Ask the Father for whatever is in keeping with the things I've revealed to you. Ask in

my name, according to my will, and he'll most certainly give it to you. Your joy will be a river overflowing its banks!

I've used figures of speech in telling you these things. Soon I'll drop the figures and tell you about the Father in plain language. Then you can make your requests directly to him in relation to this life I've revealed to you. I won't continue making requests of the Father on your behalf. I won't need to. Because you've gone out on a limb, committed yourselves to love and trust in me, believing I came directly from the Father, the Father loves you directly (John 16:23-28 MSG).

The big change from the Lord's Prayer was Jesus telling them to pray to the Father in His name. The idea of praying in Jesus's name was unheard of, even for these guys who had spent the last three years coming to believe that Jesus was the Son of God. They were used to the Old Testament model of prayer, which simply addressed God as *Adonai* or *Lord* (usually in place of the unpronounceable name of God, *YHWH*), and then close with *amen, amen*—"truly" or "so be it."

But here, Jesus told His disciples to open their prayers by addressing their Father, using Jesus's name.[8] "I tell you the truth, you will ask the Father directly, and he will grant your request because you use my name" (John 16:23 NLT). However, opening a prayer with "Father" doesn't mean you can't pray directly to Jesus or the Holy Spirit. God is not going to hear you say, "Jesus, hallowed be Your name" or "Dear Holy Spirit," and say, "Nope, you didn't use the right words." After all, all three persons are God, so all three are worthy to receive praise, honor, and worship.

> To pray in the name of Jesus is to recognize who He is and all He has done.

I open prayers with "Father" because that's what Jesus said to do. It's a richly relational term, much more personal than "God." And I end prayers by saying, "In Jesus's name" because that's what Jesus said to do. He said that's how we know our prayers will be heard. The prayer that God directs is the prayer God expects.

That's how Jesus prayed while He was on earth (John 17), and that's the kind of prayer He is saying right now on behalf of all believers (Romans 8:34). In His role as our High Priest and based on His perfect sacrifice for us (Hebrew 10:10-14), Jesus is praying to the Father for us in heaven, interceding on our behalf regularly as part of our process of sanctification. To pray in the name of Jesus is to recognize who He is and all He has done.

Even so, to pray in Jesus's name isn't a magic ticket to getting your prayers answered. You can't just tack on those three words and expect your prayer to instantly make it onto God's to-do list. What you pray for—for instance, whether it's something in keeping with His will—and the attitude with which you pray matter far more. To pray in the name of Jesus is to say, "I'm not coming to You on my own merits, Father, but on those of Jesus."

It would the wrong kind of hilarious for you to come to God based on anyone else's reputation, whether that is your pastor's, your super-religious grandmother's, or your own. Jesus opened the door for our prayers to be heard in heaven, and only Jesus could make that possible. Whether we open a prayer by addressing Father, Son, or Holy Spirit, we talk to the Father on Jesus's merits alone.

Our Heart's Interpreter

Why is it that when Jesus told His disciples to talk to the Father in Jesus's name, He didn't mention the Holy Spirit? Isn't He involved in our communication with God too? Yes, He is, but not in a way that calls attention to Himself. Jesus explained a few verses earlier:

> When the Friend comes, the Spirit of the Truth, he will take you by the hand and guide you into all the truth there is. He won't draw attention to himself, but will make sense out of what is about to happen and, indeed, out of all that

I have done and said. He will honor me; he will take from me and deliver it to you (John 16:13-15 MSG).

The Holy Spirit is a silent witness who points us to Jesus. The Spirit makes it all about the Son. Why? Because Jesus Christ is the central theme of the Bible. As the Scriptures make a big deal about Jesus, so does the Holy Spirit. But that doesn't mean that the Spirit isn't involved when we pray. In fact, I would say that He plays a crucial role in prayer. As Paul wrote:

> The Holy Spirit helps us in our weakness. For example, we don't know what God wants us to pray for. But the Holy Spirit prays for us with groanings that cannot be expressed in words. And the Father who knows all hearts knows what the Spirit is saying, for the Spirit pleads for us believers in harmony with God's own will (Romans 8:26-27 NLT).

In the larger context of this passage, Paul was describing the challenges of waiting on God's promises in a broken world. We wait with hope for Him to one day renew all things, but sometimes all we can do is groan. We can't find the words to express our deep frustration and dissatisfaction with ourselves and the world, so we grumble or murmur or sigh. Other times, we can't find the words to express our hope, gratitude, and confidence that God is working in ways we can't see or grasp. And then there are the times when we are moved to pray about something but don't know all the particulars of the situation. All of these are reasons to groan wordlessly.

> We can pray with confidence, knowing that all three members of the Trinity are involved in helping us communicate with God.

But the groaning of the Holy Spirit is different. He doesn't fret like us, because He knows the "deep things of God" (1 Corinthians 2:10). Being God, He knows God's heart and intentions. What's more, He knows exactly what and how we should pray, even when we don't. And He knows what we mean, even when we can't find the words to express what is on our mind or heart. He can take the prayers we can't find words for—our jumbled thoughts and feelings—and make them known to the Lord. That's how we can pray with confidence, knowing that all three members of the Trinity are involved in helping us communicate with God. When we see what each member of the Trinity brings to the work of prayer, it's easy to recognize that we should value all three members.

Third Great Truth: All Three Demonstrate Oneness

A third great truth about the Trinity is that there is unity among its members. The Bible is abundantly clear that there is only one God. Thus, the three persons of the Trinity are not only one in mind and purpose, but one in essence. No passage in Scripture better demonstrates this than Jesus's prayer in John 17:20-22:

> I do not pray for these alone [that is, His disciples at the time], but also for those who will believe in Me through their word [that is, all of His future followers]; that they all may be one, as You, Father, are in Me, and I in You; that they also may be one in Us, that the world may believe that You sent Me. And the glory which You gave Me I have given them, that they may be one just as We are one.

What was Jesus talking about? He was saying that the way the Father and Son (and, implied, the Holy Spirit) get along with and relate to one another is a template for the way believers ought to relate to one another. Let's explore that thought.

Relationship on Earth as It Is in Heaven

In short, fellowship ought to flow among Christians because it exists among the Father, Son, and Holy Spirit. These three members of the Trinity exist in eternal community and relational harmony. And the very purpose for which God created people was community and harmony with Him.

For eternity past, there was a family setup of Father, Son, and Holy Spirit. And they loved and were enriched by one another's fellowship. But at some point, God decided to expand on what was already enjoyed within the Trinity: He decided to make us, the pinnacle of His creation. "Let Us make man in Our image, according to Our likeness" (Genesis 1:26). He made us so that we could enjoy special relationship with Him.

> Unity in our community authenticates our Christianity.

So Jesus's prayer tells us that the ultimate basis for Christian community on earth—marriage, family, and the church—is not humanity but the Trinity. The ultimate reason for a husband and wife to look each other in the eyes and say, "I love you, I forgive you, and I'll stay with you" isn't because of some legal agreement or church-enforced document. Rather, it's an opportunity to display Trinitarian love and tenderness on a smaller scale. Unity in our community authenticates our Christianity. Jesus wants us to be one in the same way that the Trinity is one.

Unity Is Priority for the Trinity

This is why many church splits are sinful and wrong—not only because they hurt church members but because they violate the unity of the body of Christ and fail to reflect the unity among the Father, the Son, and the Holy Spirit. The whole reason we should love one another, forgive one another, be kind to one another, and mend relationships with one another is so that we honor the Trinity.

That takes relationship to the highest level, doesn't it? We were created to cultivate and maintain relationships because relationship exists in the Godhead. That's why Jesus said, "We are one: I in them, and You in Me; that they may be made perfect in one, and that the world may know that You have sent Me, and have loved them as You have loved Me" (John 17:22-23). The world will know that the Father sent the Son because of the unity among those who follow

Christ. As Jesus said elsewhere, "Your love for one another will prove to the world that you are my disciples" (John 13:35 NLT).

I heard about a man who visited a friend who worked as a guard in a mental institution. This man noticed that his friend oversaw and guarded a hundred patients alone, so he asked him, "Aren't you ever scared that they're going to get their heads together, attack you, and escape?" The guard put his arms behind his head, put his feet on his desk, and said, "The whole reason they're here is because of their inability to get their heads together and work cooperatively."

In the same way, for the church to try to represent the triune God to the world without unity is insanity. If unbelievers hear about Jesus's love and grace from Christians who then turn around and fight amongst themselves, they're going to tune us out. "I don't need to go to church—I can get this kind of drama from a soap opera."

One thing you must guard against is resisting the work of the triune God in your life, especially that of the Holy Spirit convicting you to make Jesus your Lord and Savior. Because one day, you will meet your Maker.

The question is, on whose terms will it be: yours or His? If it's on His terms, based on Jesus Christ's atoning work on the cross, you'll be glad to make God's acquaintance. But if it's on your terms—your accomplishments, your character, your merits—it doesn't matter how impressive those things are; they will never be enough to make you right before God.

God wants you to become a part of the community of the Trinity, drawn in by the Holy Spirit to receive the forgiveness purchased by the Son so you can be at peace with the Father. If you are feeling any dissatisfaction about understanding or acknowledging the Trinity, that's the Holy Spirit prompting you to embrace the full truth about Father, Son, and Holy Spirit. He's inviting you into the fellowship of that marvelous unity. Will you ask Him to open your heart's eyes so you can see the wonder and work of the Trinity today?

Chapter 14

GOOD MAN, MADMAN, CON MAN, OR GOD-MAN?

Jesus, Part 1

No other person in history has generated so much controversy and speculation, as well as written literature, as Jesus Christ. Absolutely no one! Theologians, philosophers, poets, and pundits have all weighed in concerning who Jesus is. What they often forget is that Jesus can never be overestimated. John said that if everything Jesus did had been recorded, "even the world itself could not contain the books that would be written" (John 21:25). Though it would be impossible to try to cover everything there is to know about the person of Jesus, in this chapter I want to provide a proper introduction to Him, to give you a basic idea of who He is and what He is all about.

Now, Sunday school classes are notorious for using rhetorical questions that usually have just one answer: Jesus. "Who's living in your heart?" *Jesus.* "Who's the Savior of all?" *Jesus.* One preschool teacher ran into a problem with this. She was trying to engage her young students in a lesson about Noah's ark by asking them identifying questions about animals.

"I'll describe something, and you guess what it is," she said. "I'm furry with a bushy tail and I like to climb trees." The kids stared at the teacher with blank looks. She continued, "I also like to eat nuts, especially acorns." Again, nothing. She dropped a few more hints: "I'm usually brown or gray, sometimes black, even red." No takers.

Finally she turned to a perky four-year-old who usually had the answers. "Michelle," she said, "what do you think it is?" Michelle looked at her classmates hesitantly and said, "Well, I know the answer has to be Jesus—but it sure sounds like a squirrel to me!"[1]

In a book about God, you would certainly expect a chapter or two on Jesus Christ. After all, He is the answer to humanity's question. He is God the Father's immediate answer to the problem of sin, His inevitable answer to the reality of eternity, His ultimate answer to the world's suffering, and His ongoing answer as the center of prophetic scripture. A. W. Tozer was right when he said, "We do not preach Christ with a comma after his name, as though waiting for something else; or Christ with a dash after his name as though leading to something else, we preach Christ *period.*"[2]

But who exactly is Jesus? Who was He? Was He just a good man? Was He a madman—someone who misrepresented Himself to people? Or was He the God-man? There's always been a steady stream of theories concerning Jesus Christ. I've read some pretty whacky ones—like He was a magician who practiced hypnosis, or a guru, or a wise world traveler. One theory even claims that Jesus was the husband of Mary Magdalene, with whom He sought to procreate a secret lineage to rule the world.

None of these theories hold up in the light of Scripture, and many of them are far wilder than the truth. So what is the truth about Jesus? That's a question Jesus Himself asked His disciples: "Who do men say that I, the Son of Man, am?" (Matthew 16:13). He followed with the more penetrating question, "Who do you say that I am?" (v. 15). By this time Jesus had been working with these guys for two-and-a-half years, and it was time for a test of sorts. This exam was made up of just these two questions: one general and one personal. The first question has many possible answers, but the second is pass or fail.

The disciples threw out several answers to the open-ended first question—John the Baptist, the prophets Elijah or Jeremiah. But the second question was a lot harder. And what I love is that Peter was the only one who got it right. A lot of people give Peter a hard time for being impulsive, putting his foot in his mouth, and speaking out of turn, but he got an *A* on this one: "You are the Christ, the Son of the living God" (v. 16). (Admittedly, Pete had a little help from God the Father [see v. 17], but still, he nailed it!) Peter later affirmed this truth when he wrote, "We did not follow cunningly devised fables when we made known unto you the power and coming of our Lord Jesus Christ, but were eyewitnesses of His majesty" (2 Peter 1:16).

Back in the 1960s and '70s, I was part of the cultural/spiritual phenomenon dubbed the Jesus movement. This was a great revival that began on the West Coast of the US, and its repercussions are still felt to this day. In the midst of Timothy Leary's advocating that kids experiment with LSD and "turn on, tune in, and drop out," kids up and down the coast were instead turning on to Jesus. I was one of them. I loved the emphasis the Jesus movement put on Jesus rather than on a certain denomination or flavor of Christian doctrine. And when you think about it, the Jesus movement started back in Matthew 16. That's when Peter correctly identified Jesus Christ as the Son of God and Jesus first used the word *church* to describe what He would build among His followers—a community of Christian believers all centered on Himself (v. 18).

Who Is This Guy? Let the Speculation Begin...

Now, if anyone else but Jesus were to ask the first question—*Who do men say that I am?*—it would be correctly construed as arrogant. If I said, "Who do people say that I, Skip Heitzig, am?," you would say, "Who cares? Who do you think you are to even ask such a question?" But this was Jesus, and it was entirely appropriate for Him to ask this. His identity was constantly in question even back then (see John 9:16-17).

Again, when Jesus posed this question to His disciples, He had been working with this hand-picked team for a while. They had seen His miracles, heard His messages, and watched Him live out what He had taught them. But what had they retained? What had they come to believe about His identity? The disciples had listened to Him for more than two years; now, He wanted to hear what they had to say.

So Jesus took them out of the hustle and bustle of ministry to a quiet place of R and R. The ancient Roman city of Caesarea Philippi was near the foot of Mount Hermon and the headwaters of the Jordan River. In contrast to the heat of Galilee, this was a cool, quiet, lush plateau. As the source of the Jordan, it was also a significant location in Israel's history. The river flowed out of a rock at the base of Mount Hermon, giving life to all of Israel.

Because of the beauty of the location, Caesarea Philippi was also home to about fourteen different pagan temples—centers of worship for Baal, Pan, and even Caesar Augustus (whose temple was built by Herod the Great), among others. Jesus chose this spot deliberately—not just for its beauty but because it was soaked in religious pluralism. He wanted to ask those two crucial questions against this backdrop of all things spiritual and significant so that the contrast would reveal just how unique He is compared to all the false gods people worshipped. The secular equivalent would be like going to Las Vegas to discuss the topic of gambling one's life away in pursuit of earthly pleasures.

Jesus had entered public life only a few years previous. So when He asked, "What's the buzz—who are people saying I am?," the number of different responses was impressive for such a short period of ministry. John the Baptist, Elijah, Jeremiah, some other prophets—so many answers, and all of them wrong. Did I mention that Jesus's identity has always been controversial? It goes to show you that if you're going to make a determination about Christ based on hearsay and other people's opinions, you'll probably be wrong.

I know a little bit about gossip and rumors. When I first came to Albuquerque to plant a new church, it was interesting to observe the general public's opinion of our church. As we started to grow and gain popularity, people began to say, "Who are those people meeting in that storefront? Only cults and crazies meet in storefronts."

I'll never forget how one local minister felt sorry for us and tried to give me some advice on successful church planting. He asked about when we would take the offering during Sunday morning service, and I said, "Well, we're not going to take a formal offering. We're just going to leave out a coffee can."

"What? It'll never work." He seemed genuinely perplexed. "Well, what about pledge cards? Do you have the pledge cards ready? When you have your first Sunday service, you need to pass out those pledge cards to get your budget going for the next year."

I said, "We're not going to have pledge cards, either; in fact, we probably won't even have a budget."

He slowly shook his head. "You'll never make it."

Another pastor in town decided I needed to change my youthful California surfer image, so he offered to buy me a clerical robe just to lend some credibility to my poor ministry persona. He was certain that people would take me more seriously if I wore a cassock and collar.

Over the years, people have spread all sorts of rumors about me. I wouldn't say I've necessarily partaken in Jesus's suffering because of them, but I've come to understand a little about the nature of being in the public eye. With that in mind, let's look at some of the speculation, both ancient and modern, about the identity of Jesus.

Is He the Locust and Honey Guy?

Jesus opened Himself up to gossip by the very nature of His ministry. And the rumor mills were definitely churning in Nazareth, Galilee, and Jerusalem. Some folk said that Jesus was John the Baptist, whom Herod Antipas had recently beheaded. Herod himself started this rumor. What did he see in Jesus that reminded him of John? Well, Jesus and John were cousins, right? And despite their different ministries, they had a similarity of style. John the Baptist was a fiery, no-compromise kind of a preacher, and so was Jesus.

John's first message was on repentance, and so was Jesus's. John boldly confronted the Pharisees and other leaders; so did Jesus. Add to that Herod's guilt from beheading John, and you have the perfect recipe for a gossip piece.

> Jesus advocated the most radical displays of love ever heard of.

John did some pretty outlandish things, including eating bugs and living out in the desert. He wasn't afraid to call out sin in those who committed it. But Jesus made John look mellow. Jesus advocated the most radical displays of love ever heard of—things like loving your enemies, putting yourself last, forgiving unforgivable people, and offering the other cheek when struck. He also said He was the only way to God, that anyone who ate His flesh and drank His blood would have eternal life, and that to follow Him meant to give up your personal rights and suffer.

According to Jesus, you can't love both God and money; if you harbor feelings of hatred you may as well be a murderer; and if you look at an attractive person with lust, you're guilty of having an affair. Jesus called people to pay their taxes and tithes yet also prioritize storing up treasure in heaven. His teachings revolved around loving God more than anything and loving your neighbor like you love yourself. This was revolutionary thought and speech.

Jesus even went so far as to say that if anyone believed He was who He said He was—the Son of God—they would be saved from God's righteous eternal judgment but condemned if they didn't. He overturned the tables of merchants who were fleecing temple-goers and made mud out of His spit to heal a blind man. He told us to amputate our sin, not coddle it. The picture of Jesus painted in the Bible is definitely not Sunday school Jesus, meek and mild, holding babies and collecting stray pets. So if Herod was a bit alarmed by Jesus, whether due to his own guilt over beheading John or his fear of God's justice, he can't be blamed.

Is He the Fiery Chariot Guy?

Other people wondered if Jesus was one of the Old Testament prophets come back to earth, particularly Elijah. Elijah had been dead for about 900 years by this time, but the Lord had predicted through the prophet Malachi, "Behold, I will send you Elijah the prophet before the coming of the great and dreadful day of the Lord. And he will turn the hearts of the fathers to the children, and the hearts of the children to their fathers, lest I come and strike the earth with a curse" (Malachi 4:5-6).

This prediction had worked its way into a tradition that Elijah would return, so for 400 years, the Jews had anticipated that return. At Passover, families left their door slightly ajar and set an empty seat at the table just in case Elijah were to stop by on his way to herald the coming of the Messiah. Elijah was also famous for his miracles—raising a dead boy to life, causing a three-year drought and then bringing rain, and calling fire down from heaven to burn up a bull on a water-soaked altar, among others. The people looked at all the miracles Jesus was performing and said, "This has to be the forerunner of the Messiah—a prophet just like Elijah!"

Is He the Crying Guy?

The disciples also reported that some people thought Jesus was the prophet Jeremiah. While there are definitely similarities between Jesus and Jeremiah—both were known for their compassion, and both wept over Jerusalem's failure to recognize God's truth—that's not what the buzz was about. This rumor wasn't based on Scripture but an unsubstantiated legend.[3]

According to this legend, when the Babylonians came and sacked Jerusalem, Jeremiah hid the tent of the tabernacle and the ark of the covenant in a cave on Mount Nebo (where Moses died—see Deuteronomy 34:1-5). Supposedly Jeremiah would one day return and restore those articles to their proper place in the temple, bringing glory to God and kicking off a new era of Jewish independence.

Given the widespread yearning in Jesus's day for God to lift the yoke of Roman oppression, a lot of people were hoping this legend would come to pass.

Is He an Alien? A Demoniac? A Local Boy with Delusions of Grandeur?

People's opinions about Jesus in His day were about as common as salt in the Dead Sea. The Jewish leaders and people sponsored more than their fair share. According to them, Jesus was an illegitimate child (John 8:41)[4] who was possibly demon-possessed (John 7:20). It was common back then to relegate any sort of mental health issue to demon activity, so they might have been calling Him crazy. During Jesus's trial, the Jewish leaders falsely testified against Him and accused Him of blasphemy (Mark 14:55-65). They were desperate to discredit Him, but the only allegation they got right was that He claimed to be God (John 7:28-29; 8:58; see also Matthew 22:41-46).

Although the common people loved to hear Jesus speak (Mark 12:37), they also sponsored a fair share of chatter about His identity. The people of Nazareth, Jesus's hometown, didn't buy His messianic claims. They said, "That's Joe and Mary's boy. All His brothers and sisters still live here—why is He making such a big deal of Himself?" They dismissed Jesus to the extent that He "marveled because of their unbelief" (Mark 6:6). Some of the common people called Jesus a deceiver, while others called Him good (John 7:12).

That last opinion was the most common: Jesus was a good man—a fine, honorable person. But that was it. Nothing more. He wasn't a famous prophet but simply a good teacher to whom God had given some miracle-working powers. Nicodemus, a Pharisee, described Jesus as "a teacher come from God; for no one can do these signs that You do unless God is with him" (John 3:2). Of course, Jesus *was* good, and He *was* a teacher. But He was infinitely more than these.

So, Is He Just a Good Man?

Over the years, I've heard so many different ideas about who Jesus was. I read about one group that claimed that Jesus wasn't resurrected but cloned by aliens, sort of an *X-Files* version of Jesus. I once met a guy at a doughnut shop who said, "Everybody knows we came here because of aliens." I asked him what research had led him to this conclusion, and he gave me a blank stare and offered me another cup of coffee. Such far-fetched beliefs (often rooted in pseudoscience) are trendy but treacherous. The Bible makes it clear that one day God will judge what you believed and how you lived your life, so don't you want to make sure you're staking your eternity on the truth?

The most common belief people have about Jesus today is simply that "nothing's wrong with Him; He's great!" For most people, He was a good man and wonderful teacher who spoke great words and gave a fine example—and nothing more.

An impressive group of atheists have spearheaded this belief. The French philosopher Rousseau said that Jesus exemplified Plato's theoretical perfect leader.[5] Another Frenchman, Ernest Renan, praised Jesus as the greatest man ever born—but he said that Jesus's postresurrection appearances were simply hysteria on His followers' part (or even hallucinations). English philosopher John Stuart Mill said Jesus was the pattern of perfection for humanity. The American poet Ralph Waldo Emerson, while not an atheist, thought Jesus was a great man, but not God.[6] The German theologian David Strauss, who also denied the divinity of Christ, still called Jesus "the highest model of religion."[7]

Perhaps you've heard the phrase "damned by faint praise." That becomes literal rather than metaphorical for those who deny and diminish Jesus's divinity even while complimenting Him as the highest expression of humanity. Their attempts to undercut Jesus end up leading to their own condemnation.

Is He a Liar?

The weightiest accusations against Jesus sometimes originate not with nonbelievers but among the super religious. "Some said, 'He is good'; others said, 'No, on the contrary, He deceives the people'" (John 7:12). The Greek word for "deceives" here means "to lead astray" or "to seduce." It's a strong word. And it's the emphasis of the rabbis who wrote the Jewish Talmud, a collection of commentaries from the second through fifth centuries. The portrait they painted of Jesus is alarming, to say the least.

The Talmud describes Jesus of Nazareth as the illegitimate son of Mary, whose husband (alternately called Stada or Pantera) kicked her out for adultery. As a young man, Jesus moved to Egypt to study magical arts and returned to Judea, claiming to be God and itching to start a rebellion against Rome. This kind of shoddy revisionism was already in play during Jesus's trial. As the chief priests and scribes told Pilate, "We found this fellow perverting the nation, and forbidding to pay taxes to Caesar, saying that He Himself is Christ, a King" (Luke 23:2).

After Jesus's execution, the chief priests and Pharisees, acting out of paranoia, convinced Pilate to set a guard near His tomb, saying, "Sir, we remember, while He was still alive, how that deceiver said, 'After three days I will rise'" (Matthew 27:63). They reasoned that Jesus's disciples would steal His body and claim He had been raised—"So the last deception [Jesus's apparent resurrection] will be worse than the first [Jesus's claims to be God]" (v. 64).

Speaking of deception, in the 1980s and '90s there was a group called The Jesus Seminar that met twice a year to decide, all on their own, the accuracy of what was recorded about Jesus in the Gospels. They voted on various passages, using colored beads to indicate the level of historical reliability they thought could be attributed to Jesus's statements and deeds. They were so immersed in their scholarship that they drowned any sense of objective truth. They concluded that Jesus actually said only 18 percent of the words attributed to Him in the Bible.[8] An article in *Time* summarized their findings:

The Seminar found all the Nativity descriptions to be inauthentic except for the name of Jesus' mother (Mary). No miracle working made the cut, although Jesus is generally credited with having healed some of the sick. He had a disciple named Mary Magdalene, entered a synagogue at least once and met some Pharisees. As regards the Passion and Easter: all descriptions of Jesus' trial are deemed inauthentic, along with his Palm Sunday statement that he is the Messiah.[9]

According to them, Jesus may have been a carpenter, He was probably illiterate, and He belonged to a low caste of artisans. He didn't preach salvation from sin through sacrifice. He never cured any diseases. No loaves and fishes were multiplied, no water was turned into wine, Lazarus was not raised from the dead, and certainly Jesus was not resurrected.

The self-identified scholars of The Jesus Seminar came under fire themselves for exaggerating their qualifications to judge the historical reliability of the New Testament. William Lane Craig and N.T. Wright both penned detailed criticisms of their methods and qualifications. Even liberal critics had problems with the Seminar. Garry Wills (a Pulitzer-Prize-winning Catholic journalist and author) said their methodology was less like finding "diamonds in a dunghill" and more "like finding New York City at the bottom of the Pacific Ocean."[10] The spurious results of the Seminar sounded more like the members had worked to create a Jesus based on their assumptions rather than critically test the historical record of the Bible.

> When a manmade discipline falls prey to an agenda opposed to God, truth is the first casualty.

But that's what you can expect when the fields of science, history, and philosophy attempt to displace a clear testimony of historical faith borne out over 2,000 years. When a manmade discipline falls prey to an agenda opposed to God, truth is the first casualty—but not the last. Bad ideas lead to negative consequences—wasted years and lost souls. Ironically, in trying to prove that the Bible's version of Jesus was deceptive, The Jesus Seminar itself used deception.

What a gamut of opinions about Jesus, both then and now! A myriad of ideas about His identity has surrounded Him since His earliest days, from John the Baptist to Elijah to Jeremiah to an Egyptian magician to an alien to just-a-good-man. And for so many people, any of these options are preferable over and above who He Himself claimed to be. But this was so that Scripture would be fulfilled: "He is despised and rejected by men, a Man of sorrows and acquainted with grief. And we hid, as it were, our faces from Him; He was despised, and we did not esteem Him" (Isaiah 53:3).

Who Did Jesus Say He Was?

When you consider Jesus's claims, as recorded in Scripture, they help you rule out other less satisfying options about His identity. No other major religious or philosophical leader ever made the incredible claims Jesus made. Confucius never claimed to be God. Buddha never said, "I am the way, the truth, and the life." Muhammad never called himself the Son of God. Oxford professor of religion Alister McGrath put it this way: "The challenge posed to every succeeding generation by the New Testament witness to Jesus is not so much, 'What did He teach?' but 'Who is He? And what is His relevance for today?'"[11]

Those who categorize Jesus as a good man, a Galilean peacemaker, or simply a great teacher of morals aren't thinking through what they're suggesting. A great moral teacher wouldn't make the sorts of claims Jesus made. The familiar C.S. Lewis quote says it all:

> He would either be a lunatic—on the level with the man who says he is a poached egg—or else he would be the Devil of Hell...Either this man was, and is, the Son of God: or else a madman or something worse. You can shut Him up for a fool, you can spit at Him and kill Him as a demon; or you can fall at His feet and call Him Lord and God.[12]

What you won't find in the New Testament is Jesus saying something like, "I'm a fine citizen, a great example, a moral teacher, and, hey! People like Me." He never said anything of the sort. What He did say about Himself is as lofty as can be imagined. Consider, for example, the seven great "I am" statements of Jesus:

"I am the bread of life" (John 6:35).

"I am the light of the world" (John 8:12).

"I am the door" (John 10:9).

"I am the good shepherd" (John 10:11).

"I am the resurrection and the life" (John 11:25).

"I am the way, the truth, and the life" (John 14:6).

"I am the true vine" (John 15:1).

All of these statements are rooted in Old Testament passages and images that point to God's sovereignty and provision and to the Messiah. Jesus also told a Samaritan woman, "Whoever drinks of the water that I shall give him will never thirst" (John 4:14). He told the Jewish religious leaders, "You are from beneath; I am from above" (John 8:23), and astonished (and aggravated) them by declaring, "Before Abraham was, I AM" (John 8:58). To His friend Philip, Jesus said, "He who has seen Me has seen the Father" (John 14:9). To His prosecutor Pilate, He said, "You say rightly that I am a king" (John 18:37).

The broader picture the Gospels paint of Jesus is of a good man—compassionate, gently chiding and redirecting, healing bodies and hearts, teaching an others-oriented approach to life. But these statements He made about Himself? *Radical.*

Jesus said He is the quencher of thirst, the satisfier of hunger, the light of the world, a chief citizen of heaven, older than Abraham (who predated him by millennia), the door of salvation, the exact representation of His Father, the only way to God, and the King. He also claimed to forgive sins (Mark 2:5) and have supreme authority

(Matthew 11:27; 28:18; Mark 4:39). He directly claimed to be God (Mark 14:61-64; John 5:18).

These aren't the words of merely a good man; a good man wouldn't say untrue things about himself. A madman wouldn't live a life of service and sacrifice. And a con man wouldn't suffer the ignominious death of the cross. What Jesus said about Himself reminds me of what Mr. Beaver said of Aslan in *The Lion, the Witch, and the Wardrobe*: "Who said anything about safe? 'Course he isn't safe. But he's good. He's the King, I tell you."[13]

Who Is He to You?

That brings us back to the second question Jesus asked His disciples at Caesarea Philippi: "Who do men say that I, the Son of Man, am?" (Matthew 16:13). Millions of people over the past 2,000 years have echoed Peter's answer: "You are the Christ, the Son of the living God." They have staked their souls on what Jesus said about Himself, leaving a testimony diverse in individuality but uniform in its core claim: Jesus forgives sins and changes lives.

Notice what Jesus said about Peter's response: "Blessed are you, Simon Bar-Jonah, for flesh and blood has not revealed this to you, but My Father who is in heaven" (Matthew 16:17). This was a moment of uncharacteristic insight from Peter; it happened only because he opened himself up to God's wisdom.

Now, anyone can answer the first question Jesus asked. Anyone can weigh in, correctly or not, on who Jesus is. Almost everyone who has ever heard of Jesus has settled on some opinion of Him. But our opinions must be measured against what Jesus said about Himself and against the testimony God the Father gave of His own Son (Matthew 3:17; 17:5). His knowledge and wisdom aren't subject to human influence.

The second question Jesus asked—"Who do you say that I am?" (Matthew 16:15)—invites you to take Him personally. It asks you to unpin Him from the Sunday school felt-board, take Him off the theological shelf, and liberate Him from the shackles of speculation.

According to the Bible, there is really only one reasonable answer to this question: Jesus is the Messiah—the Christ—the long-awaited Son of God who lived among us, died for our sins, rose again from the grave, and will return to judge the living and the dead. He may be your mom's redeemer and your grandfather's Savior, your girlfriend's hope and your coworker's Lord. But is He all those things to you personally? Who do you say Jesus is?

> Who you say Jesus is—good man, madman, con man, or God-man—is not a matter of opinion but of life and death.

And why does the answer to that question matter so much? As Jesus warned the Jewish leaders, "If you do not believe that I am He"—the son of God sent as a perfect, final sacrifice for sin—"you will die in your sins" (John 8:24). In His conversation with Nicodemus, Jesus laid out the wonderful, massive scope of God's rescue mission for humanity (John 3:16-17), but then said, "He who does not believe is condemned already, because he has not believed in the name of the only begotten Son of God" (v. 18). Who you say Jesus is—good man, madman, con man, or God-man—is not a matter of opinion but of life and death. Where you will spend eternity—heaven or hell—rides on your response.

Hell is an uncomfortable subject to discuss. It should be. It's not a place God designed with us in mind, but it is a real place where we will go after we die if we remain in our condemned state as sinners. Jesus spoke about hell more than anyone else in the Bible, if only because our hard hearts often require repetition for something to sink in. At the same time, Jesus spoke far more often about heaven and His coming kingdom—because that's where He wants us to be, with Him, redeemed, liberated, and joyfully serving Him and others.

I heard about an elderly man who had trouble hearing despite having a hearing aid. When he finally asked a doctor about it, the doctor took the hearing aid out and put it in the man's other ear, and the man could suddenly hear beautifully. Turns out he'd had it in the wrong ear for years. What a waste, right? But it made me think: Who have I been listening to? Have I had my hearing aid in the wrong ear? Who has helped form my view of Jesus? Over the years, I've learned the importance of listening to the right people, first and foremost Jesus Himself.

Someone once told me, "One of the reasons people find it hard to be obedient to the commands of Jesus Christ is they're uncomfortable taking commands from a stranger." But Jesus doesn't have to remain a stranger to you. You can continue to keep Him at arm's length, using philosophy or science or even theology to hold Him off, but the Bible makes it clear that doing so will condemn you before the holy God. The fact is that Jesus, who is God in the flesh, wants to have a relationship with you.

So who is shaping your view of Jesus? College professors? Friends who are ambivalent toward God? Unsaved coworkers? Social media influencers? Musicians or celebrities? Don't blindly buy into someone else's opinion about Jesus. God wants you to see Jesus for who He really is, and only He can open your eyes and your heart to do that. At that point, only you will be able to answer the question for yourself: *Who do you say Jesus is?*

Chapter 15

MARKED BY PURPOSE: THE CARPENTER WHO WAS REALLY A KING

Jesus, Part 2

Jesus of Nazareth has always fascinated me. Even during my most rebellious years of drug usage, astral projection, and spirit writing, Jesus both intrigued and frightened me. I was intrigued by His love and sacrifice but frightened of His evaluation of me. Tim Keller was right when he said, "The gospel is always more compelling to people who know their own inadequacy."[1] But when Jesus first showed up on the earth, that was hardly the case.

Two thousand years ago, no official Roman notice board carried the headline "Jewish Baby Born in Bethlehem." Nobody cared, frankly. The hot news was in Rome itself, bound up with the big names like Caesar Augustus, Governor Quirinius in Syria, and King Herod. But the fame of these individuals over the last couple millennia has paled in comparison to the fame and influence of a carpenter-turned-preacher from backwater Nazareth.

That's because Jesus of Nazareth wasn't just any peasant from Podunkville. He was—and is—God's message of hope to hurting humanity: God Himself, wrapped in flesh and blood. Paul summed up the identity of the man the Bible calls the Christ, the anointed one of God, by describing Him as "the image of the invisible God, the firstborn over all creation. For by Him all things were created that are in heaven and that are on earth, visible and invisible, whether thrones or dominions or principalities or powers. All things were created through Him and for Him" (Colossians 1:15-16).

In the last chapter we looked at who Jesus Christ is. Let's continue that theme by considering His entrance onto planet Earth.

A King Among the Critters

Growing up, my job during Christmastime every year was to set up our nativity scene. We had a nice one, with a little wooden stable, porcelain manger, and even an angel we suspended over the stable next to the star. This manger setting was always pristine, clean, and temperature-controlled, and it smelled good from the pine fronds we placed around it. In other words, compared to the original setting of Jesus's birth, it was entirely inaccurate.

Now, I'm not Grinching out on Christmas. I just think it's fascinating how much our traditions are a Disneyed-up celebration of the nativity of Christ. Over the years, we've added a little snow to the scene, brought in three visiting kings and a drummer boy, and decided to decorate a tree, which was once a symbol of pagan traditions but was redeemed in the sixteenth century by Martin Luther. And we love these traditions—we don't want anyone messing with them.

But I want to challenge you to look beyond all the tinsel and trappings to a gift of far greater worth than we could ever imagine. The reason we have a season at all is because Jesus Christ, God in the flesh, came to the planet He created. And He did so not just so that we could celebrate for a few weeks at the end of the year but so that we could see Him face to face. And to see Jesus for who He truly is transforms us. So let's do some unwrapping.

His Nativity

Ever since the other planets in our solar system were discovered, people have been fascinated by the possibility of earth being visited by aliens. In 1938, Orson Welles caused widespread panic for many US citizens in his famed radio broadcast "The War of the Worlds."

Some listeners apparently thought the earth really was being invaded by Martians. Over the years, the fear of extraterrestrials has turned to enthusiasm for them, and this enthusiasm shows no signs of letting up, even more than three-quarters of a century later.

But what about enthusiasm for what happened at Bethlehem 2,000 years ago? In his book *Mere Christianity*, C.S. Lewis named his chapter on the incarnation "The Invasion," depicting Jesus's coming to earth as an incursion on "enemy-occupied territory," with the rightful king landing in disguise. It was a great way of describing how God's arrival on earth was neither familiar nor typical.

That goes against the idea of Christmas as a preplanned good-will tour. Of course, you can still enjoy the December holiday season and celebrate the birth of Jesus in ways that bring you joy and help you focus on Him, even though Jesus wasn't actually born on December 25. Most scholars place His birth sometime around the Passover (the same season as His death).

Where did the December 25 date come from? Up until the fourth century AD, Christians had observed Christ's birth on a number of different dates—but not one of them was December 25.[2] Some say that around AD 350, Pope Julius I designated December 25 as Jesus's birthday, perhaps in an attempt to commandeer the Roman feast Saturnalia. But ultimately, there's really no reason to be concerned about when in the year we celebrate Jesus's birth. What matters is that Jesus was born at all.

And the place in which He was born was a far cry from the descriptions found in the classic hymns "O Little Town of Bethlehem" and "Silent Night." In fact, it would be more accurate to sing "O, hectic night," or "O little town of Bethlehem, how feverishly busy we see thee lie." According to Luke 2, a census was underway when Jesus was born. The Roman government legally required people to register in their ancestral hometown, resulting in a mass movement of the population. This means the tiny village of Bethlehem would have been in a state of pandemonium. Hardly a silent night!

More than ninety miles of rough terrain lay between Nazareth, where Mary and Joseph lived, and Bethlehem, where Joseph had to register. Leading a donkey loaded with provisions and his extremely pregnant wife, Joseph would have done well to make ten miles a day. Their pace was likely even slower.[3]

And don't feel too bad that they couldn't get into an inn. The inns in those days—called *caravansarai* or *kahns*—were usually made up of a central courtyard where animals were kept surrounded by slightly elevated rooms where people could rest en route to various destinations. Joseph and Mary may have done just as well to find the little stable (likely a cave enclosure). And the stone feeding trough Jesus was laid in likely could have been made up just as nicely as any crib that was available back then. His was a totally humble beginning, but there's beauty in that.

His Humility

God's entrance into this world He made shows unmatched humility. For the King of kings and Lord of lords to simply come as a baby and go through all the ups and downs of growing up is one thing. But to be born into a poor family, the first child of a teen mom and a befuddled-but-faithful carpenter? To be laid in His first moments on a bed of hay in a feeding trough, the warm stink of livestock drawn in through His first breaths?

> Jesus's life was a long arc of humble commitment to God's great desire that all mankind be delivered from the grasp of sin and death.

The King of kings wasn't attended at birth by royal representatives but by ranch animals. And this King's royal announcers weren't court officials but local shepherds. He was born in a cave and He would be buried in a borrowed tomb. Jesus's life was a long arc of humble commitment to God's great desire that all mankind be delivered from the grasp of sin and death.

His Incompatibility

God was determined to know us by becoming one of us. But the situation He was born into shows us that He was not compatible with us. Though Mary's pain turned to wonder as she held her newborn son, I can't help but wonder if she knew how hard things would get for her little boy. The fact that there was no room for them in the local inn wasn't just a temporary inconvenience but a metaphor for the world Jesus was born into.

Herod, who named himself "the Great," made a pretense of welcoming this newborn "king of the Jews" when the visiting magi informed him of the situation, but his real desire was to kill what he perceived as being a threat to his throne. He would have done anything to keep the power Rome granted him—and, in fact, he did. Herod had three of his own sons killed under pretense of treason, so it's not a shocker that he had no room in his heart for the Son of God.

Joseph was divinely warned to take his wife and son out of the country because of Herod's jealous wrath, which led to a horrible fulfillment of prophecy as Herod arranged for the murder of all boys two years old and younger in and around Bethlehem. The point is that there was no room in politics for Jesus then (much less now). That shouldn't surprise us because politics is a human game, taking the privilege and responsibility of God-given authority and abusing it for personal power and gain.

There was also no room for Jesus in religion. When the magi showed up in Jerusalem looking for the birthplace of the Messiah, the Jewish scribes they came across were fully aware of Micah 5:2, which prophesied that the Messiah would be born in Bethlehem. But there's no record that the scribes went with the wise men to seek the child; it seems they couldn't have cared less. Bethlehem was no more than a five-mile walk from Jerusalem, but they didn't move a muscle in that direction. Thirty some odd years later, a similar group of Jewish religious leaders would lead the cries for Jesus's crucifixion during His trial.

This shouldn't surprise us. Many religious leaders, even some who call themselves Christians, are fine with Jesus as long as you stick with the good man/moral teacher narrative. But sparks fly when Jesus's own claims come up: "I am the way, the truth, and the life. No one comes to the Father except through Me" (John 14:6). Did you know Jesus was actually speaking to the church, not believers, in Revelation 3:20? "I stand at the door and knock. If anyone hears My voice and opens the door, I will come in to him and dine with him, and he with Me." Too often, Jesus has to ask permission to enter the church He founded with His own blood. He is fundamentally incompatible with us because He is God.

His Personality

The Bible repeatedly makes clear the fact that the Messiah is wholly unique. The prophecies of the Old Testament point to a one-of-a-kind figure who would be born of a virgin, arrive on a very precise timeline, be called the Son of God and the Son of Man, offer Himself as a willing sacrifice, suffer and die for mankind's sins, and then be resurrected and ascend to heaven afterwards.[4]

The fulfillment of these prophecies was set into motion when the angel Gabriel appeared to Mary to announce God's plans for her and her Son (Luke 1:26-38). Gabriel told this favored virgin that the Holy Spirit would conceive a child in her. She was instructed to call Him Jesus, for "He will be great, and will be called the Son of the Highest" (v. 32). The Lord would give Him the throne of His ancestor David (that will happen in the future kingdom age), and His reign will last forever. This wasn't a Jewish baby caught in the cogs of the Roman political machine. This was the one of whom Isaiah said, "Unto us a Child is born, unto us a Son is given" (Isaiah 9:6). This unique child was both fully God and fully man.

His Humanity

When Isaiah predicted that a child would be born to us, he was emphasizing Jesus's humanity. Children are born biologically, and so was Jesus. All mammals, including humans, develop in stages of gestation from a zygote to an embryo to a fetus, and then are born into the world. Jesus was born just like any other baby. Some legends claim that Mary didn't feel pain when she delivered Him because she was without original sin (an erroneous belief she herself denied in Luke 1:46-55). But the simple truth is God entered His world the way we all did.

Now, the evangelical church, to its credit, has done a good job of defending the deity of Christ, but it has been a bit more hesitant in coming to grips with His humanity. In fact, one of the first heresies of the early church was not the denial of Jesus's divinity but His humanity. Historically, Jesus's human nature has been a controversial topic.

Around the second century, a group of mystics called the Gnostics taught that Jesus didn't have a physical human body. That led to bizarre, fanciful claims about Him—that He didn't leave footprints when He walked on the sand, or that He temporarily inhabited a body that wasn't His own, and so on. Such teachings reflected a Greek view of the world—that the material is evil and the spiritual is good.

But the Jewish view of the world was (and still is) quite different. The Jews believed that God made the world (including humans) and called it good, and that evil is a corruption of what God made good. That's why we need a redeemer—someone to rid the physical world of the effects of evil and bring us back into relationship with our Maker. That's the whole reason why "the Word became flesh and dwelt among us" (John 1:14).

John Weborg described the humanity of Jesus this way:

> There is God in the flesh, thriving in a placenta, protected by a water bag, bouncing on a donkey ride to Bethlehem where his folks had to meet the local IRS. No different than any other baby at the time. While God preferred human nature to the angelic, God asked no human favors and got

none. When the inns are full they are full. Sleep where one can. God deep in the flesh became God deep in the straw. Mary, the mother of the Creator, sustained the one who sustained all the living.[5]

His Deity

When Isaiah said, "Unto us a Son is given," he was highlighting the Messiah's divinity—His pre-existence. For a Son to be "given" to the world—as God the Father did when He sent Jesus (John 3:16)—He must have already existed. Just as Jesus Christ is the only baby ever born who didn't have a human father, He is also the only person who existed before He was humanly conceived.

That's what Jesus meant when He said, "Before Abraham was, I AM" (John 8:58). He didn't become God upon entering public ministry at age thirty. He didn't get baptized and say, "Oh, I'm God now." There are few stories in the Bible about Jesus as a boy, but even they all suggest not just His developing humanity but also His divine capacity. Luke 2:52 captures it well: "Jesus increased in wisdom and stature, and in favor with God and men." When His parents lost Him one day at twelve years old, they later found Him discussing the law with the teachers in the temple. He spoke of being about His Father's business. While Jesus completely honored Mary and Joseph, He honored God the Father more than anyone. The Gospel record repeatedly demonstrates that Jesus was fully human and fully God.

Jesus was God pre-Mary, pre-Bethlehem, pre-Isaiah, pre-Abraham, and pre-creation. That's why the incarnation had to happen: God, who exists eternally, became flesh. Paul recognized the tension of this truth when he wrote, "Great indeed, we confess, is the mystery of godliness: He was manifested in the flesh, vindicated by the Spirit, seen by angels, proclaimed among the nations, believed on in the world, taken up in glory" (1 Timothy 3:16 ESV). Jesus became flesh (John 1:14), was made "a little lower than the angels" (Hebrews 2:9), "made himself nothing" (Philippians 2:6-7 NIV), and "though He was rich, yet for [our] sakes He became poor" (2 Corinthians 8:9).

Theologians have a term for the unique merging of the divine and human natures of Christ: the hypostatic union. The Council of Chalcedon (AD 451) described Jesus's nature as the union of "full Deity and perfect humanity united without mixture, change, division, or separation in one person forever."[6] Theologians also call this Jesus's theanthropic nature. It was not a form of split personality, with the divine and human natures in conflict with each other. In the Gospel narratives, Jesus never spoke about His divine or human nature as being separate from Himself. Jesus was always and ever will be one person.

Even so, the paradoxes are wonderful and mindboggling: The one who created all the food supplies on earth and miraculously fed the hungry was Himself hungry. Jesus grew weary and yet He is our rest. He paid taxes and yet He is the King of kings. He prayed and yet He hears all our prayers. He wept and yet He dries our tears. Sold for thirty pieces of silver, He redeemed the world. Led as a sheep to the slaughter, He is the good shepherd. His death gives us life, and by dying He destroyed death. The universe is His footstool, but He became an embryo inside a womb. Great is the mystery of godliness, indeed!

> Jesus took hold of God the Father with one hand and unreconciled mankind with the other, bringing salvation by bridging the gap between us and God.

Now, why did Jesus do all this? Why bother with the pain and humility of a decaying body? As a man, Jesus was the perfect representative of humankind. He was one of us. He was born, and He experienced death. He faced temptations, pain, and annoyances, and is therefore able to sympathize with His people (Hebrews 2:9-18; 4:14-16). But as God, He was without sin, which made Him the perfect sacrifice for our sin. Moreover, His resurrection ensured His conquest over death, making His promise of our resurrection certain.

Jesus's purpose was marked out in His very name: *Yeshua*, "Yahweh is salvation." You might even say that on the cross, with outstretched arms, Jesus took hold of God the Father with one hand and unreconciled mankind with the other, bringing salvation by bridging the gap between us and God. As the God-man, Jesus now says, "Come and enjoy fellowship with your Creator. The long period of separation is over" (see Ephesians 2:14-15).

His Accessibility

Jesus is God's invitation to live the life He meant you to live. He wants you to have access to Him. Think about the nativity scene once more. There's nothing intimidating about a baby in a feeding trough, is there? A manger isn't menacing, threatening, or unapproachable. Anyone can come and feel comfortable—like the shepherds, whom society considered the lowest of the low.

You don't need ID or a visitor pass to come to Jesus, like you would if you visited the White House, Buckingham Palace, or the United Nations. You just need to realize your need for Him. This is why the rich and powerful so often struggle with accepting Jesus; in fact, Jesus said a camel had a better shot at going through the eye of a needle than the rich had at getting into the kingdom of God (see Matthew 19:24). The rich are the suppliers of earthly access, the benefactors of earthly advancement, the patrons of political gain—but their power stops at death's door. Only Jesus can give you access to God.

And God has made Himself accessible in Jesus, a truth we see displayed throughout Jesus's life. Jesus went out of His way to pass through the hated land of Samaria so He could bring the good news of the gospel to a life-worn woman. He got upset when His disciples tried to keep certain people away from Him. He always took His time with people, no matter what else was happening around Him. He stopped to talk to a woman in a crowd while en route to healing the daughter of Jairus. He paused on His way to raise Lazarus from the grave so that more people would be drawn into God's plan of salvation.

During His brief time on earth, Jesus lovingly spoke the truth to people from all walks of life, from society's most scorned to its most respected. The former generally appreciated His efforts more than the latter. And at His death, He swung wide open the door to the Father, fulfilling both the holiness required by God's law and the compassion rooted in His heart: "We can boldly enter heaven's Most Holy Place because of the blood of Jesus...For our guilty consciences have been sprinkled with Christ's blood to make us clean" (Hebrews 10:19, 22 NLT).

No other person in history has done such a thing, as pastor James A. Francis wrote:

> Here is a man who was born in an obscure village, the child of a peasant woman. He grew up in another obscure village. He worked in a carpenter's shop until He was thirty, and then for three years He was an itinerant preacher. He never wrote a book. He never held an office. He never owned a home. He never had a family. He never went to college. He never traveled two hundred miles from the place He was born. He never did one of the things that usually accompany greatness. He had no credentials but Himself. He had nothing to do with the world except the power of His divine manhood. While still a young man, the tide of popular opinion turned against him. He was turned over to His enemies. He was nailed on a cross between two thieves. His executioners gambled for the only piece of property He had on earth while He was dying—His coat. When He was dead, He was taken down and laid in a borrowed grave through the pity of a friend. And on the third day He arose from the dead. Nineteen centuries have come and gone, and today He is a centerpiece of the human race and leader of the column of progress. I am far within the mark when I say that all the armies that ever marched, and all the navies that were ever built, and all the parliaments that ever sat, and all the kings that ever reigned put together have not affected the life of man on earth as powerfully as has

that One solitary life. The explanation? He is the Son of God, the risen Savior.[7]

> When you look at all the ways our Maker has made Himself known to us, you can see how much He wants us to know Him.

Born among farmyard animals, Jesus died between common criminals. He poured His universe-creating power into a mortal frame, making Himself temporarily subject to the fickle passions of His creation. His humility demonstrated His personality, and He purchased your access to God with His own blood. Let that sink in. From our standpoint, what Jesus did doesn't make sense. His whole life flowed against the current of human nature, sometimes in a way so extreme that we would call it madness in anyone else. But what seems like madness to us turned out to be the wisdom of God.

You may have heard the word *bedlam* used to refer to a state of crazed confusion. Did you know it actually comes from the word *Bethlehem*? An old hospital in London, known as St. Mary of Bethlehem, became a city-run insane asylum, where, in its early days, you could buy a ticket to come watch and heckle the patients. *Bethlehem* got shortened to *Bet'lem* and, eventually, *bedlam*—a term synonymous with a madhouse environment.[8]

Jesus came to Bethlehem so that we could escape spiritual bedlam. It's so easy to lose sight of this truth—of the wonder of God taking on flesh to save you and me. But when you look at all the ways our Maker has made Himself known to us, you can see how much He wants us to know Him. Jesus is at the very center of God's biography, so primary in importance and impact that each of us will at some point in our lives have to consider what we think of Him. And what we decide to believe will set our lives on a permanent course as either God's enemy or His friend.

Chapter 16

HOW TO BE GOD'S FRIEND

Sometimes you hear a phrase that arrests your attention. You know the individual words, but the way they're brought together makes you stop and think. And when you do, the phrase doesn't make sense. In fact, it's actually contradictory, even though it's widely accepted. Here are a few of these phrases—oxymorons—that are pretty amusing:

- exact estimate
- act naturally
- genuine imitation
- sanitary landfill
- alone together
- small crowd
- pretty ugly
- working vacation

The top oxymoron on my list may ring true for you: Microsoft Works. Jokes aside, I believe the real number one self-contradiction of all time is this: the fact that we are invited to be God's friends. As Jesus said, "No longer do I call you servants...but I have called you friends" (John 15:15).

Friendship implies mutuality and commonality. When you're friends with another person, you enjoy each other's company. You each bring strengths to the table, and you care enough to challenge each other. You're on the same level. But how could we possibly be on the same level as God? What do we have in common? And what could we ever add to the relationship?

That's what's interesting about oxymorons: We take them for granted until we take time to pause and think about them. We like the idea of being God's friend, but then we realize what a contradiction that is on a fundamental level. As we've discovered in this book, God is in a class all by Himself. He is unique. We don't have anything to offer Him. Only God is truly holy, truly everywhere present, truly all-knowing and all-powerful and sovereign. He is not like us. So how could we possibly be friends with Him?

Some of us have just assumed we're friends with God. After all, we grew up in church, we were baptized as children, and our parents and grandparents are Christians. So we're *in*, right? Others of us have doubted that God could ever love us—*I know what kind of person I really am, so why would God want to be on friendly terms with me?* And for others of us, we've never been interested in being friends with God. *If God even exists, why would He even be aware of me? I'll just mind my business and He can mind His.*

> With God as your friend, you don't need anything else.

Of course, we've seen by now that *we* are God's business. Because of who He is, perfect in holiness and justice but also perfect in love and mercy, God cares about each one of us. Even though we will never be peers with God on any level, He still desires to have a relationship with us. That truth is mind-boggling. But what does it look like, on a practical level, to be His friend?

Fortunately, the Bible gives us an idea. We have an example in the one person who was actually given the title of God's friend: Abraham. Scripture calls him that three times (2 Chronicles 20:7; Isaiah 41:8; James 2:23). I like the passage in Isaiah the best because it was God Himself who called Abraham His friend: "But you, Israel, are

My servant, Jacob whom I have chosen, the descendants of Abraham My friend." What could be better than that?

A good friendship involves a lot more than good buddies hanging out. A true friendship goes much deeper; it commits to being a close and trusted companion in life. With God as your friend, you don't need anything else.

Consider all of God's attributes as portrayed in this book, and then imagine God employing them on your behalf—not as your private genie but as someone completely invested in your highest good. Wouldn't you rather have God as your friend and everyone else as your enemy than everyone else as your friend and God as your enemy? It's the ultimate possible relationship.

Mark Twain once traveled through Europe at the peak of his career. Wherever he went, everyone from the rich and powerful to regular folk recognized him and wanted to get close to him. This attention impressed Twain's nine-year-old daughter, who was traveling with him. At the end of the tour, she blurted out, "Daddy, you seem to know everybody but God!"

Indeed, Twain had many bones to pick with God, particularly later in his life. He became jaded and cynical about humankind—not without reason—but fell squarely into the camp that blames God for the world's evil. He had no use for the God depicted in the Bible and turned his great wit toward producing scathing comments like, "What God lacks is conviction—stability of character. He ought to try to be a Presbyterian or a Catholic or *something*—not try to be everything."[1]

Twain's cynicism reminds me of Solomon in his later years. As a young man, Solomon asked God for the wisdom to rule well, and he built the magnificent temple in Jerusalem. But somewhere along the way, he lost the plot. He disobeyed the rules God had laid out for kings, especially when he amassed 700 wives and 300 concubines, whose pagan beliefs turned his heart away from God (1 Kings 11:9). His Twain-like negativity is clear in the theme of his final biblical book, Ecclesiastes: "All is vanity" (Ecclesiastes 1:2). In this book, he described the problems every generation since Adam has had to face: injustice, poverty, hard work paid back with a pittance, the infirmities of age, and so on. But in the end, Solomon turned his thoughts back to his Maker—and here we see the difference between him and Twain:

> Let us hear the conclusion of the whole matter: Fear God and keep His commandments, for this is man's all. For God will bring every work into judgment, including every secret thing, whether good or evil (Ecclesiastes 12:13-14).

As he circled back to that bedrock truth, I wonder if Solomon thought of the words he had written years earlier: "One who has unreliable friends soon comes to ruin, but there is a friend who sticks closer than a brother" (Proverbs 18:24 NIV). It's when we push God away, rejecting that Friend who would stick closer than our own flesh and blood, that our troubles truly begin. It's then that we are at the mercy of human cruelty and fickleness without any hope for the remedy that God's Spirit working within us can provide. Remember, human beings are responsible for evil, for the self-centered corruption of what God made good. And when humans fall short, as they can't help but do, we begin to sense we were made for a deeper intimacy: We need God's friendship.

So how do you become God's friend? What are the characteristics of a human-divine friendship? Let's look at Abraham's relationship with God to figure that out.

Expect the Unexpected

We often measure the value of a friend by their willingness to support us when we show up unannounced. If someone is willing to help us when we call out of the blue, even if it's been a while since we last talked, we have a good friend. We see that with God and Abraham.

To be God's friend, you have to understand that He often shows up when you least expect it. He reveals Himself as He sees fit, in His timing. One hot afternoon, Abraham looked up from his tent door and saw three men, who we later discover were God Himself and two angels. The text doesn't make it clear at what point Abraham recognized that God was paying him a visit—right away or after a little conversation—just that Abraham offered his guests his finest hospitality: "When he saw them, he ran from the tent door to meet them, and bowed himself to the ground, and said, 'My Lord, if I have now found favor in Your sight, do not pass on by Your servant'" (Genesis 18:2-3).

Now, Abraham wouldn't have expected visitors of any kind in the scalding heat of a Middle Eastern afternoon. Travelers moved in the early morning or early evening, so when these three men showed up, Abe's wife Sarah hadn't had time to vacuum the tent or pick up his dirty socks. They had to hustle to provide properly for their sudden guests.

I had a friend years ago who would show up at my door anytime he felt like visiting. I would hear a knock, and there he was. Sometimes he would even go around to the back of the house to find where I was. But he was the kind of friend who could do that. Our friendship allowed for that kind of spontaneous behavior.

When my son was growing up, I told him, "Nathan, because we have a special relationship, you can come to me anytime. No matter what I'm doing, you can barge right in and we'll hang out." And he took me up on that. There were even a few times when he and his dinosaur barged right into a counseling session. The person I was counseling might've even been crying, but all Nate knew was that he had access. So I would ask him to sit at my desk while I talked with the person and finished the session.

Jesus used an analogy of spontaneous friendship when teaching His disciples how to pray: "Suppose you have a friend, and you go to him at midnight and say, 'Friend, lend me three loaves of bread'" (Luke 11:5 NIV). Sounds like my old buddy. I'd be hanging out or getting ready for bed, and he would come by, saying, "Dude, you got any of that Hamburger Helper left? I'm starving!" In a way, he was preparing me for how God often shows up in our lives.

You cannot predict when God will visit—that is, when He will choose to turn your life in a different direction. Often change happens after a season of relative calm, but sometimes it stacks up on top of other trials. It's often hard to know what God's purposes are when hard times come. That uncertainty takes some getting used to because it's different than knowing that God is always present, always aware of where you are and what you're going through. When God showed up at Abraham's tent, He wasn't out cruising for snacks. Among other things, He wanted to reiterate to Abraham and Sarah His promise that they would have a son.

When God shows up in our lives, He typically brings us a challenge or a change. For us, these challenges seem to come out of nowhere. But for God, they are things He has planned for us since before we ever met Him. Whatever the challenge, He knows you're ready for it, whether that's trusting Him with something hard or stepping out into an unexpected adventure in faith.

You could say that the first rule of friendship with God mirrors Isaac Newton's first law of motion: Everything continues in a state of rest unless it is compelled to change by forces acting upon it. But what we accept as scientific fact we don't necessarily love in our personal lives. How many times have you made your plans and put your feet up, confident that you have everything under control—only for it all to go sideways?

When that happens, it's like God is saying, "This is not what I have for you." If you're faced with a minor setback—some fixable aspect of your plan goes awry, for example—it's possible God is testing your flexibility and willingness to trust that even when the details aren't under your control, they are under His. But if the challenge is major—not only is your plan blown up but something seemingly worse has occurred—you may be experiencing a test of faith. Will you still let God be God now that He has taken you a different direction than you expected or wanted Him to?

Remember, blessed are the flexible, for they shall not be broken. Though this adage isn't in the Bible, it's good advice. Do you trust God even when He changes things up on you, tests you, or redirects you? Keep in mind that He might be doing anything from putting you on a safer path to getting you out of a rut.

> You must be willing to believe that when something doesn't go the way you planned or hoped, God is still working on your behalf.

Back in the thirties, a Nashville man bought a brand-new radio, took it home, and plugged it in. He tuned it to WSM— the home of the Grand Ole Opry—and then pulled off the knobs and threw them away, announcing to his family, "There's only one frequency we need in this house."

While that might be true for country music diehards, that's not the approach you can take when it comes to God and His plans for you. If you're going to trust God, you have to give Him editing rights to your life. You must be willing to believe that when something doesn't go the way you planned or hoped, God is still working on your behalf. As someone once wisely said, "God speaks to us…through the regularity with which he disappoints our plans."

You might be thinking, *Well, then, God has certainly spoken to me a lot.* I know what you mean. But when you really believe that God knows more than you do, loves you more than you can imagine, and has your best interests at heart, then you can see His sudden, unexpected interventions in your life as acts of friendship and love.

If You Want to Stand Out, Step Down

Another essential part of friendship is putting others before yourself. Ralph Waldo Emerson said, "A great man is always willing to be little."[2] Demonstrating that kind of humility toward someone is a way of confirming their value. When God and the two angels suddenly showed up at Abraham's doorstep, Abraham didn't eyeball them trying to figure out whether it was worth his time to be friendly. No, instead "he ran from the tent door to meet them, and bowed himself to the ground" (Genesis 18:2).

Bowing was a typical Middle Eastern greeting, but to bow all the way to the ground was a welcome reserved for royalty. It was an acknowledgement that someone was of a higher status than you, and in humility, you honored that by bowing low. There was even a protocol to bowing: you got down on your knees, put your hands on the ground, then gradually leaned forward till your forehead touched the ground.

Abraham also addressed his visitor as "my Lord," *Adonai* in Hebrew, and referred to himself as "Your servant" (v. 3). Now, Abraham was wealthy and well-respected and had hundreds of his own servants and workers. In today's Middle East, he would be known as a *sheikh*, a tribal ruler. Normally, people would bow when they met him. But here, he recognized that he was in the presence of someone greater than him, so he bowed down.

There's a story about a preacher who survived the Johnstown flood of 1889, a horrible event that took out a whole valley in western Pennsylvania. More than 2,200 people died, and this is still counted as one of the worst disasters in US history. This preacher loved to tell anyone he met about how he survived, as a sort of "you-can't-top-this" story. So of course, when he died and went to heaven, he was waiting for his chance. A few days after the preacher arrived, he heard about a storytelling gathering and told the apostle Peter, "Can't wait to share my story about Johnstown." Peter nodded. "It's a good one," he said, "but you should know that Noah will be in the audience."

You can't top Noah's flood story, and you can't top God's greatness. Abraham understood this. He knew he had power and influence, but he also knew that God was in the audience, so he bowed. This kind of humility is a key ingredient when it comes to having a friendship with God.

What would it look like for us to bow to the Lord? For starters, it would involve taking the focus off ourselves and putting it on Him.

We call this worship—indicating that someone, God in this case, has value beyond the ordinary. Worship is a humbling, selfless act. It shouldn't be focused on how we look, what we sound like, or what others around us are doing. Even so, we can find it hard to concentrate on God during worship. Sometimes our circumstances can so overwhelm us that they eclipse our view of the Lord and what He's doing in our lives.

Take Psalm 22:3, for example: "You are enthroned as the Holy One; you are the one Israel praises" (NIV). That sounds like standard worship material—until you read the verses surrounding it:

> My God, my God, why have you forsaken me?
>> Why are you so far from saving me,
>> so far from my cries of anguish?
> My God, I cry out by day, but you do not answer,
>> by night, but I find no rest.
>
>
> Yet you are enthroned as the Holy One
>> you are the one Israel praises.
> In you our ancestors put their trust;
>> they trusted and you delivered them.
> To you they cried out and were saved;
>> in you they trusted and were not put to shame (vv. 1-5).

Psalm 22:3 reads differently in context, doesn't it? The psalmist was wondering where God had been lately. We've all been there, where it's easy to check out and fake it, to mouth the words to worship songs with our minds in neutral. As Charles Spurgeon wrote, "I believe a very large majority of churchgoers...are merely unthinking, slumbering worshippers of an unknown God."[3]

But what if we remembered what we know about God? He is everywhere present. And in His presence, our perspective changes. We become like Isaiah, who, as we've seen, had a vision of God on His throne in heaven and said, "Woe is me, for I am undone! Because I am a man of unclean lips, and I dwell in the midst of a people of unclean lips" (Isaiah 6:5). Humbling yourself before God and worshipping Him requires this kind of perspective. No matter what is happening, He is still God. He is still seated on His throne, and He is still perfectly sovereign.

Therefore, He deserves your worship. Worship is the heart's proper response to God whereby you place Him above everything and everyone else in life. Because it's a response, it's not something you have to drum up. God made the first move: "We love Him because He first loved us" (1 John 4:19). It's also the only fitting response to God: "I plead with you to give your bodies to God because of all he has done for you. Let them be a living and holy sacrifice—the kind he will find acceptable" (Romans 12:1 NLT). Not only do you need a right response, but it must come from the heart: "The Father is looking for those who will worship him…in spirit and in truth" (John 4:23-24 NLT).

Worshipping God in this way requires humility. It means putting Him first at home, at work, in your hobbies, in your entertainment choices, and on social media, as well as putting Him above your integrity, your reputation, and even your spouse and kids. But it also means being blessed with His friendship.

Gotta Serve Somebody

Humility is so vital to friendship with God because its opposite, pride, is the greatest impediment to friendship with God. If you can get in the habit of humbly giving God control of your life, then the next step in being His friend is a lot easier: service.

Abraham immediately humbled himself before God by bowing to Him, but He didn't stay there. Let's home in on his hospitality: He said to his three guests, "Please let a little water be brought, and wash your feet, and rest yourselves under the tree. And I will bring a morsel of bread, that you may refresh your hearts" (Genesis 18:4-5). Abe ordered a lot of good food and then stood by while his guests ate (vv. 6-8), making sure they had everything they needed to relax and enjoy themselves.

Good host, right? Absolutely, but here's what I don't want you to miss: Abraham was ninety-nine years old. When we read that Abe "hurried" and "ran" and "stood by...as they ate," these were not simple activities for someone who was pushing a hundred. And it wasn't like God had told him, "All right, bring the food—but make it snappy!" Abraham moved on the double because he wanted to serve God well and right away.

Service to God from the heart brings joy. It's like when Isaac served his uncle Laban for seven years so he could marry Laban's daughter Rachel, "and they seemed only a few days to him because of the love he had for her" (Genesis 29:20). Even in the best and most loving human relationships, the shine wears off and that initial passion dissipates, and the same can often be said on our part of our relationship with God. But what sustains these relationships—including our friendship with God—is committing to serve the other person with a willing heart.

If You Love Me...

If you were to consider the defining characteristics of your main relationships in life, a word that likely wouldn't pop up is *obedience*. Maybe you obeyed your parents when you were younger, and you probably obey your boss now, but obedience isn't exactly something grown-ups do, right? As an adult, you make your own decisions, and you stand or fall by them. The thought of being obedient to someone else seems to imply you are immature, inadequate, or even incompetent. Yet Jesus said, "If you love me, obey my commandments" (John 14:15 NLT).

Why does the idea of obedience carry such negative connotations? When did it become the difference between ability and inability, maturity and immaturity, strength and weakness? Probably around the time you became an adult, obedience became reserved solely for following the orders of your boss, the police, and the military. If you think of obedience as simply following rules to avoid punishment, then it makes sense that adult peers in a mutually beneficial relationship aren't bound to obey one another.

But there's another reason to obey someone: because you love and respect them. Have you ever had a mentor (or even a parent or teacher) who you were happy to obey? Your respect for that person was so great that you wanted to please them, and the most obvious way to do that was to do what they asked of you. Now think about God. He is more reliable, more trustworthy, and more concerned about your ultimate well-being than anyone you've ever known. He is unlike any leader you've ever followed. Loyalty and obedience flow naturally out of the heart that truly knows Him.

> God is more reliable, more trustworthy, and more concerned about your ultimate well-being than anyone you've ever known.

This is why obedience is the fourth aspect of the friendship we see between God and Abraham, between the divine and the human. Abraham was called God's friend because he not only believed God's promises—he acted on them.

When God had finished His meal in Abraham's tent, He made him a promise: "I will return to you about this time next year, and your wife, Sarah, will have a son!" (Genesis 18:10 NLT). This wasn't a new promise; almost twenty-five years had passed since God first communicated it to Abe. Abraham and Sarah weren't spring chickens back then, and they certainly weren't getting any younger. But Genesis 15 tells us that Abraham "believed in the Lord, and He accounted it to him for righteousness" (v. 6). As James later noted, Abraham's trust and obedience were what earned him the title of "friend of God" (James 2:23).

The longer God's promise went unfulfilled, the crazier it sounded. But each time God reiterated that promise, Abraham said, "I believe it." Sure, he wondered *how* God was going to do it, but he didn't doubt that God *would* do it. Ultimately, all faith boils down to is the choice to take God at His word and act on it.

Now, I'm not saying that's easy; in fact, it goes against human nature. You might even say, "Well, yeah, that was Abraham. He was one of those really holy guys who had the rare faith to follow God." But look at Sarah: When she overheard God's promise that she would have a son, she laughed (Genesis 18:12). Abraham had laughed too (Genesis 17:17), but out of joy in thinking about how God was going to pull off such a wonder. Sarah laughed because she doubted that God could pull it off. She was caught up in the logical, natural view of things, which says that ninety-year-old women don't have children by their hundred-year-old husbands. Unfortunately, her doubt kept her from a deeper relationship with God.

When you're God's friend, you trust Him. And in trusting Him, you obey Him. As Jesus said, "You are My friends if you do whatever I command you" (John 15:14), and "When you obey my commandments, you remain in my love" (v. 10 NLT). These verses speak of an active, ongoing obedience; Jesus was saying, "If you keep on loving Me, you'll keep on obeying Me." And it's at that point of obedience that Jesus calls us friends.

Friendship with God includes continued obedience and conformity over the long haul, in all areas of life. You can't say, "I'll obey God in my business, but not in my marriage," just as you can't say, "I'll obey God in my marriage, but when tax time rolls around, I might not fully disclose what I earned." The key to being God's friend is to keep trusting Him and obeying Him.

When God busted Sarah for her doubting laughter, He asked her a question: "Is anything too hard for the Lord?" (Genesis 18:14). We've seen in this book that the answer is an emphatic *no*. The *all* in all-powerful really does mean "all." But I think there was a deeper question in God's query: Will you give Him access to your heart?

Evidence of God's existence and love for us is all around us, even in this dark world. We can see it in creation and even in many of our daily circumstances. But just as God didn't force His way into Abraham's tent, so God won't force His way into your heart; He only works by invitation. His friendship is different than any you've experienced before, but it's also the most important relationship you could ever pursue. Will you invite Him in and cultivate a friendship with Him, as Abraham did?

This Is the End—It's Go Time

There's a reason you're reading this book. Two, actually. First is the surface reason: you want to know more about God, you're curious about Christianity, or you're trying to get someone off your back. But the second reason is far deeper: you have intersected with God's plan for your life. Whatever your personal reasons are for reading this book, God wants to speak to you. He wants you to take what you've read here and see if it's true. Go read the Bible. Go research for yourself the problem of evil and universal fine-tuning. Then look at your life. Where is God tugging at a loose thread of doubt or unbelief?

God's truth is for every single human being. It's for the Christian who thinks he will get by on church attendance and good intentions but pushes biblical truth away. It's for the atheist who won't acknowledge that her belief is founded on the faith that there is no God even in the face of considerable evidence that an intelligent designer must exist. It's for the skeptic who finds it easier or even fashionable to ask questions without following where the answers lead.

If anything, the more we learn about God, the more we realize how little we know about Him. God can't be pigeon-holed, tucked into a tidy box that fits our notions of Him. He is not like us, and yet He urgently wants us to know Him. For some of us, this isn't news. We grew up in church, we've read the Bible, and we know the lengths to which God has gone to build a bridge of relationship with us. We rejoice in reviewing the details of His character and love for us.

But maybe for you, the idea that God wants a relationship with you is the biggest news story of all. You're beginning to see that though God is holy, perfect, and righteous and therefore must judge sin, He also loves you and made a way for you to be forgiven so that you can walk with Him through this life into eternity. He offers the only thing that will satisfy you in this life: a relationship with Him. But you must respond to His offer. Knowledge of the gift of Christ requires you to either accept it or reject it.

Maybe your questions about God continue to overshadow any possible answers you've read in this book. Because of your experiences, upbringing, or education, God has been nothing but bad news in your life. Of course, I can't explain everything that has happened to you, and I won't give you a trite answer that presumes to know God's purposes in allowing what He has allowed. Jesus Himself never offered pat responses to life's hardships. But I can offer you the same thing He offered: hope.

> Ultimately, we will never know all there is to know about God, but we can know all we need to know.

That hope is this: Whether you're a skeptic, a seeker, or a saint, God sees you, knows you, and loves you. All skeptics are humans made in God's image, and their honest search for truth is admirable. All seekers are responding in some way to the call of eternity that God has placed in every human heart. And all saints—that is, believers in Christ as Lord and Savior—battle doubt at some point. God's not put off by honest doubt as long as we, as believers, do not doubt what He says about Himself. Trust is the anchor of any healthy relationship, and God is completely worthy of ours.

Ultimately, we will never know all there is to know about God, but we can know all we need to know. At some point, seekers and skeptics have to decide whether or not to become saints. Those who choose to become saints will discover that knowing and loving God—and being completely known and loved by Him in return—is what life is all about.

You have a Maker who knows you better than you know yourself—but He has never settled for just knowing you. He wants you to know Him too. He is real, and He loves you. You are a crucial part of His story. To Him, you were worth dying for.

You've been introduced to God in these pages—a biography based on who He said He is in the Bible and what some of history's most brilliant minds have made of that self-disclosure. But maybe you have yet to really meet your Maker. In His hands are hope and life and peace—more than you could ever imagine possible, all a simple conversation away. So reach out for His friendship. He is there, and He is listening.

FOUR SIMPLE STEPS TO BECOMING GOD'S FRIEND

Recognize

Perhaps in reading this book, you've recognized something about God, yourself, or both. Maybe you've seen some aspect of God's nature or character in a new light, or learned something you didn't understand before. In learning more about Him, you've recognized something about yourself that wasn't previously clear: You need God. You're coming up short in your life, and it concerns you. You're seeing that sin is real, that it has you under control, and that God's judgment of sin is just. You don't know if you have what it takes to be God's friend, but you sure don't want to be His enemy. What can you do? First, take a deep breath. What you're experiencing is the conviction of the Holy Spirit. He is leading you back toward your Maker. Your next step is to follow His lead and make things right with God.

Repent

How do you make things right with God? It's simple. Over and over, the Bible uses a certain word to describe what all of us must do in response to God's truth: repent. Now there's a religious word if there ever was one. To repent simply means to turn from a wrong way toward a right way. It cuts through the murk and forces a response. Some reject the idea of repentance as old-fashioned and offensive, while some reluctantly embrace it, realizing that something has to give when you come face to face with the God of the universe. But no matter how you feel about it, repentance is the only thing that opens the door to having a relationship with God. As Peter put it, God "does not want anyone to be destroyed, but wants everyone to repent" (2 Peter 3:9 NLT). Repentance is the first logical step in learning about who God is.

Reveal

Once you've decided to turn from sin and turn toward God, you need to be completely open with Him. On the one hand, there's no point in hiding any dark secrets or thoughts from Him; He already knows everything about you. On the other, He still wants you to tell Him everything—so that you can know that He knows you recognize your sin and you're done with it. This is confession—which means you're letting God know all your sins because you agree with Him that sin has kept you from a relationship with Him, and you want that barrier to go away. Pour your heart out; He is listening, and He will lift the burden of your mistakes and injuries and skeletons off your soul. If you're not sure how to do that, here's a simple prayer to cover the basics of the transaction you're making with God:

> Father in heaven, I'm a sinner and I'm sick of being apart from You. Forgive me. I believe that Jesus is Your Son. I believe that He came to earth, died on a cross for my sin, and rose again from the dead. I receive Jesus as my Savior. Help me to live for Him as my Lord. I pray this in Jesus's name.

Relate

Congratulations! You just became a friend of God. You've been forgiven, your ultimate destination is now heaven, and you're ready to move forward as a new creation in Christ. You may feel a big difference, or you may not feel much at all. Either way, rest in the truth that you are safe and secure in God's love. To grow in your new relationship and your new nature, get to know God better. Read the Bible on a daily basis and start attending a church where the Bible is taught with reverence and respect. Find ways to get connected with other believers in Bible study, service, and fellowship. Make it your life's objective to one day hear Jesus say to you, "Well done, good and faithful servant; you have been faithful over a few things, I will make you ruler over many things. Enter into the joy of your lord" (Matthew 25:23).

NOTES

Introduction: Let Me Introduce You

1. Quoted in Norman L. Geisler and Paul K. Hoffman, eds., *Why I Am a Christian: Leading Thinkers Explain Why They Believe* (Grand Rapids, MI: Baker Books, 2006), 302.

2. J.I. Packer, *Knowing God* (Downers Grove, IL: InterVarsity Press, 1973), 19.

Chapter 1—can God Be Known?

1. The philosophy that emphasizes individual existence, freedom, and choice whereby humans define their own meaning.

2. Jean-Paul Sartre, "Existentialism Is a Humanism," lecture, 1946.

3. Sartre, "Existentialism Is a Humanism."

4. Shane Weller, *Modernism and Nihilism* (New York: Palgrave Macmillan, 2011), 67.

5. "On the Road with Nicolas Cage," *Details*, July 1991.

6. Bruce Springsteen, https://www.brainyquote.com/authors/bruce-springsteen-quotes (accessed March 9, 2020).

7. Ravi Zacharias, *Can Man Live Without God?* (Nashville: W Publishing Group, 1994), 21.

8. William Hermanns, *Einstein and the Poet: In Search of the Cosmic Man* (Wellesley, MA: Branden Press, 1983), 15.

9. Packer, *Knowing God* (Downers Grove, IL: InterVarsity Press, 1973), 12.

10. Tim Stafford, *Knowing the Face of God* (Grand Rapids, MI: Zondervan, 1989), 16.

11. J. B. Phillips, *Your God Is Too Small* (New York: Touchstone Books, 1952, repr. 2004).

12. Carl Jung, *Modern Man in Search of a Soul* (London: Routledge Classics, 1933), 62.

13. Augustine of Hippo, *Confessions*, Book I, Chapter 1.

Chapter 2—Is Anyone Up There?

1. Charles R. Swindoll, *Improving Your Serve* (Nashville: W Publishing Group, 1981), 183.

2. Francois Mauriac, foreword to *Night* (New York: Bantam, 1960), ix.

3. Originally reprinted in Cliff Knechtle, *Give Me an Answer* (Downers Grove, IL: InterVarsity Press, 1986), 84-85. Edited for clarity.

4. If you want to go deeper into the ontological argument that supports God's existence, I highly recommend Norman Geisler's short book *God: A Philosophical Argument* (Matthews, NC: Bastion Books, 2015). It's written as simply as an argument like this can be. Geisler defines philosophical terms and lays out various historical arguments, following them step by step, proving logically that God must exist.

5. Gottfried Wilhelm Leibniz, "Principles of Nature and Grace Based on Reason," point 7, 1714, https://www.earlymoderntexts.com/assets/pdfs/leibniz1714a.pdf (accessed January 23, 2019).

6. Norman L. Geisler, *If God, Why Evil?* (Minneapolis, MN: Bethany House, 2011), 15.

7. Ralph O. Muncaster, *Examine the Evidence* (Eugene, OR: Harvest House, 2004), 29.

8. As quoted in Norman L. Geisler and Ronald M. Brooks, *When Skeptics Ask* (Grand Rapids, MI: Baker Books, 1990), 17.

9. Geisler and Brooks, *When Skeptics Ask*, 16.

10. The debate also concerns whether the universe's expansion means that the universe is finite or infinite. If it is finite, the whole universe is taking up more space. If it is infinite, the matter in it is spreading farther apart, like two poppy seeds in a baking muffin. It's the same space, but the distance between objects is growing, and that's what is meant by expansion. Another implication of a finite universe is that at some point it will stop expanding, and like all matter, begin to contract as gravity pulls it all back together. Some call this the big crunch, the bookend to the big bang.

Chapter 3—Follow the Clues

1. C.S. Lewis, "Is Theology Poetry?" in *C.S. Lewis: Essay Collection* (London: Collins, 2000), 1.

2. Saint Augustine, *Confessions* (New York: E.P. Dutton, 1900), 194.

3. Gerald L. Schroeder, *The Hidden Face of God* (New York: The Free Press, 2001), 189.

4. Norman L. Geisler and Ronald M. Brooks, *When Skeptics Ask* (Grand Rapids, MI: Baker Books, 1990), 22.

5. National Radio Astronomy Observatory, "Very Large Array," https://public.nrao.edu/telescopes/vla/ (accessed January 31, 2019).

6. Antony Flew with Roy Abraham Varghese, *There Is a God: How the World's Most Notorious Atheist Changed His Mind* (New York: HarperOne, 2007), 75.

7. Associated Press, "There Is a God, Leading Atheist Concludes," *NBC News*, December 9, 2004, referenced in http://www.nbcnews.com/id/6688917/ns/world_news/t/there-god-leading-atheist-concludes/#.XWRZiZNKiqQ (accessed August 26, 2019).

8. As quoted in Robert Kurland, "23 Famous Scientists Who Are Not Atheists," *Magis Center*, https://magiscenter.com/23-famous-scientists-who-are-not-atheists/ (accessed March 10, 2020).

9. Robert Jastrow, *God and the Astronomers* (New York: W.W. Norton, 1978), 116.

10. C.S. Lewis, *Mere Christianity* (New York: HarperCollins, 1952), 25.

11. Frances S. Collins, *The Language of God* (New York: Free Press, 2006), 30.

12. Wernher von Braun, "My Faith," *American Weekly*, February 10, 1963, 1.

Chapter 4—Now It Gets Personal

1. Blaise Pascal, *Pensées* Part III 233, 1670, as cited in "Pascal's Wager, " *New World Encyclopedia*, https://www.newworldencyclopedia.org/p/index.php?title=Pascal%27s_Wager&oldid=1017322 (accessed August 27, 2019).

2. See Peter Stoner, *Science Speaks* (Chicago: Moody, 1958) for the really wonky version of these numbers. To account for just 48 of the 300 prophecies Jesus fulfilled, Stoner, a university chair and astronomer and mathematician, had to use electrons to estimate the number.

3. John Carl Villanueva, "How Many Atoms Are There in the Universe?," *Universe Today*, July 30, 2009, https://www.universetoday.com/36302/atoms-in-the-universe/ (accessed August 28, 2019).

4. Jonathan Merritt, "Can Former Journalist Lee Strobel Make a Convincing Case for Miracles?," *Religion News Service*, March 14, 2018, https://religionnews.com/2018/03/14/can-former-journalist-lee-strobel-make-a-convincing-case-for-miracles/ (accessed August 28, 2019).

5. While this quote is attributed to George Bernard Shaw, the original source for it is unknown.

Chapter 5—I'm God and You're Not: An Encounter with God

1. J.I. Packer, *Knowing God* (Downers Grove, IL: InterVarsity Press, 1973), 35.

2. A.W. Tozer, *The Knowledge of the Holy* (New York: HarperCollins, 1978), 1.

3. Tim Stafford, *Knowing the Face of God* (Eugene, OR: Wipf & Stock Publishers, 1989), 188-189. I also want to mention that Moses got what he wanted during the transfiguration of Jesus (Luke 9:28-36), when he and Elijah were on the mountain with Jesus, seeing Him in His glory, speaking face to face.

Chapter 6—A Cup of Coffee with God: A Short Autobiography

1. Associated Press, "'Why Believe in a God?' Ad Campaign Launches on D.C. Buses," *Fox News*, November 12, 2008, https://www.foxnews.com/story/why-believe-in-a-god-ad-campaign-launches-on-d-c-buses (accessed March 11, 2019). Edwards went on to say, "We are trying to plant a seed of rational thought and critical thinking and questioning in people's minds." Now there's a warm and comforting thought for the holiday season: Warm your lonely heart by the light and heat of a Bunsen burner approach in this season of grace and giving.

2. *Daily Mail* reporter, "'There's Probably No God...Now Stop Worrying and Enjoy Your Life': Atheist Group Launches Billboard Campaign," *Daily Mail*, January 7, 2009, https://www.dailymail.co.uk/news/article-1106924/Theres-probably-God—stop-worrying-enjoy-life-Atheist-group-launches-billboard-campaign.html (accessed March 11, 2019).

3. Packer, *Knowing God* (Downers Grove, IL: InterVarsity Press, 1973), 12.

4. John Cloud, "Can Your Name Make You a Criminal?," *Time*, January 29, 2009, http://content.time.com/time/health/article/0,8599,1874955,00.html (accessed March 13, 2019).

5. Oswald Chambers, *My Utmost for His Highest* (Grand Rapids, MI: Discovery House Publishers, 1992 edition), March 3.

6. Despite the common mistake some make of saying God behaves differently in each half of the Bible—violently in the Old Testament and with grace only in the New Testament, God is the same God throughout the Scripture. He is fierce in both testaments (Revelation 16:19), a just judge in both (James 4:12), merciful in both (Zechariah 12:10), and gracious in both. Noah found grace with God (Genesis 6:8), Abraham experienced it in spite of his many missteps (Genesis 12:3), Joseph saw it in Egypt (Genesis 50:20), as did David when he sinned (Psalm 51, among others).

7. Australian Antarctic Division contributors, "Antarctic Weather," *Australian Antarctic Division*, revised December 4, 2019, http://www.antarctica.gov.au/about-antarctica/environment/weather (accessed March 13, 2020).

8. Ezekiel 18:20-22 says, "The soul who sins shall die. The son shall not bear the guilt of the father, nor the father bear the guilt of the son. The righteousness of the righteous shall be upon himself, and the wickedness of the wicked shall be upon himself. But if a wicked man turns from all his sins which he has committed, keeps all My statutes, and does what is lawful and right, he shall surely live; he shall not die. None of the transgressions which he has committed shall be remembered against him; because of the righteousness which he has done, he shall live."

Chapter 7—The God Who Knows It All

1. Interestingly, the lyrics to the song "Knowledge Is King" include references to the Bible and the Qur'an as sources of deeper understanding about life (but if you're now waiting for my first book on '80s hip-hop to come out, you'll be waiting quite a while!).

2. Paul Reber, "What Is the Memory Capacity of the Brain?," *Scientific American Mind*, May 1, 2010, scientificamerican.com/article/what-is-the-memory-capacity. (accessed August 28, 2019).

3. Cathy Gonzalez, "The Role of Blended Learning in the World of Technology," University of North Texas *Benchmarks Online*, September 2004, https://it.unt.edu/sites/default/files/bench-marks-09-2004.pdf (accessed March 20, 2019).

4. Augustine, *Retractions*, 1.8.

5. J.I. Packer, *Knowing God* (Downers Grove, IL: InterVarsity, 1973), 5.

Chapter 8—Godisnowhere

1. Wayne Grudem, *Systematic Theology: An Introduction to Biblical Doctrine* (Grand Rapids, MI: Zondervan Academic, 1994), 173.

2. See Isaiah 13:9-11; Revelation 6:12-17; 21:27.

3. Paul quoted "Cretica" by Epimenides of Crete (sixth century BC) and "Phainómena" by Aratus, possibly of Tarsus, Paul's hometown (third century BC), respectively. They were speaking of Zeus, but Paul co-opted the truth of their art to speak truth about his God, whom the Greeks called "the unknown God" (Acts 17:23).

4. Grudem, *Systematic Theology*, 73.

5. Prophesied in Isaiah 7:14 and fulfilled in Matthew 1:23.

6. See John 14:14-21 and 16:7.

7. Herbert Lockyer, *The Last Words of Saints and Sinners: 700 Final Quotes from the Famous, the Infamous, and the Inspiring Figures of History* (Grand Rapids, MI: Kregel, 1969), 105.

8. Lockyer, *The Last Words*, 103.

9. Lockyer, *The Last Words*, 131.

10. Lockyer, *The Last Words*, 133.

11. Lockyer, *The Last Words*, 133.

12. Erin Blakemore, "Buzz Aldrin Took Holy Communion on the Moon. NASA Kept It Quiet," *History.com*, July 31, 2018, https://www.history.com/news/buzz-aldrin-communion-apollo-11-nasa (accessed April 1, 2019).

13. Buzz Aldrin with Ken Abraham, *Magnificent Desolation: The Long Journey Home from the Moon* (New York: Three Rivers Press, 2010), 27.

14. Chuck Swindoll, *Saying It Well* (Nashville, TN: FaithWords, 2012), 169-70.

15. Colonel Valentin Petrov, "Did Yuri Gagarin Say He Didn't See God in Space?," *Pravmir.com*, April 12, 2013, http://www.pravmir.com/did-yuri-gagarin-say-he-didnt-see-god-in-space/ (accessed March 31, 2019).

16. New World Encyclopedia contributors, "Nikita Khrushchev," *New World Encyclopedia*, last revised June 13, 2014, http://www.newworldencyclopedia.org/p/index.php?title=Nikita_Khrushchev&oldid=982412 (accessed April 2, 2019).

17. Swindoll, *Saying It Well*, 169-70.

18. Anecdote in *New Age Journal* vol 7, "Yuri Gagarin," 1990, *Wikiquote*, last revised January 8, 2019, https://en.wikiquote.org/wiki/Yuri_Gagarin (accessed April 5, 2019).

19. Ralph Burden, "Yuri Gagarin—Went Into Space and Found God!," *Real Life Stories*, http://www.reallifestories.org/stories/1619/ (accessed April 5, 2019).

20. The question of God's presence in suffering is a big one, but going into it at length here would move us a long way from our current topic. We'll look at this in more detail in chapters 10 and 11.

21. C.S. Lewis, *Mere Christianity* (New York: HarperOne, 1952), 40.

22. See Exodus 3–4.

23. William Evans, *The Great Doctrines of the Bible* (Chicago: Moody Press, 1949), 35.

Chapter 9—My God Is Bigger Than Your God

1. Stuart Hample and Eric Marshall, *Children's Letters to God* (New York: Workman Publishing, 1991).

2. Michael Denton, *Evolution: A Theory in Crisis* (Chevy Chase, MD: Adler & Adler, 1985), 77.

3. See also Genesis 1:27-28; Psalm 8:4-5. God made us for His glory: for example, read Isaiah 43:1-7, 20-21, Matthew 5:16, and 1 Corinthians 10:31; then read Ezekiel 36:21-32 to see how God balances His purpose for us with our use of free will by means of His glorious plan of salvation in Christ.

4. I found a site that compiles information from various sources, including the Guttmacher Institute (which began as a division of Planned Parenthood), the National Right to Life Committee, and Planned Parenthood themselves. Their numbers are for surgical abortions only; they list the Pharmacists for Life organization's estimate that there have been another 250 million chemically induced abortions since 1973. If you have the stomach for it, go watch the numbers climb at http://www.numberofabortions.com/ (accessed April 15, 2019).

5. *World Population Review*, http://worldpopulationreview.com/countries/ (accessed April 15, 2019).

6. Frances S. Collins, *The Language of God: A Scientist Presents Evidence for Belief* (New York: Free Press, 2006), 1.

7. Collins, *The Language of God*, #1.

8. Donald Grey Barnhouse, *Let Me Illustrate: Stories, Anecdotes, Illustrations* (Westwood, NJ: Fleming H. Revell, 1967), 132-133.

Chapter 10—God's Most Unpopular Attribute: Holiness

1. Yousuf Karsh, *Portraits of Greatness* (New York: T. Nelson, 1960). This book is out of print, but if you ever get a chance, take a look. Karsh's work is famous for a reason.

2. William Evans, *The Great Doctrines of the Bible* (Chicago: Moody Bible Institute, 1912), 37.

3. Discover Kyoto contributors, "Sanjūsangen-Dō," *Discover Kyoto*/NIWAKA, https://www.discoverkyoto.com/places-go/sanjusangen-do/ (accessed April 16, 2019).

4. Jerry Bridges, *The Pursuit of Holiness* (Colorado Springs: NavPress, 2006), 11.

5. In several places in Scripture, God commands His people, either directly or by implication, to be holy because He is holy and they are His: Exodus 5:29; Leviticus 11:44-45; 19:2; 20:7, 26; Leviticus 21:8.

6. Max Lucado, *The Applause of Heaven* (Nashville, TN: Thomas Nelson, 1990), 32.

7. Leighton Ford, https://www.goodreads.com/author/quotes/156809.Leighton_Ford (accessed April 24, 2019).

8. C.S. Lewis, *Letters to an American Lady* (Grand Rapids, MI: Eerdmans, 1967), 11.

Chapter 11—The Dark Side of God: Justice

1. Philip Yancey, *Where Is God When It Hurts?* (Grand Rapids, MI: Zondervan, 1997), 13.

2. C.S. Lewis, *The Problem of Pain* (New York: HarperCollins, 1996, originally published in 1940), 92.

3. Peter Kreeft, "The Problem of Evil," *Peter Kreeft*, http://www.peterkreeft.com/topics/evil.htm (accessed September 4, 2019).

4. Quoted by Michael Martin in *Atheism: A Philosophical Justification* (Philadelphia: Temple University Press, 1990), 334.

5. Quoted in Lee Strobel, *The Case for Faith* (Grand Rapids, MI: Zondervan, 2000), 38, citing The OmniPoll, conducted by Barna Research Group, Ltd., January 1999.

6. Quoted in Warren Wiersbe, *Why Us?* (Old Tappan, NJ: Revell, 1984), 23.

7. Charles Colson, *Loving God* (Grand Rapids, MI: Zondervan, 1996, orginally published in 1983), 38.

8. Lewis, *The Problem of Pain*, 4.

9. Bruce Drake, "Number of Christians Rises, But Their Share of World Population Stays Stable," Pew Research Center, March 22, 2013, https://www.pewresearch.org/fact-tank/2013/03/22/number-of-christians-rises-but-their-share-of-world-population-stays-stable/ (accessed March 14, 2020).

10. Harold Kushner, *When Bad Things Happen to Good People* (New York: Schocken Books, 2001, originally published in 1981), 58, 60.

11. Kushner, *When Bad Things Happen*, 197-198.

12. Quoted in Paul E. Little, *Know Why You Believe* (Downers Grove, IL: IVP, 4th ed., 2000), 177.

13. In heaven, our sanctification—the process of being made more like Jesus in nature and character—will be completed (Romans 8:28-30). The sinful impulses that drive us now won't even exist in us at that point. Thus, we will maintain our free will but we will actually want to choose only what pleases God because that's what pleases us—and we'll be able to do God's will without the infection and interruption of sin. That's how Jesus operated on earth, and it's how we will be heaven.

14. The apostle John described the problems the world presents: "Do not love the world or the things in the world. If anyone loves the world, the love of the Father is not in him. For all that is in the world—the lust of the flesh, the lust of the eyes, and the pride of life—is not of the Father but is of the world. And the world is passing away, and the lust of it; but he who does the will of God abides forever" (1 John 2:15-17).

15. Paul listed the works of the flesh: "adultery, fornication, uncleanness, lewdness, idolatry, sorcery, hatred, contentions, jealousies, outbursts of wrath, selfish ambitions, dissensions, heresies, envy, murders, drunkenness, revelries, and the like; of which I tell you beforehand, just as I also told you in time past, that those who practice such things will not inherit the kingdom of God" (Galatians 5:19-21).

16. I'm thankful that Paul then immediately listed the fruit of the Spirit: "The fruit of the Spirit is love, joy, peace, longsuffering, kindness, goodness, faithfulness, gentleness, self-control. Against such there is no law. And those who are Christ's have crucified the flesh with its passions and desires. If we live in the Spirit, let us also walk in the Spirit. Let us not become conceited, provoking one another, envying one another" (Galatians 5:22-26).

17. Peter gave us a heads-up on Satan's activity: "Be sober, be vigilant; because your adversary the devil walks about like a roaring lion, seeking whom he may devour" (1 Peter 5:8).

18. Oswald Chambers, *Christian Disciplines* (Grand Rapids, MI: Discovery House Publishers, 1995, originally published in 1936), 47.

19. A.E. Wilder-Smith, *Let Us Reason* (Costa Mesa, CA: The Word for Today, 2007), 211.

20. Joni Eareckson Tada, "Reflections on the 50th Anniversary of My Diving Accident," *The Gospel Coalition*, July 30, 2017, https://www.thegospelcoalition.org/article/reflections-on-50th-anniversary-of-my-diving-accident/ (accessed May 16, 2019).

21. Eareckson Tada, "Reflections."

22. Charles H. Spurgeon, *Spurgeon's Sermons Volume 05: 1859* (Woodstock, ON: Devoted Publishing, 2017), 401.

Chapter 12—How Can Three Be One?

1. This image is public domain and can be found at the site https://commons.wikimedia.org/wiki/File:Shield-Trinity-Scutum-Fidei-English.svg.

2. R.T. Kendall, *Understanding Theology* (Great Britain: Christian Focus Publishing, 1998), 28.

3. Billy Graham, "The Fruit of the Spirit," *BGEA*, 1957, posted October 28, 2011, https://billygraham.org/decision-magazine/november-2011/the-fruit-of-the-spirit/ (accessed May 22, 2019).

4. Adapted from a legend recorded in Jacobus de Voragine, "Of St. Austin, Doctor and Bishop," *The Golden Legend*, Vol. 5 (1470), http://www.intratext.com/IXT/ENG1293/_P6C.HTM (accessed May 22, 2019).

5. Barna Research Group, "Americans Draw Theological Beliefs from Diverse Points of View," Barna Group, October 8, 2002, https://www.barna.com/research/americans-draw-theological-beliefs-from-diverse-points-of-view/ (accessed June 3, 2019).

6. Kermit Zarley, "What Do Americans Believe about the Trinity?," *Patheos*, May 26, 2017, https://www.patheos.com/blogs/kermitzarleyblog/2017/05/americans-believe-trinity/ (accessed September 4, 2019).

7. Bob Smietana, "Americans Love God and the Bible, Are Fuzzy on the Details," *LifeWay Research*, September 27, 2016, https://lifewayresearch.com/2016/09/27/americans-love-god-and-the-bible-are-fuzzy-on-the-details/ (accessed May 28, 2019).

8. G. Shane Morris, "Survey Finds Most American Christians Are Actually Heretics," *The Federalist*, October 10, 2016, https://thefederalist.com/2016/10/10/survey-finds-american-christians-actually-heretics/ (accessed May 28, 2019).

9. Gordon Lewis and Bruce Demerest, *Integrative Theology* (Grand Rapids, MI: Zondervan Academic, 1987), 283.

10. Lewis and Demerest, *Integrative Theology*, 280, 283.

11. Lewis and Demerest, *Integrative Theology*, 255.

12. Justo L. González, *The Story of Christianity* (Peabody, MA: Prince Press, 2001), 63.

13. Justo L. González, *The Apostles' Creed for Today* (Louisville, KY: Westminster John Knox Press, 2007), 5.

14. Quoted in Cyril Richardson, *Early Christian Fathers* (New York: Macmillan, 1970), 70.

15. Richardson, *Early Christian Fathers*, 65.

16. "But both Him, and the Son (who came forth from Him and taught us these things, and the host of the other good angels who follow and are made like to Him), and the prophetic Spirit, we worship and adore" (Justin Martyr, *First Apology*, AD 150, ch 6).

17. Athenagoras, *Plea for the Christians* 10:2-4, AD 177, quoted in Richardson, 309.

18. Athenagoras, *Plea for the Christians*, 326.

19. Quoted in Alister McGrath, *The Christian Theology Reader*, 5th ed. (Malden, MA: John Wiley & Sons, 2017), 157.

20. Theophilus of Antioch, *To Autolycus*, Book 2.15, AD 180.

21. Charles Spurgeon, *Spurgeon's Sermons Volume 01: 1855* (Woodstock, ON: Devoted Publishing, 2017), 26.

22. Christianity is still first, though its growth is coming primarily in developing regions like South America, Africa, and Asia. See Aaron Earls, "Where Protestant Christianity Is Growing the Fastest," *LifeWay Research*, November 29, 2017, https://factsandtrends.net/2017/11/29/protestant-christianity-growing-fastest/ (accessed June 4, 2019).

23. Sura 4:171, Yusuf Ali translation.

24. Sura 24:1-21.

25. Sura 5:72-73, Sahih International translation.

26. Lewis and Demerest, *Integrative Theology*, 283.

27. And if you might be thinking, *Well, Jesus was just being polite and letting Thomas have his little moment*, think of the times Jesus was firm about His ministry, telling His mother and others that it wasn't yet His "time" (John 2:4; 7:6; 7:8; 7:30; 8:20; 13:1; 17:1; and Matthew 26:18). Remember when Jesus blasted Peter for voicing Satan's opposition to His mission (Matthew 16, Mark 8)? How about when Jesus questioned the rich young ruler's intention when calling Him "good" (Mark 10:18)? In other words, Jesus wasn't shy about letting people know when He didn't agree with their assessment of Him or His rescue operation. If Jesus didn't disagree with Thomas addressing Him as Lord and God, it's because He was acknowledging the truthfulness of the statement.

28. J.I. Packer, *Evangelism and the Sovereignty of God* (Downers Grove, IL: InterVarsity Press, 2008), 26.

Chapter 13—Two-Thirds Is Not Enough

1. A.W. Tozer, *The Pursuit of God* (Camp Hill, PA: Christian Publications, 1982), 8.

2. Dagobert D. Runes, ed., *Diary and Sundry Observations of Thomas Alva Edison* (Westport, CT: Greenwood Publishing Group, 1968), 110.

3. Lloyd John Ogilvie, *Experiencing the Power of the Holy Spirit* (Eugene, OR: Harvest House, 2001), 25.

4. See 1 Timothy 6:13 and Ecclesiastes 2:26, respectively.

5. See Deuteronomy 8:18 and John 3:16, respectively.

6. J.I. Packer, *Keep In Step With The Spirit* (Old Tappan, NJ: Revell, 1984), 57.

7. Thomas Ken, "Praise God from Whom All Blessings Flow," hymn, 1674.

8. See also John 14:13-14 and John 15:16.

Chapter 14—Good Man, Madman, Con Man, or God-Man?

1. Jack Canfield, Mark Victor Hansen, Patty Aubery, and Nancy Mitchell, *Chicken Soup for the Christian Soul* (Deerfield Beach, FL: Health Communications, 1997), 220.

2. Quoted in Albert M. Wells, Jr., *Inspiring Quotations Contemporary & Classical* (Nashville, TN: Thomas Nelson, 1988), 102.

3. Recorded in the apocryphal book of 2 Maccabees 2:1-8.

4. This was because Mary became pregnant with Jesus before she married Joseph.

5. Jean-Jacques Rousseau, *Oeuvres Complètes* tome III (Paris, 1839), 365-367.

6. Ralph Waldo Emerson, *Harvard Divinity School Address* (Cambridge, MA: July 15, 1838), https://www.historyandheadlines.com/july-15-1838-philosopher-ralph-waldo-emerson-declares-jesus-god/ (accessed July 6, 2019).

7. David Frederick Strauss, "Vergängliches und Bleibendes im Christenthum," 1838.

8. David Van Biema, "The Gospel Truth?," *Time*, April 8, 1996, 52-59.

9. David Van Biema, "The Gospel Truth?"

10. Garry Wills, *What Jesus Meant* (New York: Viking Books, 2006), xxv-xxvi.

11. Quoted in Josh McDowell, *The New Evidence That Demands a Verdict* (Nashville, TN: Thomas Nelson Inc, 1999), 138.

12. C.S. Lewis, *Mere Christianity* (New York: HarperCollins, 1952; 2001 ed.), 52.

13. C.S. Lewis, *The Lion, the Witch, and the Wardrobe* (New York: HarperCollins, 1950, 2000 ed.), 80.

Chapter 15—Marked by a Purpose: The Carpenter Who Was Really a King

1. Timothy Keller. Twitter post, January 6, 2019, 9:30 a.m., https://twitter.com/timkellernyc/status/1081966210776993794?lang=en.

2. Elesha Coffman, "Why December 25?," *Christianity Today*, August 8, 2008, https://www.christianitytoday.com/history/2008/august/why-december-25.html (accessed September 4, 2019).

3. For insight given by a traveler who hikes with pack burrows, see Russell E. Saltzman, "Biblical Travel: How Far to Where, and What about the Donkey?," *Aleteia*, January 24, 2017, https://aleteia.org/2017/01/24/biblical-travel-how-far-to-where-and-what-about-the-donkey/ (accessed September 4, 2019).

4. Respectively, Isaiah 7:14; Daniel 9:24-27; Psalm 2:1-2 and Daniel 7:13-14; Genesis 22:1-8, Exodus 12:1-51, Zechariah 12:10, and Isaiah 52:13-53:12; Psalm 16:8-11.

5. Quoted in "Christmas: Classic and Contemporary Excerpts," *Christianity Today*, December 11, 1995, https://www.christianitytoday.com/ct/1995/december11/5te048.html (accessed September 5, 2019).

6. Charles C. Ryrie, *Basic Theology: A Popular Systematic Guide to Understanding Biblical Truth* (Chicago: Moody Publishers, 1999), 284.

7. James Allan Francis, *The Real Jesus and Other Sermons* (Philadelphia: The Judson Press, 1926), quoted in Charles Swindoll and Roy Zuck, gen. ed., *Understanding Christian Theology* (Nashville, TN: Thomas Nelson, 2003), 343.

8. Pascal Tréguer, "Origin of 'Bedlam': The Hospital of St. Mary of Bethlehem," *Word Histories*, https://wordhistories.net/2017/10/07/origin-of-bedlam/ (accessed October 1, 2019).

Chapter 16—How to Be God's Friend

1. Mark Twain, *Mark Twain at Your Fingertips* (Mineola, NY: Dover Publications, 2009), 69.

2. Ralph Waldo Emerson, "Compensation" in *Essays: First Series* (1841).

3. Charles H. Spurgeon, *Spurgeon's Sermons: Volume 11: 1865* (Woodstock, ON: Devoted Publishing, 2017), 310.

Steps to Peace With God

1. God's Purpose: Peace and Life

God loves you and wants you to experience peace and life—abundant and eternal.

The Bible says ...

"We have peace with God through our Lord Jesus Christ." *Romans 5:1, NKJV*

"For God so loved the world that He gave His only begotten Son, that whoever believes in Him should not perish but have everlasting life." *John 3:16, NKJV*

"I have come that they may have life, and that they may have it more abundantly." *John 10:10, NKJV*

Since God planned for us to have peace and the abundant life right now, why are most people not having this experience?

2. Our Problem: Separation From God

God created us in His own image to have an abundant life. He did not make us as robots to automatically love and obey Him, but gave us a will and a freedom of choice.

We chose to disobey God and go our own willful way. We still make this choice today. This results in separation from God.

The Bible says ...

"For all have sinned and fall short of the glory of God." *Romans 3:23, NKJV*

"For the wages of sin is death, but the gift of God is eternal life in Christ Jesus our Lord." *Romans 6:23, NKJV*

Our choice results in separation from God.

People (Sinful)   God (Holy)

Our Attempts

Through the ages, individuals have tried in many ways to bridge this gap ... without success ...

The Bible says ...

"There is a way that seems right to a man, but its end is the way of death."
Proverbs 14:12, NKJV

"But your iniquities have separated you from your God; and your sins have hidden His face from you, so that He will not hear."
Isaiah 59:2, NKJV

There is only one remedy for this problem of separation.

3. God's Remedy: The Cross

Jesus Christ is the only answer to this problem. He died on the cross and rose from the grave, paying the penalty for our sin and bridging the gap between God and people.

The Bible says ...

"For there is one God and one Mediator between God and men, the Man Christ Jesus."
1 Timothy 2:5, NKJV

"For Christ also suffered once for sins, the just for the unjust, that He might bring us to God."
1 Peter 3:18, NKJV

"But God shows his love for us in that while we were still sinners, Christ died for us." *Romans 5:8, ESV*

God has provided the only way ... we must make the choice ...

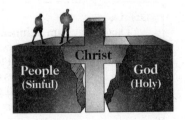

4. Our Response: Receive Christ

We must trust Jesus Christ and receive Him by personal invitation.

The Bible says ...

"Behold, I stand at the door and knock. If anyone hears My voice and opens the door, I will come in to him and dine with him, and he with Me." *Revelation 3:20, NKJV*

"But to all who did receive him, who believed in his name, he gave the right to become children of God."
John 1:12, ESV

"If you confess with your mouth that Jesus is Lord and believe in your heart that God raised him from the dead, you will be saved." *Romans 10:9, ESV*

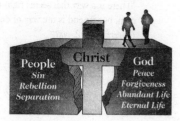

Are you here ... or here?

Is there any good reason why you cannot receive Jesus Christ right now?

How to Receive Christ:

1. Admit your need (say, "I am a sinner").
2. Be willing to turn from your sins (repent) and ask for God's forgiveness.
3. Believe that Jesus Christ died for you on the cross and rose from the grave.
4. Through prayer, invite Jesus Christ to come in and control your life through the Holy Spirit (receive Jesus as Lord and Savior).

What to Pray:

Dear God,

I know that I am a sinner. I want to turn from my sins, and I ask for Your forgiveness. I believe that Jesus Christ is Your Son. I believe He died for my sins and that You raised Him to life. I want Him to come into my heart and to take control of my life. I want to trust Jesus as my Savior and follow Him as my Lord from this day forward.

In Jesus' Name, amen.

_____   _____
Date   Signature

GOD'S ASSURANCE: HIS WORD

IF YOU PRAYED THIS PRAYER,

THE BIBLE SAYS ...

"For 'everyone who calls on the name of the Lord will be saved.'"
Romans 10:13, ESV

Did you sincerely ask Jesus Christ to come into your life?
Where is He right now? What has He given you?

"For by grace you have been saved through faith. And this is not your
own doing; it is the gift of God, not a result of works, so that no one may
boast." *Ephesians 2:8–9, ESV*

THE BIBLE SAYS ...

"He who has the Son has life; he who does not have the Son of God does
not have life. These things I have written to you who believe in the name of
the Son of God, that you may know that you have eternal life, and that you
may continue to believe in the name of the Son of God."
1 John 5:12–13, NKJV

Receiving Christ, we are born into God's family through the
supernatural work of the Holy Spirit, who indwells every believer.
This is called regeneration or the "new birth."

This is just the beginning of a wonderful new life in Christ. To deepen
this relationship you should:

1. Read your Bible every day to know Christ better.
2. Talk to God in prayer every day.
3. Tell others about Christ.
4. Worship, fellowship, and serve with other Christians in a church where
   Christ is preached.
5. As Christ's representative in a needy world, demonstrate your new life by
   your love and concern for others.

God bless you as you do.

Franklin Graham

If you want further help in the decision you have made, write to:
Billy Graham Evangelistic Association
1 Billy Graham Parkway, Charlotte, NC 28201-0001

1-877-2GRAHAM (1-877-247-2426)
BillyGraham.org/commitment